Killer Math Word Problems for Standardized Tests

(SAT, GRE, GMAT)

When Plugging Numbers into Formulas

Just Isn't Enough

Nancy L. Nolan, Ph.D.

* The SAT is a registered trademark of the College Board and Educational Testing Services (ETS). The Graduate Management Admission Test (GMAT) is a registered trademark of the Graduate Management Admission Council (GMAC). The Graduate Record Examination (GRE) is a registered trademark of Educational Testing Services (ETS). The College Board, GMAC, and ETS were not involved in the production of, and do not endorse, this publication.

Hardcover, electronic and CD-ROM versions published by:

Magnificent Milestones, Inc. USA
www.ivyleagueadmission.com

ISBN: 9781933819464

Disclaimers:

(1) This book was written as a guide; it does not claim to be the definitive word on SAT, GRE or GMAT preparation. The opinions expressed are the personal observations of the author based on her own experiences. They are not intended to prejudice any party. Accordingly, the author and publisher do not accept any liability or responsibility for any loss or damage that have been caused, or allegedly caused, through the use of information in this book.

(2) The SAT is a joint collaboration between Educational Testing Services (ETS) and the College Board, two non-profit groups that sponsor the test and decide how it will be constructed, administered, and used. Likewise, the Graduate Record Exam (GRE) is a registered trademark of Educational Testing Services and the Graduate Management Admission Test (GMAT) is a registered trademark of the Graduate Management Admission Council (GMAC). Neither Dr. Nolan nor Magnificent Milestones, Inc. is affiliated with ETS, the College Board, or the GMAC.

(3) Admission to college or graduate school depends on several factors in addition to a candidate's SAT, GRE, or GMAT scores (including GPA, recommendations, interview and essays). The author and publisher cannot guarantee that any applicant will be admitted to any specific school or program if (s)he follows the information in this book.

Dedication

For students everywhere;

may the size of your dreams be exceeded only

by your tenacity to attain them.

Acknowledgements

I am deeply indebted to the students, professors, counselors and admissions officers who have shared their perceptions and frustrations about the SAT, GRE, and GMAT. This book, which was written on your behalf, would not be nearly as powerful without your generous and insightful input.

I also want to thank my colleagues at www.ivyleagueadmission.com for providing a constant source of support, along with the best editorial help in the business.

Table of Contents

Killer Math Word Problems for Standardized Tests

(SAT, GRE, GMAT)

When Plugging Numbers into Formulas Just Isn't Enough

Chapter 1: Introduction – Killer Math Word Problems on Standardized Tests (SAT, GRE, GMAT)

Far too often, students offer the same excuse for scoring poorly on the quantitative section of the SAT, GRE or GMAT:

I understand the theory, but I can't solve word problems.

Sad to say, but in the world of standardized tests, this is analogous to saying that you know the alphabet, but you can't speak in sentences.

As you probably suspect, getting a top score on the SAT, GRE or GMAT requires far more than plugging numbers into formulas. You need to be able to apply your mathematical skills to convoluted word problems that test your ability to read clearly, interpret quickly, and determine the optimal plan of attack. Most importantly, you need to be ready for the typical tricks and traps that the test writers use over and over again to snag unsuspecting students.

This publication takes a common sense approach to preparing for the word problems that appear in the quantitative section of the SAT, GRE and GMAT. We will test your knowledge (and speed) for every topic, from basic to complex. Depending on your background and skill set, you can use this book to fill in the gaps - and to find creative ways to solve killer problems without breaking a sweat.

From our perspective (after reviewing numerous versions of these exams), the quantitative section is designed to test your ability to *solve problems*, rather than your mathematical knowledge. The questions lean heavily toward word problems that apply mathematical formulas in real-world applications, such as calculating:

- interest on a loan
- a price or salary increase
- travel times and speeds
- work schedules

Word problems are challenging because they do not give you a simple equation to solve. Instead, you must translate the verbal information into a mathematical relationship and solve for an unknown. To do so, you must know what you are being asked – and be able to find the answer quickly and accurately. Because the questions are not presented in any particular order or context, you must know when plugging in numbers is – and is not – enough.

From our experience, students who achieve a top score on the SAT, GRE and GMAT take a three-prong approach to the quantitative section of the exam. They understand:

- the underlying mathematical concepts
- the tricks and traps the test writers employ
- how to USE the information in 1 and 2 to solve practical word problems

Without a doubt, steps 2 and 3 are the difference between a good score and a great one. Sadly, they are also the areas in which most test prep programs fall embarrassingly short. This publication is designed to fill the critical gap between theory and application. We are going to teach you how to tackle the different types of math word problems that appear on standardized tests…. and how to handle the typical tricks, traps, and pitfalls that the test writers will use to confuse you.

Before we begin, here is a quick summary of how this publication is organized:

1. **Chapter 1** presents a set of general strategies for the quantitative section of the SAT, GRE, and GMAT which can be applied to all types of questions and problems. It also offers a few time-saving techniques for the day of the exam.

2. **Chapters 2 – 28** offer detailed explanations of the different types of word problems that you will likely encounter on the tests, including the underlying theory behind each type. In each chapter, we will also present specific tricks that the test writers use to complicate the problems and to confuse unsuspecting students. Finally, we also offer numerous examples of each type of problem, which range from easy to difficult to nearly impossible. Regardless of your background or skill set, we want you to be prepared for what you will likely face on the day of the exam.

3. **Chapter 29** offers a 50-problem final exam for you to take under controlled testing conditions. After you master the different types of problems on the SAT, GRE and GMAT, you can use the mock exam to test your skills and identify the areas in which you may need additional practice.

General Tips for the SAT, GRE and GMAT

Before we begin, here is our own obligatory list of common sense things to do before you take a standardized test:

1) Be familiar with the types of questions in each section. Refresh your skills in basic mathematics and geometry. Practice on our test questions until you are comfortable with every question type.

2) Know how long you have to complete each section and pace yourself accordingly.

3) Don't waste time reading the instructions on the test day. We include the specific instructions for the quantitative section of the exam in this publication. Read them thoroughly and make sure you understand them. This will save you several minutes on the actual day of the test.

4) Develop an optimal strategy to suit the specific challenges of the computer-adaptive test (CAT) version of the exams, which ask fewer questions than the old paper version. On the CAT, the first question in any given section will be of average difficulty. If you answer it correctly, your next question will be slightly more difficult. If you answer it incorrectly, your next question will be slightly easier.

On a practical basis, how does this affect you? Unlike other standardized tests, all problems on the CAT are not worth the same - the difficult questions are weighted more heavily than the easier questions. If you get the first few questions wrong, the software will not allow you to advance to the more difficult ones. As a result, your performance on the first few questions in each section of the CAT has a significant influence on your final score. Give them the time and effort they deserve.

Finally, unlike the paper version of the exam, you cannot skip a question or go back to an earlier question on the CAT. Once you click the 'answer confirm' box, your answer can not be changed.

5) Answer every question, even if you are clueless about how to approach it. In many cases, you are better off guessing than wasting a ton of time on a question or problem that you aren't able to solve. The test questions will vary widely in their level of difficulty. Further, each student brings a unique set of strengths and skills to the exam, which will influence his/her performance. Some questions are designed to be extremely difficult for all students. On such a highly-timed test, they should not consume a disproportionate amount of your time.

6) Keep track of time as you work on each section of the test. Although we will teach you many strategies for different types of questions, you must work quickly and efficiently to apply them to as many questions as possible.

7) Don't try to cram a lot of studying into the last few days before the test. Your best bet is to prepare a few hours a day for several weeks before the exam and to relax (or try to relax) the day or so before the actual test.

8) Arrive at the test center a few minutes early with all of your essential supplies (photo ID card, admission ticket, sharpened #2 pencils, watch, comfortable clothing, snack). Avoid chatting about the test during the breaks; this usually just increases your self-doubt and your test-taking anxiety.

9) Few applicants know how they did on the test when they leave the test center. Most feel badly, but this is usually just burnout from the stress of the long day. Don't panic and cancel your score unless:

a) You were seriously ill on the test day (and it affected your performance)
b) You were seriously unprepared and plan to remedy that before taking the test again

8

General Tips for the Quantitative Section of the SAT, GRE, and GMAT

The math topics on the SAT, GRE, and GMAT include arithmetic, basic algebra and geometry (no proofs). Trigonometry and calculus are NOT included. According to the test writers, they try to eliminate biases that favor candidates with specific strengths and backgrounds.

Although the test writers vary their questions from year to year, certain topics tend to appear with similar frequency on the SAT, GRE, and GMAT. Recent exam questions fell into the following categories:

Ratios, Rates, Percentages	25%
Word Problems	25%
Number Properties	25%
Geometry	20%
Other	5%

Here's the great news for students; from our experience, nearly every test question has a simple solution and can be solved with a minimum of calculations. The trick is to correctly assess each question and apply the correct strategy.

Strategy 1. For standard multiple choice questions, students have an advantage, because the correct answer is right in front of them. For these questions, elimination strategies are paramount. First, be aware that the SAT, GRE, and GMAT list all answer choices in ascending order:

        a.   3
        b.   9
        c.   12
        d.   36
        e.   72

At first glance, this might not seem like particularly useful information. But let's put it into several contexts that reveal its hidden power. First, let's assume that these five answers were for a problem that asked you to calculate the amount of money that someone had left over after buying back-to-school supplies. Let's also assume that you reach this problem with only a few minutes left in the math section, but you think it's worth a shot.

If you are going to approach the problem by plugging the answer choices into an equation, start with the middle answer, which is 12. Why (other than that you hope it is the right answer)? Because even if 12 is wrong, you will have narrowed your answer choices from 4 possibilities to 2.

If 12 is too large to be the right answer, you will automatically know that the correct answer will be either a or b. Likewise, if 12 is too small to be correct, you will know that the right answer to the problem is d or e. Even f you run out of time and wind up guessing, you have dramatically increased your odds of getting the right answer.

Strategy 2. The drawback of multiple choice questions is that the test writers can usually anticipate the errors that you are likely to make in your calculations (such as forgetting to take a square root or to raise a number to a power). A common trick is to include these "mistakes" as incorrect answer choices, to try to mislead you. When you finish the problem, you are excited to see that the answer you calculated was one of the answer choices. In your mind, it must be right, but it's dead wrong! You unknowingly fell into the "likely error trap."

Example; the problem asks you to solve for x:

$(x + 5) - (4/2)(6/3) = 12$

        a. -2
        b. 4/5
        c. 8
        d. 11
        e. 13

This is a particularly easy problem; the correct answer is Choice D, or 11. But the other answer choices were not chosen randomly. If you made a mistake at the end and added 1 instead of subtracting 1, you would have gotten an answer of 13, which is answer choice e. If you forgot to subtract the quantity (4/2)(6/3) from (x + 5), you would have gotten –2, which is answer choice a. The other answer choices are other results that you could have gotten if you had made a less likely (but still possible) mistake.

On an easy problem like this, the tactic may not be an issue for you. But, rest assured, the test writers also use the SAME sneaky answer choices on the harder questions. If you get tired and sloppy, they might lure you into a trap. (If the question asks for the x-intercept, you can be fairly certain that the y-intercept will be one of the wrong answer choices!)

Strategy 3. Now, let's get down to some actual quantitative traps and pitfalls. According to mathematical rules, when both sides of an inequality are multiplied or divided by a negative number, the inequality is reversed:

Example: If $x > y$ and $c < 0$, then $cx < cy$

If we plug in simple numbers for x, y and c (such as 4, 3 and -2, respectively), the concept is easy to understand:

$4 > 3$ and $–2 < 0$ Hence, $(-2)(4) < (-2)(3)$ or $-8 < -6$

Unfortunately, this concept is rarely tested on its own, but in the context of a more difficult problem. A typical "trap" that students fall into is failing to reverse the inequality sign. Be aware of this pitfall for this type of problem. As we've already warned, the wrong answer that you get when you make this mistake will likely be one of the five answer choices.

Strategy 4. Beware of questions in which a single "trick" word, such as **not**, **except** or **but**, changes your entire approach to the problem. Let's look at another typical example.

Which of the following numbers CANNOT be even?

a.   The sum of two odd numbers
b.   The sum of an odd number and an even number
c.   The product of two even numbers
d.   The product of an odd number and an even number
e.   The sum of two even numbers

Here, we have an easy problem that is needlessly complicated by the odd wording of the question stem. If a number cannot be even, then it must be odd. Hence, we must find the one answer choice that MUST be odd. By plugging in numbers to test each answer choice, we can quickly determine that Choice B, the sum of an odd number and an even number, is the only one that cannot produce an even number. It is therefore the correct answer.

Strategy 5. If you've tried everything else (substitution, back-solving, etc.) and you STILL can't solve a problem, don't sweat it. *Just guess.* Your chances for success are 20% for multiple choices questions, and even higher if you can eliminate a few incorrect answer choices.

When evaluating the possible answers, immediately rule out the ones that are obviously wrong:

Example: the question asks you to determine a length, and the answer choice is negative.

Example: the question defines the answer as an integer, but the answer choice is a fraction between zero and one.

Example: the question asks you to calculate the area in which a circle intersects with a square (which is very tiny), and the answer choice is larger than the size of one of the actual figures.

In all of these situations, at least one (or more) answer choices can immediately be ruled out. The more choices you can eliminate, the greater your odds of guessing correctly.

Strategy 6. On any question, if the quantities are expressed in different forms, make them look alike. Eliminate parentheses and factor out expressions. In geometry formulas, convert a given measurement (such as an area, perimeter or volume) to the formula that it represents. Many times, the test writers will provide data in different forms as a trap. One (or more) of the incorrect answer choices will be answers that you will get if you fail to convert your units properly.

Strategy 7. Unless a question specifically states that a number is an integer, don't assume this is the case. Many times, students must solve problems by substituting numbers for variables to see what "fits." Unless you are specifically told that the variable is a positive integer, always check a positive number, a negative number and a fraction in the equation(s) to see what happens. Note the difference between the following two examples, in which a seemingly insignificant difference in wording makes all the difference in the world.

Example 1: For all k not equal to zero, which of the following are true?

I. $k^2 > k$
II, $4k > 2k$
III. $k + 6 > k$

    a.   I only
    b.   II only
    c.   III only
    d.   I and II only
    e.   I, II and III

Example 2: For all positive integers, which of the following are true?

I. $k^3 > k$
II, $4k > 2k$
III. $k + 6 > k$

    a.   I only
    b.   II only
    c.   III only
    d.   I, and II only
    e.   I, II and III

At first glance, these two examples seem identical; in actuality, they are quite different. In Example 1, we are asked to determine which of the statements are true for all k not equal to zero, which INCLUDES negative numbers and fractions. If we simply plug in positive numbers in place of k, we would conclude that all three statements were correct. However, if we substitute values such as ½ and –6 in place of k, we quickly discover that the only statement that is true for positive numbers, negative numbers and fractions is III. Hence, Choice C is correct.

In contrast, Example 2 only requires students to test positive integers in each equation. When we do, we discover that all three of the statements are correct. In this case, the correct answer is Choice E.

Strategy 8. Although function problems are usually quite easy on standardized tests, many students are needlessly intimidated by the odd notation that the test writers use. Don't be surprised to see all sorts of unusual keyboard symbols in the formulas, such as

X # Y
a * b
m ^ n

The strange symbol just means there is a relationship between the two variables. Your job is to clarify that relationship and to solve the actual equation. To do so, all you need to do is plug numbers and see what happens.

<u>Example</u>: The operation @ is defined for all non-zero p and s by the equation p @ s = p/s. If so, then the expression (p @ s) @ r is equal to:

    a. p/sr
    b. s/pr
    c. psr
    d. pr/s
    e. r/ps

This problem, which seems intimidating, is actually very easy to solve. All we need to do is divide the quantity p/s by r. (p @ s) @ r = (p/s) / r = (p/s)(1/r) = p/sr. Hence, the correct answer is Choice A.

Strategy 9. Be prepared to interpret the graphs of different types of linear and quadratic equations. The test writers will test these concepts in several ways. Sometimes, they will show you a graph of a line and ask which one of the answer choices could (or could not) be a point on that line. To find the answer, you will just need to use the formula for the slope of the line.

Other times, the test writers will ask you to determine the x or y intercept of a line simply from a set of points. These questions are rarely too difficult, but they often include traps:

If the writers ask for you to determine the x-intercept of a line, they will undoubtedly include the y-intercept as one of the answer choices. Likewise, if the calculation is a simple subtraction, don't be surprised if the writers include negative numbers in the calculations, to try to confuse you about the way the line should be drawn. It's a silly mistake, but if you are feeling pressed for time, you may fall into the trap.

<u>Example 1</u>: A line with the equation y = 14x – 28 crosses the x-axis at the point with the coordinates m, n. What is the value of n?

    a. -28
    b. -2
    c. 0
    d. 2
    e. 7

The test writers have complicated the problem by asking you to find a coordinate of a single point (m, n) on the line. Upon further inspection, though, they are simply asking us to find the y-intercept, which is where the line crosses the x-axis. To do so, we simply need to solve the equation for x, when y equals 0. The correct answer is 2, or Choice D. (To no one's surprise, the incorrect answer choices are all numbers you would get if you misinterpreted the question.

Strategy 10. Use our tried-and-true method for solving word problems, which are the focus of this publication.

1. Read the question quickly and carefully.
2. Identify what you are being asked.
3. Eliminate all extraneous information.
4. Organize your facts.
5. Decide what calculations you need to perform.
6. Do them in the correct order.
7. Check your answer (and units) to ensure that it makes sense

As you probably suspect, we have dozens of additional strategies for different types of word problems. To master them, read on!

Chapter 2: Word Problems Using Basic Arithmetic

When they prepare for the SAT, GRE, or GMAT most students gloss over fundamental topics such as basic arithmetic. After all, for such an important test, it seems foolish to waste any serious time reviewing the basic operations that you learned in grade school, such as addition, subtraction, multiplication, and division. Yet the quantitative sections of these exams DO test these concepts in the form of mathematical word problems. Consequently, we would be remiss if we did not include a chapter with several relevant examples.

Most of the arithmetic word problems on the SAT, GRE, and GMAT are practical in nature – and are relatively easy to solve. They will ask you to calculate how much something costs, or the amount of time that is required to complete a series of tasks. Others, however, include traps and pitfalls, such as tricky wording, extraneous details, and confusion about what you are actually being asked. To begin our discussion of word problems, those that involve basic math are a logical place to start.

You've known – and used - these concepts for years, so we won't belabor the point here. Instead, we'll jump right to heart of the matter, which are actual word problems. At your convenience, try the following problems, which test your knowledge of addition, subtraction, multiplication, and division. To duplicate actual test conditions, you should spend no more than 90 seconds on each one.

At the end of the chapter, we provide a detailed answer for each problem, along with a short discussion of the typical tricks and traps that the test writers will use to try to confuse you.

Example 1: Basic Math

Carla owed her university $585 in tuition. When she receives her paycheck of $116, she pays it all to the university, along with $219 that she has borrowed from a friend. Later in the day, Carla wins $947 in the lottery, and immediately pays off the rest of her tuition bill and her friend. How much money does Carla have left?

    a. $250
    b. $362
    c. $478
    d. $697
    e. $728

Solution: The easiest way to solve this problem is to keep a running total of what Carla has. When she pays the first part of her tuition bill, she winds up owing $250 ($585 – $116 – $219 = $250). Then, after Carla wins the lottery and settles up with both the school and her friend, she has $947 – $250 – $219 = $478. Choice C is correct.

Example 2: Basic Math – Plus Fractions

Jim's ticket won a lottery prize worth $433,890 after taxes. Jim decides to keep one-third of the amount and to divide the remainder equally among his two parents and three sisters. How much money will his two parents receive from Jim?

    a. 14,463
    b. 28,926
    c. 57,852
    d. 115,704
    e. 289,260

Solution: If Jim keeps one third of the lottery money, then the portion he gives to his family must equal 2/3 of $433,890, or $289,260. This amount will later be split among five people, two of whom are Jim's parents. Their portion is therefore 2/5 of $289,260, or $115,704. Choice D is correct.

Example 3: Basic Math – Thinking Through a Proportion

The Ice View Highway, which links City A and City B, provides two rest areas every twelve miles. How many rest areas would a car pass if it traveled one-half of the 4,356 miles of Ice View Highway, starting at the origin of the highway?

    a.   182
    b.   356
    c.   363
    d.   726
    e.   789

Solution: There are two ways to solve this problem. First, let's do it by simple multiplication and division. The first step is to must calculate the total distance that the car travels, which is 4356/2 = 2178 miles. Second, we must determine how many 12-mile segments are in this distance: 2178/12 = 181.5. Finally, we must multiply the number of 12-mile segments by the number of rest areas per segment, which is (181.5)(2) = 363. Choice C is correct.

Alternatively, we can solve this problem by using a proportion. If there are 2 rest areas every 12 miles, there will be x number of rest areas on 4356/2, or 2178 miles of highway. Mathematically, this translates to the following proportion: 2/12 = x/2178, solving for x = 363. Choice C is correct.

You're probably thinking, the first method was incredibly tedious; why did you include it? To show you that there is more than one way to tackle a problem and get the right answer. If you aren't comfortable with proportions, or you didn't want to use one, you could easily solve the problem using basic arithmetic.

Example 4: Mathematical Comparisons

David visited his grandmother in the hospital, where there were two places for him to park. Lot A charges $5.00 for the first hour of parking and 75 cents for each additional half hour. Lot B, on the other hand, charges a flat rate of $19.75 for an entire day of parking. Assuming that David will park his car for 7 hours that day, what will be the *additional* cost of parking in Lot B?

    a. $3.00
    b. $3.75
    c. $5.75
    d. $11.00
    e. $11.70

Solution: To solve, simply calculate the total amount to park in Lot A vs. Lot B for 7 hours. For Lot A, the cost is $5.00 + (0.75)(12) = $14.00. Lot B, on the other hand, costs $19.75. The difference is $5.75, which is Choice C.

Example 5: Problems with All Variables

At a local nursing home, X gallons of orange juice are needed per week per patient. At that rate, how many weeks will Y gallons of orange juice serve Z patients?

    a.   XZ/Y
    b.   YZ/X
    c.   X/YZ
    d.   Y/XZ
    e.   Z/XY

Solution: The easiest way to solve this problem is to substitute numbers for the variables. Let's assume that X = 2 gallons for one patient for one week. Let's also assume that Y = 20 and Z = 5. Hence, we have 5 patients, who will each drink 2 gallons per week. How long will 20 gallons last?

Time (in weeks) = (20 gallons)/{(5 patients)(2 gallons per patient)} = 20/10 = 2 weeks. Mathematically, this equals Y/XZ. Choice D is correct.

Sample Word Problems Using Basic Arithmetic: EASY - MODERATE

1. Sara is completely broke when she receives a $74 parking ticket. When Sara's brother gives her $125 for her birthday, she pays the ticket and buys $26 in gas. How much money does Sara have left?

    a. $25
    b. $26
    c. $51
    d. $99
    e. $101

2. On her way to the Post Office, Claire spent 10 minutes in her car, 11 minutes at the drugstore and another 11 minutes talking on her cell phone to her boyfriend. If she arrived at the Post Office at exactly 11:04 am, what time did Claire leave for the Post Office?

    a.   10:22 am
    b.   10:32 am
    c.   10:33 am
    d.   10:34 am
    e.   10:35 am

3. A wholesaler shipped seven dozen roses to a flower shop for use in a window display. If Jane takes three roses for her own use, and nineteen are discarded because they are wilted, but Barb adds back an additional half-dozen roses to the group, how many roses were available for the window display?

    a.   61
    b.   64
    c.   68
    d.   71
    e.   74

4. Jason has 1,489 nickels in a large jar in his bedroom. If he adds 324 nickels on Monday, and adds another 112 nickels on Tuesday, but removes 117 nickels on Wednesday, how much money (in dollars) does Jason have left in the jar on Thursday, assuming that there are no other additions or subtractions?

    a. $90.40
    b. $94.80
    c. $108.80
    d. $180.80
    e. $188.00

5. A cattery has 85 Persian cats, 411 Siamese cats and 103 Calico cats. For a treat, the owner of the cattery purchases 88 lbs of catnip, to be distributed evenly among all of the cats. Assuming there are no other types of cats in the cattery, how much catnip (in ounces) would each cat receive?

    a.   2.35
    b.   5.80
    c.   6.80
    d.   11.60
    e.   23.50

6. On spring break in Florida, Jennifer bought six shirts as souvenirs for her friends, which cost $14.50 each. If Jennifer works at a donut shop for $5.85 per hour, how many hours will she have to work to pay for the shirts (assuming no taxes or other deductions are withheld from her paycheck)?

      a. 5.85
      b. 6.00
      c. 8.70
      d. 14.50
      e. 14.87

7. Every time Carla travels west on highway B, she must pay a $3.00 toll. Every time she travels east on the same road, she receives a $2.00 credit. If Carla travels west on highway B seventeen times during April and she travels east on highway B twelve times during the same period, what is Carla's net gain/loss from traveling on highway B?

      a. $5 loss
      b. $24 loss
      c. $27 loss
      d. $24 gain
      e. $27 gain

8. Diane has 18 errands to run, which take 14 minutes each, before she can go home. If Diane needs to be home by 5:00 pm, what is the latest time that she can start the errands?

      a. 11:40 am
      b. 11:48 am
      c. 12:40 pm
      d. 12:48 pm
      e. 1:40 pm

9. Sheila can wear her 100% linen suit four times before she needs to have it dry cleaned. She wears the suit to church every Sunday and to meetings at her bridge club on the first Tuesday of every month. If it costs $8.00 for each individual cleaning, and Sheila does not wear the suit on any other occasions, how much will Sheila pay to dry clean the suit each year?

      a. $48.00
      b. $64.00
      c. $96.00
      d. $104.00
      e. $128.00

10. Eve's boyfriend asked her to buy five items at the grocery store, which only accepts cash. They include a frozen pizza that costs $3.25, a bottle of juice that costs $4.89, a pound of butter that costs $2.89, a six-pack of root beer that is marked down from $3.59 to $3.19 and two packs of gum that cost 89 cents each. If Eve also wants to buy a magazine for herself that costs $3.50, how much money does she need to have with her?

      a. $16.00
      b. $18.61
      c. $19.01
      d. $19.50
      e. $19.90

11. Sara had to mail a package on the day that the Post Office increased its rates. The cost is 55 cents for the first ounce and 34 cents for each additional ounce. How much did Sara pay to mail a package that weighed three quarters of a pound?

    a. $3.74
    b. $3.95
    c. $4.08
    d. $4.29
    e. $4.63

12. An oven timer rings whenever the internal temperature reaches 425 °F. On a typical shift, the alarm rings five times every ten minutes. In a ten-hour shift, how many times will the alarm ring?

    a.   150
    b.   300
    c.   600
    d.   1500
    e.   3000

13. Donna and David both decided to participate in a race for charity. Donna had eleven sponsors who promised to donate $5 for every mile that she ran. David had fifteen sponsors who promised to donate $3 for every mile that he ran. If Donna ran six miles and David ran five miles, how much ADDITIONAL money did Donna raise for the charity than David?

    a. $105
    b. $210
    c. $225
    d. $330
    e. $555

14. Dan brought his car to the mechanic to have his engine fixed. The mechanic quoted him the following prices for parts: $350 for a new alternator, $150 for the battery and $25 for miscellaneous parts. Assuming that the minimal charge for labor is $45 per hour (rounded to the nearest half-hour) and that the shop can complete all repairs in 3.5 hours, what is the minimum amount that Dan will have to pay to have his car fixed?

    a. $157.50
    b. $525.00
    c. $682.50
    d. $705.00
    e. $727.50

15. Kathy is buying a notebook computer on an installment plan. She can pay for it over a period of 6 months or 15 months. If the notebook costs $1850, how many *additional* dollars would she have to pay each month to pay for it over 6 months rather than 15 months (assuming there are no finance charges)?

    a. $103
    b. $123
    c. $185
    d. $203
    e. $308

16. After announcing the availability of the Forever stamp, the US Post Office recorded $2,313,716.10 in sales for the stamps at the Glendale office in a single day. Assuming that the stamps cost 41 cents each, how many Forever stamps did the Glendale office sell that day?

    a. 564,321
    b. 948,624
    c. 746,360
    d. 5,643,210
    e. 9,486,246

17. Dina drove 240 miles round trip to visit her family for Thanksgiving. If her car averages 30 miles per gallon of gas and Dina paid an average price of $2.85 per gallon of gas, how much did she spend for gas on her trip?

    a. $22.80
    b. $24.00
    c. $32.85
    d. $42.75
    e. $85.50

18. The Glenview Airport offers two parking lots: long-term and short-term. Long-term parking costs a flat rate of $7.00 per day. Short-term parking costs $1.00 for the first two hours, and 50 cents for each additional hour. If a visitor plans to park for 6 hours at the airport, what will be the additional cost of parking in long-term parking versus short-term parking?

    a. $1.00
    b. $3.00
    c. $4.00
    d. $6.00
    e. $7.00

19. Joe rented a moving truck for $50 per day plus an additional charge for mileage. If Joe kept the truck for five days, traveled 600 miles during that time, and was charged a total of $550 for the rental, what was the charge for each mile?

    a. 25 cents
    b. 30 cents
    c. 50 cents
    d. 75 cents
    e. 85 cents

20. Carrie added M coins to her large collection, which gave her a total of N coins. Then, Carrie sold M – 180 of her coins to a local collector. How many coins did Carrie have left?

    a. M - N + 180
    b. N + M - 180
    c. N - M + 180
    d. N - M - 180
    e. (M + N – 180)/2

Sample Word Problems Using Basic Arithmetic: AS HARD AS IT GETS

21. A flea market vendor in Florida sold two types of earrings: a good hoop that costs $20 per pair and a bronze cross that costs $12 per pair. On a busy Sunday, the flea market vendor sold 600 pairs of gold hoop earrings and collected a total of $36,000 in revenues. Assuming that no other products were sold, and that the vendor collected no sales tax on any of the earrings, how many TOTAL pairs of earrings did he sell that Sunday?

    a.   1800
    b.   2000
    c.   2400
    d.   2600
    e.   3000

22. Two students played a game of catch on the roof of the chemistry building, which was 1,750 feet high. Unfortunately, after a bad throw, the ball fell to the ground and bounced several times. With each consecutive bounce, the ball reaches a height that is the same fraction of the height it reached on its previous bounce. If the ball reaches a height of 897 feet after its fifth bounce, what is this fraction?

    a.   1/8
    b.   1/6
    c.   3 / 4
    d.   5/6
    e.   7/8

23. At a wedding reception, twelve guests sat together at a round table. At the end of the meal, before they left, each guest at the table kissed all of the other guests goodbye. What was the total number of kisses?

    a.   24
    b.   55
    c.   66
    d.   78
    e.   132

24. Cara and her three roommates bought an old house for $395,000 and embarked on a series of structural and cosmetic renovations. Over the course of a year, they invested $105,500 on upgrades and repairs and listed the house for sale with a local realtor. If they sold the house for $675,000 and paid the realtor a 7% sales commission, how much of the profits did each girl receive (assuming that they split the profits evenly)?

    a. $20,925.00
    b. $31,812.50
    c. $63,625.00
    d. $95,437.50
    e. $127,250.00

25. Over the course of a busy shift, three cashiers at a grocery store gave each other money from their cash drawers to avoid running to the bank. After Cashier 1 gave $15 to Cashier 2 and Cashier 2 gave $12 to Cashier 3, Cashier 1 had $22 more than Cashier 2 and $30 more than Cashier 3. Originally, how much more did Cashier 1 have than Cashier 3?

    a. $25
    b. $27
    c. $33
    d. $43
    e. $47

Answer Key for Word Problems Using Basic Arithmetic

1. To answer this question, subtract the amount of money that Sara spent from the total amount she had available. 125 – 74 – 26 = 26   Choice A is correct. The trap in this question is the inclusion of alternative answer choices that match the answers you WOULD have gotten if you had subtracted incorrectly.

2. Add the minutes that Claire spent in the car; then, subtract them from the time she arrived at the Post Office. 10 + 11 + 11 = 32 minutes en route. 11:04 – 32 minutes = 10:32 am. Choice B is correct.

3. First, determine the total number of roses. Then, add and subtract according to the details in the question stem. If we do, we get: 12(7) = 84 roses - 3 – 19 + 6 = 68.   Choice C is correct. This problem requires you to add and subtract a string of numbers. As long as you convert the "dozen" terms to individual roses, and keep the signs correct when you add, you will obtain the right answer.

4. This is a simple addition and subtraction problem, with a final conversion to dollars at the end. When we add and subtract the terms, we get: 1489 + 324 + 112 – 117 = 1808 nickels x ($1.00/20 nickels) = $90.40. Choice A is correct.

5. To solve, we must calculate the total number of cats in the cattery, which is 85 + 411 + 103 = 599 cats. Then, we must convert the amount of catnip to ounces, which is 88 lb x 16 oz/lb = 1408 oz.   Finally, we must divide the total amount of catnip evenly among the total number of cats, which is 1408 / 599 = 2.35 ounces. Choice A is correct.

6. First, we must calculate the total amount that Jennifer spent on the shirts, which is $14.50 x 6 = $87.00 spent. Then, we divide this amount by her hourly pay to determine the number of hours she must work to pay for the shirts: 87/5.85 = 14.87 hours. Choice E is correct.

7. To solve, we must calculate the amount of money that Carla pays in tolls to that amount that she receives in credits. Her tolls = 17 (3) = $51. During the same period, Carla gets back 12 (2) = $24. The difference is $51 - $24 = $27, which is a loss. Choice C is correct.

8. First, we must calculate the total number of minutes that Diane needs to complete her errands, which is 18 x 14 = 252 minutes, or 4.2 hours, which is 4 hours and 12 minutes. Therefore, Diane must leave home by 12:48 pm to complete the errands by 5:00 pm.   Choice D is correct.

9. To solve, we must first calculate the total number of times that Sheila wears the suit each year, which is 52 + 12 = 64. Then, we must calculate the total number of times that she needs to have it cleaned per year, which is 64/4 = 16. If the cost per cleaning is $8.00, then Sheila's annual cost of dry cleaning it will be (16)($8.00) = $128. Choice E is correct.

10. To solve, we must add the amounts that Eve will spend at the store, which are $3.25 + 4.89 + 2.89 + 3.19 + 2(0.89) + 3. 50 = $19.50. Choice D is correct. There were several traps in this question, though. First, the test writers offer two numbers for the cost of root beer ($3.59 vs $3.19). The $3.59 figure is extraneous information that was included to confuse you – it is not part of the calculation. Additionally, the cost of gum must be doubled because

Eve is buying to packs, rather than one. Needless to say, the incorrect answer choices include the totals that you would have gotten if you had made these common mistakes.

11. First, we must convert the weight of the package from pounds to ounces. In this case, 0.75 pounds X (16 ounces/1 pound) = 12 ounces. The total cost is $0.55 for the first ounce and $0.34 for the 11 additional ounces, or 55 + 11 (34) = $4.29 total cost to mail a 12-ounce package. Choice D is correct.

12. If the alarm rings five times every ten minutes, then it rings 5(6) times, or 30, times per hour. On a ten-hour shift, it will ring 5(6)(10) times, or 300 times. Choice B is correct.

13. The problem asks us to calculate the difference between the amount of money raised by Donna and David. Eleven sponsors paid $5 for each mile that Donna ran. Since she ran six miles, Donna raised (11)(5)(6) = $330. In David's case 15 sponsors paid $3 for each mile. Since he ran five miles, David raised (15)(3)(5) = $225. Therefore, Donna raised $105 more than David. Choice A is correct.

14. The cost of repairs = Total cost of parts + Total cost of labor. The total for the parts is $350 + $150 + $25 = $525. The total cost for labor = ($45) (3.5) = $157.50. The total cost to fix the car is $525 + $157.50 = $682.50, or Choice C.

15. To solve, we just determine the difference in monthly payments. 1850/6 = $308.33 per month. 1850/15 = $123.33 per month. 308.33 – 123.33 = $185 difference. Choice C is correct.

16. To answer, simply divide the total amount of sales by the cost per stamp: $2,313,716.10/0.40 = 5,643,210. Choice D is correct.

17. 240 miles/30 miles per gallon x $2.85 per gallon = $22.80. Choice A is correct.

18. Short-term parking for 6 hours costs $1.00 + 4(0.50) = $3.00. Long-term parking costs $7.00, which is $4.00 more. Choice C is correct.

19. The total charge ($550) for the truck was based on the number of days Joe rented it plus the cost per mile.

$550 = ($50 per day)(5 days) + (600 miles)(X per mile)
600x = 300
X = 0.50 or 50 cents per mile . Choice C is correct.

20. As always, the fastest way to solve this problem is to substitute numbers for the variables. Then, we can convert the relationship back to letters. Let's say M = 200 and N = 500. Therefore, (M – 180) = 20.

When Carrie sold the coins, she reduced her collection by the following amount: 500 – (M – 180) = 500 – M + 180. Converting this back to letters, she had N – M + 180 coins left. Choice C is correct.

21. This problem is relatively straightforward, but it requires multiple steps to solve. And, as you probably suspect, the more calculations you are asked to make, the greater the likelihood that you will make a mistake – or fall into a common trap. First, we must examine the information we have been given – and what we are being asked. Then, we can map out the fastest and simplest strategy to solve it.

In this problem, we know the total revenue, which is based on the sale of two products, a gold hoop earring and a bronze cross earring. We need to know how many TOTAL pairs of earrings were sold.

First, we must determine the amount of the total revenue came from the gold hoop. In this case, the vendor sold 600 pairs of gold earrings at $20 per pair, for a total of $12,000. Therefore, the rest of the $36,000 in sales – which is $24,000 – came from the sale of the bronze cross earrings.

Since the bronze cross earrings sold for $12 per pair, we can simply divide to determine the number of pairs that were sold: $24,000/$12 = 2000 pairs of bronze cross earrings.

Finally, the TOTAL number of pairs sold on Sunday was the sum of the two types: 600 pairs of good hoop earrings + 2000 pairs of bronze cross earrings= 2600 total pairs. Choice D is correct.

22. The easiest way to solve this problem is to try the individual answer choices. When we do, we find that Choice E (7/8) is correct. Each bounce is 7/8 the height of the previous one.

Fifth bounce 897 feet
Fourth bounce: 1,025 feet
Third bounce: 1,172 feet.
Second bounce: 1,340 feet
First Bounce: 1,531 feet
Original height: 1,750 feet

23. The trick to answering this question correctly is to avoid counting the kisses twice. If we number the guests 1 - 12, we can summarize the kissing as follows:

Guest 1 kisses 2, 3, 4, 5, 6, 7, 8, 9, 10, 11, and 12 (11 kisses)
Guest 2 kisses 3, 4, 5, 6, 7, 8 9, 10, 11, and 12 (10 kisses)
Guest 3 kisses 4, 5, 6, 7 ,8 ,9, 10, 11, and 12 (9 kisses)
Guest 4 kisses 5, 6, 7, 8, 9, 10, 11, and 12 (8 kisses)
Guest 5 kisses 6, 7, 8, 9, 10, 11, and 12 (7 kisses)
Guest 6 kisses 7, 8, 9, 10, 11, and 12 (6 kisses)
Guest 7 kisses 8, 9, 10, 11, and 12 (5 kisses)
Guest 8 kisses 9, 10, 11, and 12 (4 kisses)
Guest 9 kisses 10, 11, and 12 (3 kisses)
Guest 10 kisses 11 and 12 (2 kisses)
Guest 11 kisses 12 (1 kiss)

Thus, the total number of kisses is 11 + 10 + 9 + 8 + 7 + 6 + 5 + 4 + 3 + 2 + 1 = 66. Choice C is correct.

24. In this case, we must pay careful attention to what we are being asked, which is to calculate each girl's share of the profits, which is the net sales price less the expenses.

First, we must calculate the total amount of money that they invested in the house, which is $395,000 + $105,500 = $500,500. Second, we must determine the net sales price, which is $675,000 minus a 7% sales commission: (675,000)(0.93) = $627,750.

Third, we must determine the profit on the transaction, which is $627,750 - $500,500 = $127,250. Finally, we must divide this value by 4 to determine each girl's individual share, which is $31,812.50. Choice B is correct.

25. To solve this problem, let's assume that Cashier 1 ends her shift with $100. Then, we know that Cashier 2 and Cashier 3 end their shifts with $78 and $70 in their cash drawers, respectively. We can now work backwards to determine how much money each cashier had at the beginning of the shift.

C 1	C 2	C 3	
100	78	70	End of shift; C1 has $22 more than C2 and $30 more than C3
115	63	70	During the shift, C1 gave $15 to C2; let's reverse it
115	75	58	During the shift, C 2 gave C3 $12; let's reverse that
115	75	58	The amount of money each Cashier had at the beginning of the shift

In both cases, we conclude that Cashier 1 initially had $30 more than Cashier 2 and $47 more than Cashier 3. Choice E is correct.

Chapter 3: Divisibility and Remainders

For most students, the concept of a remainder is fairly simple; it is the number "left over" when a quantity is not evenly divisible by another. In recent years, the SAT, GRE, and GMAT have made a specific point of testing student's knowledge of divisibility and remainders with needlessly complicated word problems. For that reason, we think it is sufficiently important to devote an entire chapter to these popular types of questions.

Example 1. Divisibility

How many positive integers less than 95 are evenly divisible by 10, 6 and 5?

    a. 0
    b. 1
    c. 2
    d. 3
    e. 4

Solution: The best way to tackle it is to consider each divisor separately, beginning with the largest one (in this case, 10):

The positive integers less than 95 that are evenly divisible by 10 are 90, 80, 70, 60, 60, 40, 30, 20, and 10

Next, eliminate those that are NOT divisible by the next largest divisor, which is 6. When we do, we are left with 90, 60, and 30.

Finally, eliminate any of the remaining numbers that are NOT divisible by 5. In this case, 90, 60, and 30 are all divisible by 5. Hence, there are 3 positive integers that are evenly divisible by 10, 6, and 5. Choice D is correct.

Example 2. Remainders

Which of the following is the smallest integer that leaves a remainder of 3 when divided by 7?

    a. 14
    b. 43
    c. 50
    d. 87
    e. 99

Solution: For most remainder problems, the fastest way to solve them is to examine the answer choices in the order they are presented. In this case, the problem asks us to find the smallest integer, so we will start with Choice A, which is the smallest answer choice.

We will divide the answer choice (14) by 7 and see if it leaves a remainder of 3. If so, we have our answer. If not, we will check all of the answer choices until we find the correct one. In this case:

14: $14/7 = 2$. No remainder
43: $43/7 = 6\text{-}1/7$.
50: $50/7 = 7\text{-}1/7$
87: $87/7 = \textbf{12-3/7}$.

Thus, the correct answer is Choice D.

Example 3: Divisibility w/ Remainders

What is the least positive integer that is divisible by both 2 and 5 and leaves a remainder of 2 when divided by 6?

    a.   8
    b.   14
    c.   20
    d.   50
    e.   62

Solution: There are actually several traps in this seemingly easy question. First, the words *least positive integer* seem to imply that the answer will be the smallest of the answer choices, which is rarely the case. Likewise, if the question asks you to find the greatest or maximum value of something, the correct answer will rarely be the largest answer choice presented. It is simply a ploy that the test writers use to try to tempt the students who are guessing.

The second trap is the inclusion of an answer choice that meets *some* of the requirements of the question, but not all of them. Choices A and B are not divisible by 5, but they *do* have a remainder of 2 when they are divided by 6. Choice D is a popular choice, because it DOES meet all of the requirements, but it is not the *least* positive integer that does so.

Our advice for questions like this is to attack the two conditions separately. First, eliminate answer choices that are not evenly divisible by 2 and 5. They are obviously wrong, because they violate the first condition in the problem. Then, starting with the *smallest* answer choice (because the question asks for the *least* positive integer), test the remaining answers until you find one that fits. Stop there; the first answer that fits is the correct choice. In this case, the correct answer is Choice C, or 20.

Example 4. Convoluted Problems w/ Prime Numbers

What is the sum of the prime numbers between 30 and 50?

    a.   87
    b.   131
    c.   168
    d.   199
    e.   232

Solution: To us, this problem is the definition of tedium; it's only purpose is to slow you down, make you review the definition of prime numbers, and add. But that's what you need to do to ace a standardized test, so here goes. A prime number is evenly divisible only by itself and one. For the range of numbers between 30 and 50, the following are prime: 31, 37, 41, 43, and 47. Their sum is 199. Choice D is correct.

Sample Word Problems: Divisibility and Remainders: EASY - MODERATE

1. How many positive integers less than 75 are evenly divisible by 3, 5 and 6?

        a.   1
        b.   2
        c.   3
        d.   4
        e.   5

2. What is the largest integer that will divide evenly into 97 and 117?

        a.   1
        b.   7
        c.   9
        d.   11
        e.   13

3. Which of the following is the smallest integer that leaves a remainder of 1 when divided by 8?

        a.   131
        b.   137
        c.   145
        d.   153
        e.   168

4. What is the least positive integer that is divisible by both 2 and 9 and leaves a remainder of 4 when divided by 5?

        a.   18
        b.   36
        c.   45
        d.   49
        e.   54

5. What is the largest integer that will divide evenly into 57 and 399?

        a.   7
        b.   13
        c.   17
        d.   19
        e.   21

6. How many positive integers less than 100 are evenly divisible by 4, 6, 8 and 12?

        a.   1
        b.   2
        c.   3
        d.   4
        e.   5

7. What is the product of the prime numbers between 10 and 20?

        a.   60
        b.   3,536
        c.   4,199
        d.   46,189
        e.   508,079

8. If 5,625 is divided by 55, what is the remainder?

        a.   5
        b.   10
        c.   15
        d.   25
        e.   30

9. When 102 is divided by x, the remainder is 2. What is the smallest positive integer value of x?

    a. 4
    b. 6
    c. 8
    d. 10
    e. 20

10. If 86,868,686 is divided by 6,868, what is the remainder?

    a. 2222
    b. 3434
    c. 4343
    d. 6832
    e. 12648

11. What is the sum of the largest 5 prime numbers that are less than 100?

    a. 393
    b. 413
    c. 419
    d. 443
    e. 449

Sample Word Problems: Divisibility and Remainders: AS HARD AS IT GETS

12. A number (x) is divisible by 2, 3, and 5.   What is the smallest three-digit number that is divisible by 2, 3, 5, and 3x?

    a. 120
    b. 150
    c. 180
    d. 210
    e. 300

13. When x is divided by 17, the remainder is 9. What is the remainder when 5x is divided by 17?

    a. 3
    b. 7
    c. 9
    d. 11
    e. 13

14. When 35 is divided by the positive integer P, the remainder is 2. For how many different values of P is this true?

    a. 1
    b. 2
    c. 3
    d. 4
    e. 5

15. What is the least positive three-digit integer that is divisible by both 5 and 11 and leaves a remainder of 3 when divided by 6?

      a.   55
      b.   100
      c.   110
      d.   150
      e.   165

Answer Key for Word Problems: Divisibility and Remainders

1. The question asks us to determine how positive integers less than 75 are divisible by 3, 5 and 6. First, we will list the integers that are evenly divisible by our largest number, which is 6: 6, 12, 18, 24, 30, 36, 42, 48, 54, 60, 66, 72. (Note: Because they are all multiples of 6, they are also divisible by 3.)

In this group, we must then select the numbers that are ALSO evenly divisible by 5, which are 30 and 60. Our correct answer is Choice B. There are two positive integers less than 75 that are divisible by 3, 5, and 6.

2. The fastest way to solve this problem is to try each of the answer choices. When we do, we discover that the largest one that divides evenly into 63 and 117 is 9. Choice C is correct.

3. The easiest way to solve this problem is to try the answer choices in the order they are presented. When we do, we discover that $137 = 8(17) + 1$. Choice B is correct.

4. To solve this problem, we must check our answer choices against both criteria in the problem: they must 1) be divisible by 2 and 3 AND 2) they must leave a remainder of 4 when they are divided by 5. Choices C and D are not divisible by 2, so we do not need to examine them further. Of the remaining choices, only Choice E (54) meets both criteria. .

5. The easiest way to solve this problem is to try each answer choice. The largest one that divides evenly into 57 and 399 is 19, which is Choice D.

6. The question asks us to determine how positive integers less than 100 are evenly divisible by 4, 6, 8, and 12. First, we will list the integers that are evenly divisible by our largest number, which is 12: 12, 24, 36, 48, 60, 72, 84, and 96. (Note: Because they are all multiples of 12, these numbers are also evenly divisible by 6.)

Next, we eliminate numbers from this group that are NOT evenly divisible by 8, which leaves us with 24, 48, 72, and 96. (Note: Because they are all multiples of 8, they are also evenly divisible by 4.)

Thus, there are 4 positive integers that meet the criterion: they are 24, 48, 72, and 96. Choice D is correct.

7. The prime numbers between 10 and 20 are 11, 13, 17, and 19. Their product is $(11)(13)(17)(19) = 46,189$. Choice D is correct.

8. $55 \times 102 = 5610$. Thus, the remainder is 15. Choice C is correct.

9. The fastest way to solve this problem is to try the answer choices. When we do, we discover that Choice D is correct. 102/10 = 10 with a remainder of 2.

10. We can solve this problem by dividing the two quantities:

86868686/6868 = 12648.323529. 0.323529 x 6868 = 2222. Choice A is correct.

To check: 12648 x 6,868 =   86866464 + 2222

11. To solve, we must simply count back from 100 and add together the 5 largest prime numbers:

90 – 100: prime numbers include 97
80 – 90: prime numbers include 87, 83,
70 - 80: prime numbers include 79, 73, and 71

The largest prime numbers less than 100 are therefore 97 + 87 + 83 + 79 + 73 = **419**. Choice C is correct.

12. The first step is to find the smallest number that is evenly divisible by 2, 3, and 5, which is 30. Thus 30 = x. Our second step is to find the smallest three-digit number that is divisible by 2, 3, 5, and 90, which is 3x. The fastest way is to check the answer choices in order. When we do, we discover that Choice C, 180, is correct.

13. To solve this problem, simply choose a number that meets the original condition: it leaves a remainder of 9 when it is divided by 17. In this case, the number **26** meets the condition.

Next, let's submit the number 26 to the second condition and see what happens. (26)(5)/17 = 130.

130 = (17)(7) + 11. 130 leaves a remainder of 11 when it is divided by 17. Choice D is correct.

14. To solve, we will list the possibilities that meet the criterion in the problem:

35/3 = 11, with a remainder of 2
35/11 = 3, with a remainder of 2

Thus, there are 2 values of P for which the criterion holds.

15. To solve this problem, we must start by listing the three-digit multiples of 11. When we reach one that is *also* a multiple of 5, we can check to see if it meets the second criterion in the problem.

110 is the first three-digit multiple of both 5 and 11. But, it leaves a remainder of 2 when divided by 6.

Next, we must check 165, which meets both criteria; it is a multiple of both 5 and 11. It leaves a remainder of 3 when divided by 6. (27 x 6 = 162. 162 + 3 = 165.) Hence, the correct answer is 165, which is Choice E.

Chapter 4: Fractions and Decimals

A fraction is simply a mathematical expression in which one number is divided by another number (2/3, 5/6, and 77/5 are all fractions).

On a practical basis, a fraction is a way to express division (if $10.00 is divided evenly by 5 people, they will each receive 10/5, or $2.00 dollars).

Likewise, fractions can be used to compare two quantities (if a class contains 50 students, of which 17 are male and 33 are female, then the fraction 17/50 compares the number of *male students* in the class to the *total number* of students).

If we divide the numerator of a fraction by the denominator and present the result in its simplest form, we have a **decimal** (1/10 = 0.1, 2/5 = 0.4, 65/100 = 0.65).

Typically, the SAT will include several word problems to test your ability to work with fractions and decimals in a practical manner. You will be expected to add, subtract, multiply, divide, and *simply* them quickly and accurately. Additionally, many problems will require you to convert fractions to decimals and vice versa.

The same rules hold true for fraction and decimal problems as for other types of word problems:

- Read the question quickly and carefully.
- Identify what you are being asked.
- Eliminate all extraneous information.
- Organize your facts.
- Decide what calculations you need to perform.
- Do them in the correct order.
- Check your answer (including the units) to ensure that it makes sense.

Word Problems with Fractions & Decimals: EASY - MODERATE

1. A home improvement store bought 300 generators before a major hurricane and sold 240 of them in a single day. What fraction of the 300 generators did not sell?

        a.   1/6
        b.   1/5
        c.   1/4
        d.   1/3
        e.   2/5

2. Gina decides to save money by making her bridal outfit from scratch.   She buys 5 yards of a beautiful silk fabric that costs $35 per yard. After studying her pattern, Gina concludes that she will need 6/4 yards of the fabric for her dress, 5/2 yards for her jacket, and 1/3 yard for her veil. How many yards of material will Grace have left over?

        a.   2/5
        b.   1/2
        c.   2/3
        d.   1
        e.   5/2

3. Tim took 96 minutes to repair the engine of a customer's car. What fraction of an 8-hour work day does this represent?

    a. 1/12
    b. 1/8
    c. 1/6
    d. 1/5
    e. 3/16

4. Doris left her $600,000 in equal installments to her three sons. A week after Doris's death, one of her sons died before he could receive his inheritance. Instead, his portion of Doris's estate was divided equally among the man's four daughters. What fraction of Doris's original estate did each of the four granddaughters receive?

    a. 1/12
    b. 1/8
    c. 1/6
    d. 1/5
    e. 1/4

5. Ken listed his car for sale on EBay for $8,000 but did not receive any bids. Later, he re-listed it for $6,400. What fraction of the original price does this represent?

    a. 2/3
    b. 3/4
    c. 4/5
    d. 5/6
    e. 7/8

6. Gayle arranged four types of stones in a decorative rock garden. She used 5- ¼ pounds of gray stones, 12 -1/4 pounds of red stones, 25- 1/5 pounds of white stones and 44-1/2 pounds of blue stones. What was the total weight of the stones in the rock garden?

    a. 78- 3/5 pounds
    b. 78 – 1/5 pounds
    c. 86- 3/5 pounds
    d. 87 – 1/5 pounds
    e. 88 – 1/5 pounds

7. At the beginning of her shift, Kate had 60-½ dozen cans of Pepsi. At the end of her shift, 54-1/3 dozen cans remained. How many cans of Pepsi did Kate sell during her shift?

    a. 54
    b. 74
    c. 648
    d. 652
    e. 726

8. Brad decided to fill the gas cans for three of his elderly neighbors: Jim, Bill and Marge. If Jim needs 4 ½ gallons of gas, Bill needs 6 -2/5 gallons, and Marge needs 3 gallons, how much will Brad have to spend to fill all three gas cans, assuming that gas costs $3.95 per gallon?

    a. $13.90
    b. $48.91
    c. $51.86
    d. $54.91
    e. $58.86

9. A seamstress bought a beautiful bolt of silk material to use to make wedding dresses. If the bolt contains 55 yards of material and each dress requires 6-1/5 yards, how many dresses can the seamstress make from a single bolt of the material?

      a.   7
      b.   8
      c.   9
      d.   10
      e.   11

10. How many quarters of a yard are in 75/5 yards?

      a.   60
      b.   125
      c.   150
      d.   175
      e.   375

11. A shopkeeper reduced the price of a refrigerator from $1000 to $500. A week later, he reduced the sales price by an additional 15%. What was the new price for the refrigerator?

      a. $350
      b. $375
      c. $400
      d. $425
      e. $450

12. Eighteen seconds is what fraction of eighteen minutes?

      a.   1/6
      b.   1/10
      c.   1/18
      d.   1/30
      e.   1/60

13. Sara's CD collection includes 235 titles. Of these, 125 are classic rock, 25 are punk and 38 are rap. The remaining CDs are gospel recordings. What fractional part of Sara's CD collection is gospel music?

      a.   1/6
      b.   1/5
      c.   1/4
      d.   2/5
      e.   3/8

14. A computer science curriculum includes 8 courses on hardware and 4 courses on software. The remaining ¼ of the courses are on web design. What fraction of the courses is devoted to software?

      a.   1/4
      b.   1/3
      c.   2/5
      d.   1/2
      e.   5/8

15. At the end of a night, a waitress calculates the total amount of tip money to be $346.84. After giving the busboy 5% of the total amount, she must divide the remainder into five equal shares and place *two* of those shares into an envelope. How much will the waitress place in the envelope?

    a. $62.43
    b. $65.90
    c. $124.86
    d. $131.80
    e. $138.74

16. After making preserves with her grandmother, Gayle had enough to fill 28.5 jars. If each full jar contained 23.1 oz, how many total pounds of preserves did Gayle have?

    a. 32
    b. 41
    c. 46
    d. 56
    e. 65

17. Three sisters took their mother for a nice dinner on Mother's Day. The total for four meals was $185.30. If the girls plan to leave a 20% tip and split the bill three ways, what dollar amount will each sister owe?

    a. $46.32
    b. $55.59
    c. $61.76
    d. $68.32
    e. $74.12

18. How many 6 ounce rib eye steaks are in a carton of steaks that weighs 48 pounds? (Assume that all of the steaks are rib eye and that they account for the total weight of the box)

    a. 96
    b. 108
    c. 128
    d. 146
    e. 196

19. To make enough brownies for a Girl Scout troop, Mrs. Wilson must mix 30 pounds of batter. Her tiny mixer at home, however, can only handle batches of 24 ounces. How many times will Mrs. Wilson have to run her mixer to produce the entire 30 pounds of brownie batter?

    a. 6
    b. 15
    c. 16
    d. 20
    e. 24

20. Joe's monthly budget includes $1,200 for rent, $400 for his car payment, $150 for insurance, $250 for utilities, and $200 for groceries. Assuming that Joe' monthly take-home pay is $3,300, what fraction of it is left for discretionary spending?

    a. 1/5
    b. 1/4
    c. 1/3
    d. 2/5
    e. 2/3

Word Problems with Fractions & Decimals: AS HARD AS IT GETS

21. The denominator of a fraction is three times as large as the numerator. If 5 is added to both the numerator and denominator, the value of the fraction is ¾. What was the numerator of the original fraction?

        a.   1
        b.   2
        c.   3
        d.   4
        e.   5

22. For the repeating decimal 0.04321043210432104321....., what is the 49th digit to the right of the decimal point?

        a.   0
        b.   1
        c.   2
        d.   3
        e.   4

23. The number of female doctors at Mercy Hospital is twelve less than three times the number of male doctors. Also, eight fewer than one-quarter of the doctors at the hospital are surgeons. If 50 of the doctors are surgeons, how many of the doctors are female?

        a.   24
        b.   60
        c.   61
        d.   171
        e.   183

24. A race horse is owned by two accountants and an attorney, each of whom has an equal share. If one of the accountants sells one-third of his share to the attorney, and the other accountant keeps one-half of his share and sells the rest to the attorney, what fraction of the race horse will the attorney own?

        a.   1/6
        b.   1/9
        c.   2/9
        d.   11/18
        e.   11/36

25. If $0.00C = S^{-1}$, $0.000D = T^{-1}$, and $E = CD$, what is the value of $(ST)^{-1}$ (assuming that S, T, C, D, and E are all integers)?

        a. $E \times 10^{-3}$
        b. $E \times 10^{-4}$
        c. $E \times 10^{-5}$
        d. $E \times 10^{-6}$
        e. It cannot be determined from the information given.

Answer Key: Word Problems with Fractions & Decimals

1. The home improvement store sold 240/300 generators, which means that (300 – 240)/300, or 60/300 did not sell. 60/300 can be reduced to **1/5**. Choice B is correct.

2. First, we must determine how much fabric Gina will need to sew her entire outfit, which is 6/4 + 5/2 + 1/3 yards. To add these fractions together, they must all have the same denominator. In this case, the least common denominator (which is evenly divisible by 2, 3, and 4) is 12, which makes our equation:

18/12 + 30/12 + 4/12 = 52/12 = 4- 4/12 yards = 4 -1/3 yards.   Now, we must determine how many yards of fabric Gina will have left over. If she has purchased 5 yards of the fabric, she will have 5 – 4- 1/3 = **2/3** yards left over. Choice C is correct.

As far as the price of the fabric ($35 per yard), you didn't need to know it. It's completely extraneous information.

3. An 8-hour work day contains 8(60) = 480 minutes. If Tim took 96 minutes to repair the engine, then we can represent the fraction of the day he used as 96/480 = **1/5**. Choice D is correct.

4. Doris's sons each inherited 1/3 of her $600,000 estate, or $200,000. One of the $200,000 shares was subsequently divided among one of the son's four daughters, who each received $200,000/4 or $50,000. The question asks us to determine what fraction of the *original estate* each girl received, which is $50,000/$600,000 = **1/12**. Choice A is correct.

5. If the original price was $8,000 and the new price is $6,400, then the relationship can be represented by $6,400/$8,000 = 8/10 = **4/5**. Choice C is correct.

6. To solve, we must add the total weights of the stones: 5-1/4 + 12-1/4 + 25-1/5 + 44-1/2. First, we will convert the mixed number to fractions, which become 21/4 + 49/4 + 126/5 + 89/2. Second, we must add these fractions together, which requires them to have the same denominator. In this case, the least common denominator (which is evenly divisible by 2, 4, and 5) is 60, which makes our equation: 315/60 + 735/60 + 1512/60 + 2670/60 = 5232/60 = 87-12/60 = **87-1/5 pounds**. Choice D is correct.

Alternatively, you can convert the numbers to decimals and add. (5.25 + 12.25 + 25.2 + 44.5 = 87.2 = 87-1/5)

7. To solve this problem, we simply need to subtract the number of remaining cans of Pepsi (54-1/3 dozen) from the original number of cans (60-1/2 dozen). First, we must convert each value from "dozens" to single cans. 60-1/2 dozen = (60)(12) + (1/2)(12) = 720 + 6 = 726. 54-1/3 dozen = (54)(12) + (1/3)(12) = 648 + 4 = 652. Finally, we must subtract the remaining cans from the original number to determine the number of cans sold: 726 – 652 = **74 cans sold**. Choice B is correct.

8. To solve, we must first add the individual gallons of gas that each person needs: 4-1/2 + 6-2/5 + 3-0/2. To do so, we will convert the mixed number to fractions, which become 9/2 + 32/5 + 6/2. Second, we must add these fractions together, which requires them to have the same denominator. In this case, the least common denominator (which is evenly divisible by 2 and 5) is 10, which makes our equation: 45/10 + 64/10 + 30/10 = 139/10 = 13.90 gallons. Finally, we must multiply the number of gallons Brad needs by the price per gallon of gas: (13.90 gallons)($3.95 per gallon) = **$54.91**. Choice D is correct.

9. To answer this question, we must divide the total amount of material (55 yards) by the quantity needed to make a single dress (6-1/5 yards).   When we do, we find that the seamstress has enough material to make 8 =87/100 dresses. Since she cannot sell a fraction of a dress, we must round our answer down to **8 dresses**. Choice B is correct.

10.75/5 yards is equal to 15 yards. Each yard is equal to 4 quarters of a yard. Therefore, the number of quarter yards in 75/5 yards is (15)(4) = **60.**   Choice A is correct.

11. The trick to this question is to ignore the initial reduction from $1000 to $500, which is extraneous information. What we are being asked to determine is a 15% reduction of a refrigerator that is marked at $500. Our answer is 500 - (500)(0.15) = 500 – 75 = **$425.** Choice D is correct.

12. Eighteen minutes = (60)(18) = 1080 seconds. 18 /1080 = **1/60.** Choice E is correct.

13. In this case, we are given the total number of CDs (235), which is divided into four smaller categories: classic rock (125), punk (25), rap (38), and gospel music (unknown number of CDs). We are asked to find the *fractional part* of the collection that is gospel.

To solve, we must first identify the number of CDs that are gospel. We do this by subtracting the other types of CDs from the total number in Sara's collection: 235 – 125 – 25 – 38 = 47. Then, we must convert this number into a fraction which represents the number of gospel CDs to the total number of CDs, which is 47 / 235. Finally, we must reduce this fraction to its lowest terms, which is **1/5.** Choice B is correct.

14. 12 courses (8 + 4) comprise ¾ of the curriculum, which means that there are 16 total courses. Of these, 4, or **1/4,** are on software. Choice A is correct.

15. 346.84 – 17.34 = 329.50 / 5 = 65.90 x 2 = **$131.80.** Choice D is correct.

16. 28.5 x 23.1 = 658.35/16 = **41.14** pounds. Choice B is correct.

17. First, we must add the amount of the tip to the bill: $185.30 x 0.2 = $37.06. Total cost = $222.36. Each share is 222.36 / 3 = **$74.12.** Choice E is correct.

18. We can solve this using a proportion. 1 steak / 6 oz = x steaks / 768 oz, so x = **128.** Choice C is correct.

19. We can solve this using a proportion. 1 batch / 24 oz = x batches / 480 oz, so x = **20** times. Choice D is correct.

20. Total expenses = 1200 + 400 + 150 + 250 + 200 = 2200. 2200/3300 = 2/3, which leaves **1/3** for discretionary spending. Choice C is correct.

21. This problem is easy to solve if you stay calm, read carefully, and set up your equation correctly. First, let x be the original numerator. The original fraction is therefore x/3x. The new fraction is (x + 5)/(3x + 5), which equals ¾. We must solve the equation for x. When we cross-multiply, we get: 4x + 20 = 9x + 15, or x = **1.** Choice A is correct.

22. The repeating pattern is 04321, which includes 5 digits. The 49th digit is therefore the fourth digit in the series, which is **2,** or Choice C.

23. This problem tests your knowledge o f both fractions and algebraic equations. To solve, we must first assign our variables.

X = # of males doctors
3x - 12 = female doctors
Total doctors = x + 3x – 12

1/4(x + 3x - 12) – 8 = 50
X + 3x – 12 – 32 = 200
4x = 244
X= 61 male doctors
3x – 12 = 3(61) – 12 = **171** female doctors. Choice D is correct.

24. First, let's draw a simple diagram of the original ownership structure:

Accountant 1	Accountant 2	Attorney
1/3	1/3	1/3

Next, we will document the changes in ownership with each transaction. First, one of the accountants sells one-third of his 1/3 share to the attorney, which has the following effect:

Accountant 1	Accountant 2	Attorney
2/9	3/9	4/9

Next, the other accountant sells the attorney one-half of his 1/3 share, but keeps the other ½, which has the following effect:

Accountant 1	Accountant 2	Attorney
2/9	1/6	11/18

At this point, the attorney owns **11/18** of the race horse, while the two accountants own the remaining 7/18. Choice D is correct.

25. The easiest way to solve this problem is to substitute actual numbers for the variables. Let's assume that S = 200 and T = 5000. If we plug these numbers into the formulas given, we can calculate C and D:

1/200 = 0.005. C = 5
1/5000 = 0.0002. D = 2

Now, we can calculate **1/ST**, which is 1/(200)(5000) = (0.005)(0.0002) = **0.000001**

At first blush, it may seem that answer Choice C (E x 10^{-5}) is correct, because it contains the "right" number of decimal places. And it *would* be correct if E was any digit less than 10. But E = CD = 10, which makes Choice D (E x 10^{-6}) the correct answer. (If we substitute 10 for E, 0.000000E = 0.000001.)

Chapter 5: Percent

By definition, the word percent means "part of 100." On a practical basis, 20% means 20 out of 100, or 20/100, or 0.20. In SAT, GRE and GMAT word problems, students will need to convert numbers from fractions and decimals to percent (and vice versa). You will also be expected to use percents in practical situations, such as taxes, sales commissions, and price increases (and reductions). A brief review:

To change a **percent to a decimal**, divide by 100 (move the decimal point two places to the left):

54% = 0.54
3% = 0.03
189% = 1.89

To change a **decimal to a percent**, multiply the number by 100 (move the decimal point two places to the right) and add the % sign:

0.67 = 67%
3.45 = 345%
0.0034 = 0.34%

To change a **percent to a fraction**, remove the % sign and divide by 100:

80% = 80/100 = 4/5
400% = 400/100 = 4
0.6% = 0.6/100 = 6/1000 = 3/500

To change a **fraction to a percent**, multiply by 100 and add the % sign:

3/5 = 300/5 = 60%
8/2 = 800/2 = 400%
0.5/10 = 50/10 = 5%

Formula for Percent

The SAT will also include word problems that use percentages in practical situations. In most cases, they can easily be solved using the standard formula: **Percent = Base x Rate**

Base vs. Percent

For many students, the hardest part of these problems is determining which number is the base, and which number is the percent. As a general rule, the base is the number that appears FIRST in the sequence of events. It is the:

Cost of an item before the retailer marks it up or adds sales tax
Price of an item before the retailer offers a discount
Original number you have BEFORE any change occurs

In contrast, the percentage is a number that is *added to (or subtracted from)* the base, depending on what is happening in the problem. It is the amount tax, discount, or markup that is added to (or subtracted from) a price

Thankfully, there is an easy way to keep the two values straight. In word problems, the **percent** will be associated with the verb *is/are* and the **base** will be associated with the word *of*.

Example 1: In the sentence, "Half *of* the girls *are* Juniors," the girls are the **base** and the Juniors are the **percent**.

Example 2: In the sentence, "Fifteen is half of thirty," thirty is the **base** and fifteen is the **percent**.

Before you try our practice problems, we'd like to present the most common tricks and pitfalls you are likely to see on the SAT, GRE or GMAT (in some way, shape, or form, the test writers WILL include these concepts).

Example 1: Using the Basic Percent Formula

If Joe buys a car for $30,600 and the sales tax rate in his state is 6%, what is the total price he will pay for the car?

    a. $1800
    b. $1836
    c. $31,836
    d. $32,436
    e. $32,836

Solution: This is as easy as percent problems get on standardized tests. To solve it, we simply plug the correct values into the percent formula. In this case, the Base is $30,600 and the Rate is 6%, so our equation becomes:

Percent = Base X Rate
Percent = ($30,600)(0.06) = $1,836 tax.

Joe's total cost for the car will therefore be $30,600 + $1,836 = $32,436. Choice D is correct.

Example 2: Paying Attention to the Details

The most common way that the test writers can complicate seemingly "easy" questions is by changing a single word, which totally changes what you are being asked. If you are in a hurry when you reach the question, or if you simply misread it, you will likely get the wrong answer. Even worse, you will *think* you got it right, because the answer you calculated shows up as one of the five answer choices. Note the two examples below, which are typical percent problems.

Example 1: What positive integer is 40% less than 15,600?

    a.   4,680
    b.   6,240
    c.   6,864
    d.   8,680
    e.   9,360

Example 2: What positive integer is 40% of 15,600?

    a.   4,680
    b.   6,240
    c.   6,864
    d.   8,680
    e.   9,360

Solution: If you glanced quickly at these questions and didn't see the difference, then you fell into the trap. In Example 1, you must find the number that is 60% **of** 15,600, which is *40% less*. The correct answer is Choice E, or 9,360. Example 2, however, is asking you to find 40% **of** 15,600, which is 6,240, or Choice B.

On a mathematical basis, these questions are no-brainers. The trick is to read them carefully, to catch which calculation you must make. Under serious stress, even good students can fall into the trap.

Example 3: Finding the Original Whole

After a 65 percent increase, the student body at Brandywine College was 15,860. How many students were enrolled at the college before the increase?

    a.   5,551
    b.   7,920
    c.   9,612
    d.   10,309
    e.   21,411

Solution: There isn't anything terribly difficult about this question, IF you understand how to work with percentages. In this case, we can simply "convert" the information we are given into an easy and straightforward formula.

First, we must define our variable x as the unknown quantity, which is the original enrollment at the college. According to the question stem, the total number of students (15,860) is 65% higher than the original number. Hence, 15,860 = 1.65X. If we solve for x, we find that the original number of students was 15,860/1.65 = **9612**. Choice C is correct.

Alternatively, we can solve this problem using the basic equation Percent = Part X Whole. In this case, however, the unknown x is the Part, and the new enrollment (15,860) is the Whole. Our equation becomes: 165% = Part X 15,860. When we solve it, we find that the Part, which is the original number of students, is 9612.

Example 4: Multiple Increases or Decreases in %

A software company discounts its old version of web design software to 50% of its original price. Two months later, when the software has still not sold, the company lists it on eBay at a price that has been reduced by an additional 20%. By what overall percentage has the price been reduced?

    a.   55%
    b.   60%
    c.   70%
    d.   75%
    e.   80%

Solution: In this case, we are asked to calculate the *overall* % increase or % decrease of a price. In the final calculation for such problems, the correct denominator is the ORIGINAL whole, not the intermediate one. And, of course, the wrong answers you would get if you used the incorrect denominator will likely be included as answer choices.

The most common mistake for this question is to simply add the two % and assume that you have the answer (50% + 20% = 70%). Wrong!

Simply plugging in a few easy numbers will show us the error. Assume that the software originally cost $100. The first 50% discount reduces its price to $50. The second discount is 20% of $50, or $10, which reduces the price to $40. To calculate the *overall percentage* that the software has been reduced, we must use the original denominator of $100: $60 / $100 = 60%. Choice B is correct.

Example 5: When Prices Change in Opposite Directions

Susan purchased a new condo when she moved to Los Angeles. Two years later, after a devastating correction in the housing market, she sold it to her neighbor Nathan for 40% less than she originally paid for it. Nathan did a few quick fixes and re-sold the condo to Janice for 20% more than he paid Susan for it. The price that Janice paid for the condo was what percentage of the original price that Susan paid?

    a.   28%
    b.   40%
    c.   65%
    d.   72%
    e.   80%

Solution: The "trap" that many students fall into is simply subtracting 40% and adding back 20%, which leaves an overall loss of 20%. Accordingly, they choose Choice E – which is incorrect. For questions that deal with multiple changes in percentages, the denominators are different for each step. Why? The first change is a reduction of the original price; the second change is an increase of a smaller amount.

Here is the correct approach to the problem. Because the problem works with percentages, we will use 100 as the original price. (We are free to use any number, but since percentages are involved, 100 is the least confusing choice.)

If Susan paid $100 for her condo, then she sold it to Nathan for $60, which is 40% less. Nathan sold the condo to Janice for 20% more than what HE paid for it, which was $60. Nathan therefore sold the condo for $60 + (0.2)($60) =

$72. The question asked us to determine what percentage of Susan's original price Janet paid for the condo. In this case, the correct answer is 72/100, or 72%, which is Choice D.

To gain experience – and build your confidence – try the following work problems. Detailed explanations are included at the end of the chapter.

Word Problems: Percent: EASY - MODERATE

1. Before the prom, a local boutique sold 98 prom dresses from its original selection of 392. What percentage of the selection did NOT sell?

    a.   20%
    b.   25%
    c.   75%
    d.   80%
    e.   90%

2. A buffet table contains 7 entrees, 3 soups and 2 specialty salads. The remaining ¼ of the items are desserts. What percent of the items on the buffet table are specialty salads?

    a.   3.125%
    b.   6.25%
    c.   12.5%
    d.   16.67%
    e.   20%

3. Eight hundred people answered a newspaper ad to audition for American Idol. Forty percent of them were assigned Whitney Houston songs. Of this 40%, one-quarter of the people sang "I Will Always Love You." How many people sang "I Will Always Love You?"

    a.   40
    b.   60
    c.   80
    d.   120
    e.   160

4. A year ago, Julie had 62 recipes for her country cookbook. This year, she has 329 recipes. What percentage increase does this number represent?

    a.   4.306%
    b.   43.06%
    c.   430.6%
    d.   4306%
    e.   none of the above

5. If 110 of the 220 students in Algebra class are from Hawaii and 22 of the students are from Canada, what percentage of the students is from neither Hawaii nor Canada?

    a.   30%
    b.   35%
    c.   40%
    d.   45%
    e.   60%

6. Jason inherited $8 million from his paternal grandfather. Today, he placed the entire amount in account that earns 9 1/2% simple annual interest. Assuming that Jason leaves the money in the account and does not withdraw any of the interest, how much will he have (principal + interest) exactly one year from today?

    a. $8,000,760
    b. $8,007,600
    c. $8,076,000
    d. $8,760,000
    e. $8,950,000

7. A year ago, the local police issued 1432 speeding tickets at a particular intersection. This year, after decreasing their patrol in this area, they only issued 91 tickets at the same intersection. What percent decrease does this represent?

    a.   6.35%
    b.   9.36%
    c.   63.5%
    d.   93.65%
    e.   936.5%

8. A stock decreases in value by 20 percent. By what percent must the stock price increase to reach its former value?

    a.   20%
    b.   25%
    c.   30%
    d.   40%
    e.   50%

9. In reading a thermometer, a nurse mistakenly recorded a temperature of 97 degrees instead of 102 degrees. What was the percentage error (to the nearest hundredths of a percent)?

    a.   0.49%
    b.   0.51%
    c.   4.90%
    d.   5.00%
    e.   5.15%

10. If the 6% hotel tax on a room is $4.32, what was the total price of the room (including tax)?

    a. $70.32
    b. $72.00
    c. $76.00
    d. $76.32
    e. $78.00

11. Two individual price reductions of 10% and 15% are equal to a single price reduction of:

    a.   12.5%
    b.   20%
    c.   24.5%
    d.   25%
    e.   27.5%

12. A plasma television that costs $1650 is reduced in price by 50%. If the price is raised back to $1650, what % increase does this represent?

    a.   50%
    b.   75%
    c.   100%
    d.   150%
    e.   200%

13. A restaurant depletes its supply of mustard every 25 days. If its use increases by 75%, how many days would the same amount of mustard last?

    a.   6.25
    b.   12.5
    c.   14.3
    d.   43.75
    e.   75

14. In geometry class, 35% of the students are athletes and 15% of the athletes run track. What percentage of students in the geometry class are athletes who run track?

    a.   5.25%
    b.   10%
    c.   12.5%
    d.   20%
    e.   50%

15. Kathy earns a 25% commission on all jewelry sales in her department and a 15% commission on all luggage sales. If she sells $3,250 in jewelry and $5,175 in luggage in a given month, what will be the total amount of Kathy's commissions?

    a. $776.25
    b. $812.50
    c. $1263.75
    d. $1588.75
    e. $2106.25

16. A business executive and his client are charging their dinner tab on the executive's expense account. The company will only allow them to spend a total $50 for the meal. Assuming that they will pay 7% in sales tax for the meal and leave a 15% tip, what is the most their food can cost?

    a. $39.55
    b. $40.63
    c. $41.63
    d. $42.15
    e. $43.15

17. Barbie's salary is $720 per week after a 20% raise. Before Barbie's raise, her supervisor Connie's salary was 50% greater than Barbie's. If Barbie and Connie receive the same dollar amount raise, what is Connie's salary after the raise?

    a. $860
    b. $900
    c. $960
    d. $1020
    e. $1200

18. Jake earns a base salary of $700 per week plus a 15% commission on sales. In a week in which Jake sold $12,400 worth of merchandise, what was his total weekly pay (before taxes)?

    a. $824
    b. $1860
    c. $1940
    d. $2500
    e. $2560

19. After careful negotiations, the Zippy Insurance Company agreed to pay 75% of Chad's accident expenses, after deducting $100 in non-covered items and a $325 administrative fee. If Chad's expenses totaled $14,625, how much did he receive from Zippy Insurance?

    a. $10,650
    b. $10,950
    c. $11,650
    d. $11,960
    e. $12,650

20. In the past year, Karen's book collection increased from 114 to 328. What percentage increase does this number represent?

    a. 2.1%
    b. 2.8%
    c. 21.4%
    d. 28.8%
    e. 214%

Word Problems: Percent: AS HARD AS IT GETS

21. Sally receives a commission of W% on a sale of Z dollars. What is her commission?

    a. 1/WZ
    b. WZ
    c. W/Z
    d. WZ/100
    e. 100WZ

22. In a college lecture hall, 60% of the students have tattoos. In a second class that is twice the size of the first, 20% of the students have tattoos. What percent of both classes are students *without* tattoos?

    a. 30%
    b. 33-1/3%
    c. 40%
    d. 50%
    e. 66-2/3%

23. A group of eight friends celebrated New Year's Eve at their favorite restaurant. At the end of the evening, they paid a $40 tip to their server, which was 15% of the total bill. If the total cost of the evening (meal plus tip) was divided equally among the friends, what did each person pay?

    a. $28.33
    b. $33.33
    c. $35.33
    d. $38..33
    e. $40.33

24. Dave and Dina paid $365,000 for their first house. If they had waited, the sales price would have increased by 6% the first year, 8% the second year, and 4% the third year. What would Dave and Dina have paid for the house if they had waited and purchased it at the end of the third year?

    a. $386,900
    b. $416,100
    c. $417,852
    d. $430,700
    e. $434,566

25. For administrative purposes, a local university divides its activities among five separate colleges. According to the university charter, the College of Arts and Sciences is entitled to 80% of the university's office workers, while the remaining four colleges (Agriculture, Engineering, Health Science and Business) must divide the remaining office workers equally. If the College of Arts and Sciences merges with the College of Health Science, they will have 340 total office workers. How many office workers did the university originally employ?

    a. 400
    b. 420
    c. 450
    d. 500
    e. 680

26. What number is 1,650% greater than 12?

    a. 19.8
    b. 21
    c. 198
    d. 210
    e. 1,980

27. If e + 6f is equal to 160 percent of 15f, what is the value of e/f?

    a. 3
    b. 9
    c. 12
    d. 18
    e. 24

28. Luke purchased a new Lexus for $65,000. The value of the car decreases by 12% each year. How many years must elapse before the Lexus is worth $20,571?

    a. 6
    b. 7
    c. 8
    d. 9
    e. 11

29. There are 375 more Democrats than Republicans in Wheeling County. If there are P Republicans, then, in terms of P, what percentage of Wheeling County residents are Republicans?

    a. 100P/(2P + 375)%
    b. 3P − 375%
    c. 2P(3P − 375)/100%
    d. 100/(2P + 375)%
    e. (P − 375)/(2P + 375)%

30. A gourmet food shop charges $150 for a 2-pound tin of caviar, which is 45% more than the amount that the store paid for it. During the holiday season, store employees can purchase any remaining tins of caviar at 20% off the store's cost. How much would it cost an employee to purchase a 2-pound tin of caviar during the holiday season?

    a. $54.00
    b. $66.00
    c. $72.76
    d. $82.76
    e. $88.00

31. At a local couture shop, the owner assigned prices for her new spring items at the beginning of January. At the end of each month, she discounted each item's price by 5% until it sold. If the price of a ball gown was X at the beginning of January, what would its price be on June 15?

    a. 0.6983X
    b. 0.7000X
    c. 0.7351X
    d. 0.7738X
    e. 0.8145X

32. A scientist placed ten bacteria cells in a glass jar. Every minute, the bacteria double in volume. After 20 minutes, the bacteria completely filled the glass jar. How many minutes did it take for the jar to be 25% full?

    a. 4
    b. 5
    c. 10
    d. 18
    e. 19

Answer Key: Percent Problems

1. The boutique sold 98/392, or 25% of the dresses. Therefore, 75% of the dresses did not sell. Choice C is correct.

2. 7 + 3 + 2 = 12 items = ¾ of the total number of items. Hence, the overall total is 16. 2/16 = 1/8 = 12.5%. Choice C is correct.

3. 800 x 0.4 = 320. 320 x 0.25 = 80. Choice C is correct.

4. 329 - 62 = 267/62 = 4.306 x 100 = 430.6% increase. Choice C is correct.

5. 110/220 = ½ = 50%. 22/220 = 1/10 = 10%. Therefore, 50% + 10% = 60% are from Hawaii & Canada. Therefore, 40% are not. Choice C is correct.

6. $8,000,000 x 0.095 = $760,000 interest. Total = $8,760,000. Choice D is correct.

7. 1432 – 91 = 1341. 1341/1432 x 100 = 93.65% decrease. Choice D is correct.

8. Let's solve this by using $100 as the initial price of the stock: The 20% decrease reduced the stock price to $80. For the stock to reach $100 again, there must be a $20 increase. $20 is what % of $80? 20/80 x 100 = 25%. Choice B is correct.

9. 97/102 = 0.951. The % error = 1 – 0.951 = 4.90%, which is Choice C.

10. If 0.06x = $4.32, then x = $72. Total price = $76.32. Choice D is correct.

11. Two price reductions = 0.9 x 0.85 = 0.765, which is 24.5%. Choice C is correct.

12. The increase from $825 to $1650 would be 100%. Choice C is correct.

13. The mustard would be used 1 ¾ (or 7/4) times as fast, which would deplete the supply in 4/7 the usual amount of time.   25 (4/7) = 14.3 days. Choice C is correct.

14. In this case, we simply multiply the numbers together to find the percentage of students   in both groups: 0.35 x 0.15 = 5.25%. Choice A is correct.

15. Kathy's total monthly commission is the sum of ($3250(0.25) and ($5175)(0.15), which is $812.50 + $776.25 = $1588.75. Choice D is correct.

16. The total bill, which can be no more than $50, include the cost of the meal, 7% sales tax and a 15% tip. If we let x = the cost of the food, then the tax = 0.07x. The tip is 15% of the total cost of the food and the 7% tip. Algebraically, we can represent the tip as 0.15 (x + 0.07x) = 0.1605x.

Since the total bill can be no more than $50, our final equation for the meal is:

Meal + Tax + Tip = 50, or x + 0.07x + 0.1605x = 50. Solving for x, the cost of the meal must be less than $40.63.
     Answer Choice B is correct.

17. First, we must find Barbie's original salary. 720 = 1.20x, x = 600. Thus, Barbie's raise was 720 – 600 = $120.
     Now, we must find Connie's original salary. $600 + 0.5(600) = 900. Now, we must add Connie's raise: 900 +
     120 = $1020. Choice D is correct.

18. First, let's calculate Jake's commission for the week, which is 12,400(0.15) = 1860. Now, we can calculate his total weekly pay: 700 + 1860 = $2560.   Choice E is correct.

19. First, we must subtract the deductions from the total: 14625 – 100 – 325 = 14,200. Chad received 75% of this amount, or $10,650. Choice A is correct.

20. 328 – 114 = 214/100 = 214% increase. Choice E is correct.

21. This is a deceptively easy problem to solve, yet most students are intimidated by the use of letters instead of numbers. To solve it, simply plug in a few numbers, consider your solution, and choose the answer choice that matches it.

Let's assume that W = 5% and Z = $100. Sally's commission would be ($100)(0.05) = $5.00. At first blush, this may seem like answer choice B, which is WZ, but it is not. When we converted the 5% to 0.05 we divided the 5 by 100; hence, the solution was actually WZ/100, which is Choice D.

For students who ARE comfortable working with variables, you can obtain the same answer by simply plugging the letters into the formula. If Sally receives a W% commission, then:

W% = W/100
(W/100) (Z) = WZ/100

47

(*Note*: Please see Chapter 18 for additional examples of problems with all variables.)

22. To solve, we must plug in random numbers for the class sizes and solve for the percentage. Let's assume that the first class has 100 students.

First class = 100. 60% = 60 students with tattoos
Second class = 200. 20% = 40 students with tattoos

100/300 = 33-1/3% of students have tattoos. Therefore, the percentage without them is 66 -2/3%. Choice E is correct.

23. This problem isn't difficult, but tedious. First, we must determine how much of the tip each friend paid, which is $40/8 or $5. Then, we must calculate the total amount of the bill, knowing that the $40 tip was 15%. Our equation becomes: 15/100 = 40/x. Solving for x, 15x = 4000, x = $266.67.

Next, we must divide this total by 8, which is the portion attributable to each friend: $266.67/8 = $33.33.

Finally, we must add the amount of the food and tip for each person, which is $5.00 + $33.33 = $38.33. Choice D is correct.

24. Once again, this problem isn't difficult, but time consuming because we must make multiple calculations -and use the correct price each time.

At the end of year one, the new price would be ($365,000)(1.06) = $386,900.
At the end of year two, the new price would be ($386,900)(1.08) = $417,852.
At the end of year three, the new price would be ($417,852)(1.04) = $434,566.08.

Choice E is correct.

25. First, we must document the fractional portion of the staff that is allocated to each college.

AS: 80/100 = 4/5 = 16/20.
EG: (1/4)(1/5) = 1/20
ENG: (1/4)(1/5) = 1/20
HS: (1/4)(1/5) = 1/20
BUS: (1/4)(1/5) = 1/20

Next, we must add together the fractions for the Colleges of Arts and Sciences and Health Sciences: 16/20 + 1/20 = 17/20 = 0.85 = 340 workers.

Finally, we must use this number to calculate the original number of workers: 0.85/340 = 1/X. X = 400 original workers. Choice A is correct

26. 12 + 16.5 (12) = 210. Choice D is correct.

27. According to the problem,

e + 6f = (1.60)15f
e + 6f = 24f
e = 18f
e/f = 18. Choice D is correct.

28. Each year the car decreases by 12%. We can solve the problem by recording the depreciation in a simple chart:

Original value $65,000
First year ($65,000)(0.88) = $57,200

Second year ($57,200)(0.88) = $50,336
Third year ($50,336)(0.88) = $44,296
Fourth year ($44,296)(0.88) = $38,980
Fifth year ($38,980)(0.88) = $34,302
Sixth year ($34,302)(0.88) = $30,186
Seventh year ($30,186)(0.88) = $26,564
Eighth year ($26,564)(0.88) = $23,376
Ninth year ($23,376)(0.88) = **$20,571**. Choice D is correct

29. For the sake of simplicity, let's assume that there are 100 Republicans in Wheeling County, which makes P = 100.

Republicans (P)   100
Democrats (P + 375)   475
Total (2P + 375)   575

The number of residents who are Republicans is therefore 100 / 575, or P/(2P + 375). If we convert this to a percentage, we get 100P/(2P + 375). Choice A is correct.

30. By definition, $150 = 1.45x, which means that the store paid $103.45 for each tin of caviar. At the end of the season, employees can buy the tins for 80% of this price, which is ($103.45)(0.80)= $82.76. Choice D is correct.

31. For the sake of simplicity, let's let X = 100

Original price 100
End of Jan 90 (100)(0.95) = 95
End of Feb (95)(0.95) = 90.25
End of March (90.25)(0.95) = 85.74
End of April (85.74)(0.95) = 81.45
End of May (81.45)(0.95) = 77.38

The price on June 15, the price would be **0.7738X.** Choice D is correct.

32. The easiest way to solve this problem is to work backwards. If the bacteria double in volume every minute, then at 19 minutes, the jar was half full. And, working backwards another step, the jar was **25%** full at **18** minutes. Choice D is correct.

Chapter 6: Word Problems with Ratios & Proportions

In Chapter 4, we defined a fraction as a mathematical expression in which one number is divided by another number (2/3, 5/6, and 77/5 are all fractions). A **ratio** is simply another word for a fraction.

On a practical basis, a **ratio** can be used to compare two quantities (if a class contains 20 students, of which 7 are male and 13 are female, then the ratio 7/20 compares the number of *male students* in the class to the *total number* of students).

Ratios can be presented in one of three ways (in each case below, the expression reads "3 to 5:"

3 to 5
3:5
3/5

A **proportion** is a mathematical statement in which two ratios are equal:

$10/25 = 2/5$
$0.050/0.50 = 1/10$
$80/4 = 20/1$

By definition, for the ratio A/B = C/D, AD = BC

Examples: $12/15 = 4/5$ $(12)(5) = (15)(4)$ $3/6 = 14/28$ $(3)(28) = (14)(6)$

The SAT, GRE and GMAT may test your knowledge of ratios and proportions by simply presenting an equation in which three of the terms are known - and you must calculate the fourth term. But it is FAR more likely that they will expect you to apply your knowledge to word problems in which you must set up and solve your own equations.

A typical trap on standardized tests is to include terms – and answer choices - that use different units. When you solve these problems, make sure that your units within a ratio and proportion are the same – also check to be sure that your final answer is the same unit of measure as the five answer choices. One (or more) of the incorrect answer choices will usually be answers that you will get if you fail to convert your units properly.

The test writers have other traps in store for you with ratios and proportions. Here are the most common ones to look for.

Example 1: Different Units

On the blueprint for a football stadium, 1 foot represents 1/4 mile. If the architect makes an error of 1/8 inch in reading the blueprint, what will be the corresponding error in the actual stadium?

    a.   7.50 feet
    b.   12.50 feet
    c.   13.75 feet
    d.   27.50 feet
    e.   55.00 feet

Solution: This is a classic example of an easy problem that is presented in multiple units. To make the units consistent, we can use a simple proportion:

1 foot / 1/4 mile = 1/8 inch / x

Noting that the answer choices are presented in terms of feet, we will convert all of our numbers to feet and solve for x. Since 1 mile = 5,280 feet, our equation is:

1 foot / 1320 feet = 1/96 feet / x
$x = 1320/96 = 13.75$ feet, or Choice C.

Example 2: Adding to (and Subtracting from) the Parts of a Ratio

Example A: When American Idol auditions were held in New York City, the judges allowed an equal number of men and women to take the stage. At the end of a grueling day, the ratio of female to male singers who advanced to the next round was 3 to 2. At the very end of the day, the judges had a change of heart and agreed to add one additional female singer and one additional male singer to the group that advanced. What is the new ratio of female to male singers?

  a.   3:2
  b.   4:3
  c.   5:4
  d.   6:5
  e.   It cannot be determined from the information given.

Example B: When American Idol auditions were held in New York City, the judges allowed an equal number of men and women to take the stage. At the end of a grueling day, the ratio of female to male singers who advanced to the next round was 3 to 2. At the very end of the day, the judges had a change of heart and agreed to add one additional female singer and one additional male singer to the group that advanced. If the total number of singers who advanced was 32, what was the original number of men chosen to advance?

  a.   8
  b.   10
  c.   12
  d.   18
  e.   20

Solutions: If you do nothing else in this chapter, make SURE that you understand the difference between these two problems. It is a key concept that the SAT, GRE and GMAT present on nearly every exam.

Although you can multiply and divide ratios (or parts of them), you cannot simply add or subtract from them, UNLESS you know something about the quantities that they represent. In Example A, the test writers do not tell us anything about the original number of singers (male or female) or how many of them advanced to the next round. We simply have a ratio. Hence, the correct answer is E, we cannot determine the final ratio without additional information.

Example B is a different story, because we have been given enough information to solve the problem. In the original scenario, the 3:2 ratio of female to male singers applied to a population of 32 – 2, or 30. Hence, the original 30 selected to advance included 18 women and 12 men (a 3:2 ratio). The correct answer for the original number of men chosen to advance is Choice C, 12.

Example 3: Ratios That Represent Different Quantities.

A pet shop owner purchased a delightful selection of Siamese, Bengal, and Persian kittens for her store. If the ratio of the number of Siamese kittens to Bengal kittens is 3:5, and the ratio of the number of Bengal kittens to Persian kittens is 1:4, what is the ratio of the number of Siamese kittens to Persian kittens?

  a.   1/20
  b.   3/20
  c.   1/8
  d.   5/20
  e.   3/5

Solution: This convoluted problem, which compares ratios that represent different quantities, is a favorite of the test writers. To find the correct answer, students must re-state each ratio so that each one has the same whole. Only then can they be compared properly.

To find the ratio of Siamese kittens to Persian kittens, we must re-state both ratios so that the number of Bengal kittens is the same in both.

Siamese to Bengal = 3:5
Bengal to Persian = 1:4

In this case, the numbers corresponding to Bengal kittens are 5 and 1, respectively. The easiest way to re-state the ratios is to use their least common multiple of 5 and 1, which is 5.

Siamese to Bengal = 3:5
Bengal to Persian = 5:20

The ratios are now stated in a form in which the same number (5) refers to Bengal kittens. The ratio of Siamese to Bengal to Persian kittens is 3:5:20. The ratio of Siamese kittens to Persian kittens is 3:20, which is Choice B.

Example 4: "Possible" Ratios

A Toyota dealer has 34 Corollas on the lot. The only color choices are blue or black. Which of the following is a possible ratio of blue to black Corollas on this particular car lot?

        a.   5/17
        b.   2/13
        c.   5/13
        d.   7/17
        e.   7/10

Solution: In recent years, the SAT, GRE and GMAT writers have introduced a new type of question to determine if students understand the underlying premise of a ratio. In this case, by definition, the sum of the numerator and denominator **must** be a factor of 34, which is the total number of Corollas on the lot. This limits the possibilities to 1, 2, 17 and 34. The correct answer choice, E, is the only one in which the terms add up to one of these factors (7/10, the sum is 17). The others are mathematically impossible.

Example 5: Direct and Inverse Variation

Two quantities vary directly if they change in the same direction. If one goes up, the other one also increases. Likewise, if one goes down, the other also decreases. Ratios are useful tools for solving problems in which quantities vary directly.

Increasingly, though, the SAT, GRE and GMAT are including questions in which quantities vary inversely, which means that they change in opposite directions. As the first quantity increases, the second one decreases (and vice versa). There are several practical situations in which the variables vary inversely:

- People working together to complete a job. The more workers who contribute, the less time they will need to complete the job.

- People consuming food, water, or drugs. The more people who consume the item, the less time it will last.

- The driving speed and the time it takes to complete a journey. The faster someone drives, the sooner (s)he will reach his/her destination.

Here is a typical example:

A hospital has enough orange juice to feed 150 patients for 8 days. If 30 of the patients do not drink orange juice, how many days will the supply last?

        a.   6.4
        b.   9.6
        c.   10
        d.   12
        e.   40

Solution: In this case, the number of patients times days is a constant. We simply need to set up an equation to determine how long the orange juice will last if only 120 patients (150 – 30) drink it, which we will call x.

(150)(8) = 120(x)
X = 10 days   Choice C is correct.

Example 6: Problems with All Variables

If A school buses can carry B students, how many buses will be needed to carry C students?

    a.   BC/A
    b.   ABC
    c.   1/AC
    d.   AC/B
    e.   B/AC

Solution: Don't be thrown by the use of letters instead of numbers – the problem is still a basic proportion, in which we must determine the value of an unknown x. The question asks us to determine the number of buses needed for C students, knowing that A buses are needed to carry B students.

Our proportion, therefore, is A/B = X/C.
X, therefore, equals AC/B, which is Choice D.

Alternatively, you can solve the problem by substituting numbers for the variables. Let A = 10, B = 100, and C= 200.

10/100 = x/200x
X = (200)(10)/100, which is AC/B.

Now that you have reviewed the underling concepts, reinforce your skills by solving these mathematical word problems. Detailed solutions are presented at the end of the chapter.

Word Problems: Ratios & Proportions: EASY - MODERATE

1. If it takes a robot thirty-six minutes to travel the 18 blocks between the police station and the fire house, how long will it take the same robot (in minutes), traveling at the same rate per block, to travel from the police station to the train station that is 64 blocks away?

    a.   10
    b.   32
    c.   128
    d.   648
    e.   2304

2. Three hundred entertainers will perform at a talent show. The group contains only singers and dancers. If the ratio of singers to dancers is 2:1, how many dancers are there?

    a.   50
    b.   100
    c.   150
    d.   175
    e.   200

3. If it takes 12 people to serve 500 meals at the soup kitchen, how many people will be required to serve 14,280 meals?

    a.   29
    b.   290
    c.   343
    d.   1190
    e.   11,900

4. Which of the following expresses the ratio of 12 ounces to 6 pounds?

    a. 1/16
    b. 1/12
    c. 1/8
    d. 1/6
    e. ¼

5. The asking prices of two cars are in the ratio of 8:9. If the two cars together cost $85,000, what does the cheaper car cost?

    a. $35,000
    b. $40,000
    c. $42,000
    d. $42,500
    e. $45,000

6. The results of a beauty pageant are determined by a personal interview, a swimsuit competition, an evening gown competition, a talent show and a quiz about current events. If the personal interview counts twice as much as each of the other selection criteria, what fraction of each contestant's final score is determined by the personal interview?

    a. 1/8
    b. 1/6
    c. ¼
    d. 1/3
    e. 2/5

7. Carly has $38 dollars left over after spending 4/9 of her birthday money. How much money did Carly receive for her birthday?

    a. $48.40
    b. $59.10
    c. $68.40
    d. $76.00
    e. $85.50

8. A jeweler has 62 garnet rings in stock. The only color choices for the bands are gold and silver. Which of the following is a possible ratio of gold to silver bands for this selection of rings?

    a. 12/31
    b. 12/54
    c. 27/35
    d. 27/62
    e. 12/13

9. A hallway that is 90 feet long is divided into two sections that are in the ratio of 3:2. What is the length of the shorter section?

    a. 9
    b. 18
    c. 21
    d. 27
    e. 36

10. A tour bus at Disney World holds 124 people. If the park requires one adult for every five children on the tour bus, how many children can fit on the bus?

    a. 20
    b. 22
    c. 24
    d. 30
    e. 32

11. In a large lecture hall containing 550 female students, 27 were on birth control pills, 110 were taking antibiotics, and 220 were taking antihistamines. The remaining 193 students were not taking any medication. In simplest terms, what is the ratio of female students taking birth control pills to the total number of students in the lecture hall?

    a. 1: 100
    b. 1 : 193
    c. 1: 27
    d. 1 : 20
    e. 1 : 5

12. Grace and Edna own a small business that earned $48,000 in profits last year. If they agreed to split the profits in a 9:4 ratio, with Grace getting the larger share, how much did Edna earn from the business?

    a. $10,453.67
    b. $11,896.23
    c. $14,769.23
    d. $21,453.23
    e. $33,230.70

13. The amount of sugar in a cake batter varies directly as the weight of the batter. If there are 42 pounds of sugar in a one-ton quantity of batter, how many pounds of sugar would there be in 325 pounds of batter?

    a. 3.412
    b. 6.825
    c. 13.650
    d. 27.30
    e. 54.60

14. David drives to work on the interstate. The time it takes him to reach his office is inversely proportional to his rate of speed. If he drives at 75 mph, it takes him 30 minutes. How long (in minutes) will it take David if he drives 45 mph?

    a. 18
    b. 45
    c. 50
    d. 75
    e. 112.50

15. Kelly wants to have her favorite picture enlarged to the size of a wall poster. The original picture measures 2 inches by 3 inches. If the shorter side of the poster will be 4 feet long, how long (in inches) will the longer side be?

    a. 6
    b. 36
    c. 64
    d. 72
    e. 78

16. Jake found a great deal on discontinued paint at Home Depot. When he brought the paint home, he discovered that the four cans he purchased were enough to paint three quarters of his bedroom. How many additional cans of paint will Jake need to buy to complete his bedroom and to paint three additional rooms that are the same size as his bedroom?

    a.   13
    b.   16.7
    c.   17.3
    d.   19
    e.   19.3

17. If Q is 25% of R and S is 30% of R, what is the ratio of Q to S?

    a.   3/20
    b.   1/5
    c.   11/20
    d.   3/4
    e.   5/6

18. w, x, y, and z are all positive integers. Which of the following proportions is NOT equivalent to the others?

    a. $y/w = z/x$
    b. $z/y = x/w$
    c. $w/y = x/z$
    d. $w/z = x/y$
    e. $x/w = z/y$

19. If the square of D varies directly with the cube of E, and E = 2 when D = 5, what does D equal when E is 3?

    a.   2.75
    b.   3.12
    c.   8.43
    d.   9.18
    e.   84.37

20. If U varies inversely with the square root of V, and U is 16 when V is 36, what is the value of U when V is 144?

    a.   2
    b.   8
    c.   64
    d.   128
    e.   324

Word Problems: Ratios & Proportions: AS HARD AS IT GETS

21. The ratio of professors to students at a private college is 1:12. If 36 new students are admitted, there will be 16 times as many students as professors. What is the new number of students at the college?

    a.   124
    b.   132
    c.   136
    d.   144
    e.   148

22. At the Cordon Bleu, 25% of culinary majors will eventually decide to specialize in dessert preparation. Of those who select this specialty, the ratio of men to women is 5:2. If 35% of Cordon Bleu's entering class is culinary majors, and if the number of women who are specializing in dessert preparation is 60, how many students are in the entire class?

    a. 840
    b. 1,200
    c. 1,680
    d. 2,400
    e. 3,360

23. A baker makes her famous chocolate frosting by mixing extra dark fondant with Brazilian chocolate liqueur. In a 3000g batch of frosting, the ratio of fondant to liqueur is 5:3. In a 2000g batch of the same frosting, the ratio is 6:4. If the baker mixes these two batches of frosting together into a bigger bowl, how many grams of extra dark fondant will the combined batch contain?

    a. 1,200
    b. 1,875
    c. 3,075
    d. 3,600
    e. 4,275

24. If A girls can build a web site in B hours, how many hours will it take them to build the site if three of the girls cannot participate?

    a. A – (B/3)
    b. AB/3
    c. A/(B - 3)
    d. B/(A – 3)
    e. AB/(B – 3)

25. At the campus bookstore, students can buy three candy bars for M cents. How many can they buy for N dollars?

    a. 300N/M
    b. 300M/N
    c. 300/MN
    d. MN/300
    e. 30/MN

26. A jar contains 50 candies that are either Hershey Kisses or Special Dark Bars.   Which of the following could NOT be the possible ratio of Hershey Kisses to Special Dark Bars?

    a. 1:4
    b. 3:7
    c. 2:3
    d. 7:8
    e. 12:13

27. Three roommates compared the balances in their individual savings accounts at the end of the summer. The ratio of Samantha's savings to Christina's savings is 3 to 8. The ratio of Samantha's savings to Barbara's savings is 4 to 11. What is the ratio of Christina's savings to Barbara's savings?

    a. 24/88
    b. 33/88
    c. 24/44
    d. 32/33
    e. 33/32

28. The ratio of W to V is twenty-five times the ratio of V to W. Which of the following terms is equal to V/W?

    a.   1/25
    b.   1/5
    c.   5/1
    d.   25/1
    e.   125

Answer Key: Word Problems - Ratios & Proportions

1. We can solve this using a proportion. 36/18 = x/64.   x = 128 minutes. Choice C is correct.

2. For a 2:1 ratio, the whole is 3. 2/3 of 300 = 200 singers;1/3 of 300 =100 dancers. Choice B is correct.

3. We can solve by using a proportion. 12/500 = x /14,280.   x= 342.7 = 343. Choice C is correct.

4. 6 pounds = 96 oz. 12/96 = 1/8. Choice C is correct.

5. An 8/9 ratio means the total is 17. 8/17 x 85,000 = $40,000. Choice B is correct.

6. The contest is judged on the results of 5 events. One of them, the personal interview, counts as two of the other events. Hence, it is worth 2/6 of the overall score, with each of the other 4 events being worth an additional 1/6. The correct answer is 1/3, or Choice D.

7. 5/9 of the birthday money = $38.   Thus, we can set up a ratio to determine the original whole: 5/9 = 38/X. Hence, X = $68.40, which is Choice C.

8. The sum of the numerator and denominator must be a factor of 62, which is the total number of rings in stock. This limits the possibilities to 1, 2, 31 and 62. The correct answer choice, C, is the only one in which the terms add up to one of these factors (27/35, the sum is 62). The others are mathematically impossible.

9. For a ratio of 3:2, the whole is 5. The shorter section is therefore 2/5 of the whole. 2/5 of 90 = 36, which is Choice E.

10. If there is one adult for every five children, we must divide the capacity of the bus by 6, 124/6 = 20.6. Therefore, there can be no more than 20 children on the tour bus (4 groups, each of which contains one adult and 20 children). Choice A is correct.

11. 27 / 550 = 1 / 20.   Choice D is correct.

12. 9x + 4x = $48,000, or 13x = 48000, so x =3692.3. Edna's share = 4x = $14,769.23. Choice C is correct.

13. 42 / 2000 = x / 325. x = 6.825 lb. Choice B is correct.

14.75 / 45 = x / 30, so x = 50 minutes. Choice C is correct.

15. We can solve this by using a ratio: 2/48 = 3/x, so x = 72 inches. Choice D is correct.

16. We can solve this using a proportion. If 4 cans covered ¾ of one room, how many cans are needed to cover 3-1/4 rooms? 4 / 0.75 = x / 3.25. Solving for x = 17.3 additional cans. Choice C is correct.

17. Q = 0.25R. S = 0.3R. Thus, Q/S = 0.25/0.30 = 5/6. Choice E is correct.

18. Choice D is correct. In all of the other answer choices, the proportions reduce to: xy = wz.

19. According to the problem, $D^2 = kE.^3$ We also know that E = 2 when D = 5, which enables us to solve for our constant, k.

(5)(5) = k(2)(2)(2), or k =25/8. Now, we can solve for x when E = 3:

$D^2 = kE^3$
$D^2 = (25/8)(E^3)= (25/8)(3)(3)(3) = 675/8 = 84.37$
D = 9.18. Choice D is correct.

20. By definition, U = k/√V, so 16 = k/√36, or 16 = k/6, or k =(6)(16) = 96. Thus, U = (96)/√144 = 96/12 =8.   Choice B is correct.

21. The hardest part about this question is setting up the equation we need to solve it. First, it's important to acknowledge one key point: the # of professors (x) remains the same. We also know that the original number of students is 12 times this number, or 12x. Therefore, the number of new students is 12x + 36. Finally, we also know that 12x + 36 = 16x. Solving for x, we find that the number of professors (x) = 9. Therefore, the original number of students = (9)(12) = 108 and the new number of students = 108 + 36 = 144. Choice D is correct.

22. First, let's work with what we know, which is that 60 women will major in dessert preparation. We also know that the ratio of men to women in dessert preparation is 5:2, which means that there are (60)(5)/2 =150 men who have chosen this specialty.

By definition, these students (60 + 150 = 210) are 25% of the culinary majors at the school. Therefore, the total number of students who are culinary majors must be: 210/25 = x/100, X = 840.
Finally, these 840 students represent 35% of the entering class. Hence, the total number of entering students is: 840/35 = x/ 100, X = 2400.   Choice D is correct.

23. The question asks us to determine the total amount of extra dark fondant in the final batch of frosting. By definition, the total amount of frosting in the combined batch is 3000g + 2000g = 5000g.

Now, we must calculate the portion of this amount that is extra dark fondant. To do so, we must calculate the amount in each of the two individual batches and add them together.

In the first batch, which is 3000g, the ratio of fondant to liqueur is 5/3. Hence, the amount of fondant in the first batch is (3000g)(5/8) = 1875 grams.

In the second batch, which is 2000g, the ratio of fondant to liqueur is 6/4. Hence, the amount of fondant in the second batch is (2000g)(6/10) = 1200 grams.

Therefore, the total amount of extra dark fondant in the final batch is 1875g + 1200g = 3075 grams.   Choice C is correct.

24. The fewer girls who participate, the longer it will take to build the site. Hence, this problem is one in which the

variables vary inversely. Let x = the amount of time it will take to build the site with 3 fewer girls. Our equation, therefore, is: (A)(B) = (B – 3)(X)

X = AB/(B – 3) Choice E is correct. (*Note*: Please see Chapter 18 for additional examples of problems with all variables.)

25. We can solve this problem by solving a basic proportion, in which our unknown quantity is X. In this case:

M/3 = 100N/X
X = 300N/M

To check our answer, we can plug-in a set of random number for M and N. Let's assume that M = 90 and N = 9. Thus, students can buy 3 candy bars for 90 cents. If so, how many can they buy with $9.00.

X = 300(9.00)/ 90 = 2700/90 = 30

If candy bars cost 30 cents each (3 for 90 cents), then students can buy 30 candy bars for $9.00 (which is equal to 300N/M). Choice A is correct.

26. For the ratios to "work," the total number must be a multiple of 50 (2, 5, 10, or 25).

   1:4: total is 5 (10 of one type and 40 of another)
   3:7: total is 10 (15 of one type and 35 of another)
   2:3: total is 5 (20 of one type and 30 of another)
   7:8: total is 15, which is NOT a multiple of 50. Choice D is correct.
   12:13: total is 25 (10 of one type and 40 of another)

27. Samantha/Christina = 3/8
Samantha/ Barbara = 4/11

Christina/Barbara = (Christina/Samantha) x (Samantha/Barbara) = 8/3 x 4/11 = **32/33**. Choice D is correct.

28. W/V = 25V/W
W = 25V^2/W
W^2 = 25V^2
W^2 = 25V^2
1/25 = V^2/W^2
1/5 = V/W. Choice B is correct.

Chapter 7: Algebra Word Problems with Integers

Most word problems on the SAT, GRE, and GMAT require a mastery of basic algebra, in which common words must be translated into mathematical relationships.

The following are the most common translations that you will be required to make:

Addition (+): add, sum, plus, more, increase, greater, excess, enlarge, rise, grow

Subtraction (-): less, difference, subtract, diminished, reduced, remainder, minus, decrease, drop

Multiplication (x): product, times, of

Division (/): divide, quotient, ratio, half

Here are several practical examples of "English to algebraic" translation:

| Eighty seven diminished by x equals 12. | $87 - x = 12$ |

| If the sum of x and 12 is divided by three, the quotient is 8. | $(x + 12)/3 = 8$ |

| Five x is eight more than twice x. | $5x = 2x + 8$ |

| Three times the quantity of x – 3 divided by eighteen is eleven. | $3(x - 3) / 18 = 11$ |

| Eighteen is six less than five x diminished by three. | $18 = (5x - 6) - 3$ |

The SAT, GRE and GMAT will test your ability to write - and solve – original equations that accurately represent the information that is presented in the question stem. Although there are many different types of problems (including those in Chapters 7 - 28), they all require the same general approach:

1. Read the problem carefully; make sure that you understand what it is asking you to find
2. Circle or underline the variable or unknown
3. Use the information in the problem to write an equation that will enable you to solve for the unknown. In your equation, call the unknown x.
4. Complete the mathematical operations in the proper order
5. Check your work
6. Confirm that your answer is one of the five answer choices

This chapter will cover the most common types of word problems with integers.

Example 1. Consecutive Integers

The sum of five consecutive integers is 325. What is the middle integer?

    a. 63
    b. 64
    c. 65
    d. 66
    e. 67

Solution: In this problem, we know that 5 consecutive numbers, when added together, equal 325. We will let the smallest of the 5 numbers = x. Therefore, the second, third, fourth and fifth consecutive numbers are equal to x + 1, x + 2, x + 3, and x + 4, respectively.

Mathematically, we can represent their relationship by the following equation:

$x + (x + 1) + (x + 2) + (x + 3) + (x + 4) = 325$
$5x + 10 = 325$

x = 315/5 = 63.
The middle number is x+2, or 65, which is Choice C.

Example 2. Consecutive Even or Odd Integers

If x + 15 is an even integer, the sum of the next three even integers is:

      a.   x + 57
      b. 3x + 45
      c. 3x + 51
      d. 3x + 57
      e. $(x + 15)^3$

Solution: In this case, we are asked to find the sum of three consecutive even integers.

If (x + 15) is even, then the next consecutive even integer is (x + 17). The following consecutive even integer is (x + 19) and the next consecutive even integer is (x + 21).

Therefore, the sum of the next three even integers is:

(x + 17) + (x + 19) + (x + 21) = 3x + 57. Choice D is correct.

Example 3. Tricky Relationships … and Translations

If three less than eleven times a whole number is equal to 140, what is the number?

      a. 11
      b. 13
      c. 14
      d. 17
      e. 19

Solution: The SAT, GRE and GMAT are notorious for word problems that express simple relationships in a convoluted manner. This is a typical example. To solve, just translate what you read on the page to a mathematical equation.

In this case, we will let x = the whole number we are trying to find. Once we define our variable, the problem easily converts to a simple equation:

11x – 3 = 140
11x = 143
x= 13. Choice B is correct.

Example 4. Practical Scenarios

When Sara and Claire got dressed for the prom, they checked out each other's makeup collections.   If Sara has six more than three times number of tubes of lipstick than Claire has, and Claire has eighteen tubes of lipstick, how many tubes does Sara have?

      a. 21
      b. 24
      c. 54
      d. 60
      e. 66

Solution: We can write a simple equation to calculate the answer. First let's define our unknown, x, as the number of tubes of lipstick that Sara owns.

According to the problem, x = 3(18) + 6 = 60 tubes of lipstick.   Choice D is correct.

As you will see in the coming chapters, Example 4 merely scratches the surface of the type of algebra word problems that may appear on the SAT. For your convenience, we will cover one topic at a time, to give you the optimal chance to develop a working strategy for each one.

To test your skills on this chapter's topic - algebra work problems with integers - try the following problems. Detailed solutions are at the end of the chapter.

Algebra Word Problems with Integers: EASY - MODERATE

1. For three consecutive integers, three times the sum of the first and second is 27 more than twice the third. What is the smallest of these three integers?

     a. 6
     b. 7
     c. 8
     d. 9
     e. 11

2. The sum of two numbers is 18. When three times the larger number is subtracted from 5 times the smaller number, the difference is 2. What is the larger number?

     a. 7
     b. 8
     c. 9
     d. 10
     e. 11

3. The larger of two numbers is 11 more than the smaller. Double the small number equals 14 more than the small number. What is the small number?

     a. 24
     b. 25
     c. 26
     d. 35
     e. 36

4. If 25 less than eight times a number is equal to 215, find the number.

     a. 20
     b. 25
     c. 30
     d. 35
     e. 40

5. Five consecutive even integers have a sum of 370. What is the largest of the five integers?

     a. 70
     b. 76
     c. 78
     d. 80
     e. 82

6. The sum of two numbers is 48. Their difference is 12. What is the smaller number?

     a.   18
     b.   22
     c.   26
     d.   30
     e.   36

7. One number is six times a smaller number. If four times their difference is equal to 60, what is the larger number?

     a.   - 3
     b.   2
     c.   3
     d.   4
     e.   18

8. The difference between two positive consecutive integers, when each is squared, equals 29. What is the smaller number?

     a.   12
     b.   13
     c.   14
     d.   15
     e.   16

9. The difference between $(X + Y)$ and $(X - Y)$ is 12. Find the smaller of the two numbers if XY is 90.

     a.   2
     b.   3
     c.   5
     d.   6
     e.   10

10. If y is 5 less than 4 times x, what is the value of x?

     a. $(y - 5)/4$
     b. $(y + 5)/4$
     c. $4y + 20$
     d. $4y - 20$
     e. $4/5\ y$

11. The sum of two numbers is 238. Their difference is 46. What is the smaller number?

     a.   96
     b.   104
     c.   136
     d.   142
     e.   150

12. If B = 12 x 15 x 34, then all of the following answer choices are integers EXCEPT:

     a.   B/18
     b.   B/30
     c.   B/32
     d.   B/36
     e.   B/72

13. A prime triple is a set of three consecutive prime numbers in which the first and last number differ by six. Which of the following is NOT a prime triple?

    a.   (41, 43, 47)
    b.   (7, 11, 13)
    c.   (13, 17, 19)
    d.   (23, 27, 29)
    e.   (67, 71, 73)

14. If 20/X is an odd integer, which of the following could X equal?

    a.   2/3
    b.   1/3
    c.   2/5
    d.   2/7
    e.   4/3

Algebra Word Problems with Integers: AS HARD AS IT GETS

15. The mean of fourteen consecutive integers is 27-1/2. If the integers are arranged in increasing order, what is the mean of the largest seven integers?

    a.   24
    b.   25
    c.   31
    d.   34
    e.   35

16. M is the set of positive and negative integers that are multiples of 5. M = (......-15, -10, -5, 0, 5, 10, 15......). Integers A and B are members of set M. Which of the following expression is NOT a member of set M?

    a.   AB
    b.   A/B
    c.   A + B
    d. $A^2 + B^2$
    e.   A – B

17. The sum of the first V positive integers is W. What is the sum of the next V positive integers?

    a. VW
    b. (V + W)/V
    c. $V + W^2$
    d. $W + V^2$
    e. $W^2 – V^2$

18. The cost for a pen and notebook at the campus bookstore is $10.50.   If the notebook costs $10.00 more than the pen, what does the pen cost (assuming there is no sales tax)?

    a.   25 cents
    b.   50 cents
    c.   75 cents
    d. $1.00
    e. $1.50

19. When Joe sold his business, he gave 75% of the $675,000 profits to his three partners and kept the rest for himself. Partner A received four times the amount that Partner B received, while Partner C received twice as much as Partner A and B received together. How much did Partner A receive?

     a. $33,750
     b. $46,023
     c. $135,000
     d. $184,091
     e. $337,500

20. K-Mart and Wal-Mart bought different size square buildings for their new stores. The length of K-mart's store is four times as long as the length of Wal-Mart's store. If the sum of the perimeters of both storefronts is 6,000 feet, what is the area of the K-Mart store (in square feet)?

     a.   60,000
     b.   72,000
     c.   144,000
     d.   720,000
     e.   1,440,000

21. A realtor earns X dollars for every condo she sells, plus Y dollars for every half-hour she works. In one week, the realtor worked eleven hours and sold six condos. How many dollars did she earn that week?

     a.   11X + 6Y
     b.   11X + 12Y
     c.   22X + 6Y
     d.   6X + 22Y
     e.   6X + 22Y

22. In 2006, Dell Computer suffered a decline in desktop computer sales that amounted to 25% of the desktops sold in 2002 less 15,000. If the number of desktops sold in 2002 less the decline in desktop sales in 2006 amounted to 1,200,000 units, how many desktop computers did Dell sell in 2002?

     a.   948,000
     b.   1,185,000
     c.   1,245,000
     d.   1,580,000
     e.   1,896,000

Answer Key: Word Problems w/ Integers

(*Note*: Some of these problems can also be solved by using two equations – and two variables. Please see Chapter 19 for techniques and strategies)

1. The three consecutive integers are x, x + 1 and x + 2. From the problem, we can write the following equation:

$3 \{x + (x + 1)\} = 2 (x + 2) + 27$
$6x + 3 = 2x + 31$
$4x = 28$
$x = 7, x + 1 = 8\ x + 2 = \mathbf{9}.$ Choice B is correct.

2. First, let's define our variables. We will let x = the smaller number and 18 – x equal the larger number. Five times the smaller number is therefore 5x. Three times the larger number is 3(18 – x).

Further, we know that the difference between these two quantities is equal to 2. We must therefore solve the following equation:

$5x - 3(18-x) = 2$, so $5x - 54 + 3x = 2$, or $8x = 56$, or $x = 7$ and $18 - 7 = \textbf{11}$. Choice E is correct.

3. Let x = the smaller number. Therefore, the larger number = $x + 11$. We also know that:

$2x = (x + 11) + 14$
$2x = x + 25$
$x = \textbf{25}$. Choice B is correct.

4. This can be solved by a simple equation: $8x - 25 = 215$. $x = 30$. Choice C is correct.

5. From the data in the problem, we can write the following equation: $x + (x + 2) + (x + 4) + (x + 6) + (x + 8) = 370$, so $5x + 20 = 370$, so $5x = 350$, $x = 70$. $x + 8 = \textbf{78}$. Choice C is correct.

6. First, let's define our variables. We will let one number = x. Therefore, the second unknown is $x - 12$. The sum of these two numbers is 48. Hence, our equation becomes:

$x + (x - 12) = 48$
$2x = 60$
$x = 30$
$x - 12 = 18$
The smaller number is **18,** which is Choice A.

7. Let's call the two numbers x and $6x$. We also know that $4(x - 6x) = 60$. If we solve for x, we find:

$4x - 24x = 60$
$-20x = 60$
$x = -3$
$6x = -18$. The larger number is **–3**. Choice A is correct

8. In this case, the fastest way to solve this problem is to plug in the answer choices and test them. When we try Choice C, we get the right answer. $(15)(15) - (14)(14) = 225 - 196 = \textbf{29}$.

9. The easiest way to solve this problem is to try each answer choice. We know that the product of X and Y is 90; the problem asks us to identify the *smaller* of the two numbers. Therefore, we will substitute each answer choice into the formula $(X + Y) - (X - Y) = 18$ to see which combination gives us the correct an answer.

When we try Choice D, we discover that it works. $(6)(15) = 90$. Additionally, $(15 + 6) - (15 - 6) = 12$. Additionally, $(15)(6) = \textbf{90}$. The correct answer is 6, or choice D.

10. According to the problem, $y = 4x - 5$. If we solve for x, we find $x = \textbf{(y +5)/4}$. Choice B is correct.

11. First, let's define our variables. We will let one number = x. Therefore, the second unknown is $x - 46$. The sum of these two numbers is 238. Hence, our equation becomes:

$x + (x - 46) = 238$
$2x = 284$
$x = 142$
$x - 46 = 142 - 46 = \textbf{96}$. Choice A is correct.

12. First, we must calculate the numeric value of B, which is $12 \times 15 \times 34 = 6120$

Next, we must check each answer choice to see which one does not produce an integer:

B/18= 6120 / 18 = 340 = integer
B/30 = 6120 / 30 = 204 = integer
B/32 = 6120/ 32 = **191.25** = not an integer. Choice C is correct.
B/36 = 6120 / 36 = 170 = integer
B/72 = 6120 / 72 = 85 = integer

13. Choice D is not a prime triple because **27** is not a prime number.

14. The simplest way to solve this problem is to try each answer choice; the correct one will produce an odd number.

20/(2/3) = 60/2 = 30
20/(1/3) = 60/1 = 60
20/(2/5) = 100/2 = 50
20/(2/7) = 140/2 = 70
20/(4/3) = 60/4 = 15. Choice E is correct.

15. If the mean of fourteen consecutive integers is 27-1/2, then seven of the integers are less than 27-1/2 and the other seven are larger. The seven largest integers must be 28, 29, 30, 31, 32, 33 and 34. The average of these seven numbers is **31**. Choice C is correct.

16. To solve this problem, we can simply plug in random numbers for A and B and check each answer choice. When we do, we discover that the Choice B is the only one that yields an answer that is not an integer that is a multiple of 5 (5/15, 10/25, etc.).

17. To solve, let's substitute a few random numbers for the variables. Let's let V = 7. Then, W = 1 + 2 + 3 + 4 + 5 + 6 + 7 = 28.

The sum of the next 7 integers would be 8 + 9 + 10 + 11 + 12 + 13 + 14 = 77.

The answer choices require us to relate this sum (77) to the initial values of V and W, which are 7 and 28, respectively. Mathematically, $77 = 28 + 49 = W + V^2$. Choice D is correct.

18. Most students read this problem too quickly and simply choose Choice B, 50 cents. Not so fast. This problem contains a psychological trick that can easily convince you to select the wrong answer.

First, let's define our variables. We will let the cost of the pen = x. Therefore, the cost of the notebook = x + $10.00. If the cost of both items is $10.50, our equation becomes:

Cost of Pen + Cost of Notebook = Total Cost
x + (x + $10.00) = $10.50
2x + $10.00 = $10.50
2x = $0.50
X = **$0.25** = Choice A

19. First, let's define our variables. To avoid working with fractions, we will let Partner B's share = x. Therefore, Partner A's share = 4x and Partner C's share = 2(x + 4x) = 2(5x) = 10x.

Partner A's Share + Partner B's Share + Partner C's share = $675,000(0.75)
1x + 4x + 10x = $506,250
15x = $506,250
X = $33,750 = Partner B's share
4x = Partner A's share = 4($33,750) = **$135,000**. Choice C is correct.

20. This problem is easy to solve, but it requires multiple steps. It also requires a working knowledge of geometry, which we will cover later in this publication.

First, let's work with what we know, which is the length of each store.

We will let the length of Wal-Mart = x. Therefore, the length of K-Mart = 4x.

The perimeter of Wal-Mart is 4x, while the perimeter of K-Mart is 16x. Since the sum of the perimeters = 6000 feet, our equation becomes:

4x + 16x = 6000 ft.
20x = 6000 ft.
X = 300 feet = the length of Wal-Mart
Therefore, the length of K-Mart is 4(300) = 1200 feet

The area of K-Mart is (1200 feet)(1200 feet) = **1,440,000** square feet. Choice E is correct.

21. The easiest way to solve this problem is to substitute numbers for the variables. Let's assume that X = 1000 and Y = 20. Total earnings =Condo sales + Hourly Pay = 6(1000) + (2)(11)(20) = 6X + 22Y. Choice E is correct.

22. First, let's define our variables:

X = the number of desktops sold in 2002
Y = the decline of desktop sales in 2006

Thus, we can write the following two equations:

Y = x/4 – 15,000, or 4y = x – 60,000
X –Y = 1,200,000, or y = (x - 1,200,000)

If we combine the equations, we can solve for X:

4(x - 1,200,000) = x – 60,000
4x - 4,800,000 = x – 60,000
4,740,000 = 3x
X = **1,580,000** desktops sold in 2002. Choice D is correct.

Note: In Chapter 19, we will present other word problems that can be solved by writing two equations.

Chapter 8: Interest on Financial Investments

In the world of finance, the amount of money that a person invests is called principal, while the money that a bank pays the person for investing it is called interest. The rate (or interest rate) is the percentage used to compute the amount of interest that a bank pays on any given deposit.

By definition: **Interest = Principal x Rate x Time (or I = PRT)**

Unless otherwise specified, the interest is simple interest per year (no compounding).

On the SAT, GRE and GMAT, the interest problems can be relatively straightforward. You will be given three of the four quantities (interest, principal, rate, time) for a given scenario and asked to calculate the fourth quantity. Most of the time, however, the test writers will throw a predictable curve ball to test your understanding of these basic concepts - and the relationship among them. Here are the most common examples,

Example 1: Using the Basic Rate Equation

Frank puts $5,000 into a college savings account that pays 4.25% simple annual interest. If he leaves the money in the account for 3.5 years, what is the total amount that Frank will have?

    a. $5,014.88
    b. $5,063.75
    c. $5,743.75
    d. $7,437.50
    e. $7,543.75

Solution: Interest = Principal x Rate x Time. In this case, we have simple annual interest and we are asked to calculate the total amount at the end of 3.5 years:

Total = $5,000 + ($5,000)(0.0425)(3.5) = $5,000 + $743.75 = $5,743.75   Choice C is correct.

Example 2: Working Backwards With the Interest Equation

Maria put $4390 into a Platinum CD at her local bank, which she left untouched for six years and nine months, when she withdrew the entire amount, plus all of the simple annual interest she had earned. If the total balance in Maria's account was $6175, what simple rate of annual interest did she earn?

    a. 3.82%
    b. 4.62%
    c. 5.52%
    d. 6.02%
    e. 7.12%

Solution: In this case, we know the beginning and ending amounts and are being asked to calculate the rate of simple annual interest that was earned over 6.75 years. To solve, we will use the basic equation:

Interest = Principal x Rate x Time. The trick is to work backwards from our final total to determine the rate of interest that was paid. In this case, our total of $6157 represents the initial deposit of $4390 PLUS the interest earned.

Mathematically, $6175 = $4390 + PRT = $4390 + ($4390)(X)(6.75), so 6175 = 4390 + 29632.50X, or X =1785/29632.5 = 0.0602 = 6.02% Choice D is correct.

Example 3: Two Different Investments

Samantha deposited a total of $25,000 in a bank CD and a money market account. The bank CD offers a 7.5% annual return, while the money market account offers a 5.25% annual return. If Samantha earns $400 more per year from the CD than the money market account, how much did she invest in the CD?

    a. $10,569
    b. $11,011
    c. $11,569
    d. $13, 431
    e. $13, 989

Solution: Here, we are asked to calculate how much of the $25,000 Samantha placed into one of two investments. Let x = the amount in the bank CD and 25000 – x = the amount in the money market.

In this case, we know the interest rates on the two products and the difference between them. So, we can use this information to set up an equation to solve for the initial amount of money invested. The trick is to include the additional $400 in earnings on the correct side of the equation (since the CD earns her $400 more, we must add it to the OTHER side of the equation to make the quantities equal).

Principal x Rate x Time of CD = Principal x Rate x Time of Money Market
x(0.075)(1) = (25000 – x)(0.0525)(1) + 400
0.075x = 1312.5 – 0.0525x + 400
0.1275x = 1712.5
x =$13,431.37 in the CD.   Choice D is correct.

Example 4: Determining How Much Money to Invest to Achieve a Desired Income

Dave's grandmother has $50,000 invested at 5%. How much must she invest at 8% to earn $15,000 in interest from her investments annually?

    a. $31,250
    b. $62,500
    c. $156,250
    d. $312,500
    e. $625,000

Solution: In this problem, the interest payments from both investments must equal $15,000 per year. To solve, we will let x = the amount of money that Dave's grandmother will invest at 8%.

Our equation becomes:

5%($50,000) + 8%(x) = $15,000
(0.05)($50,000) + (0.08)(x) = $15,000

2500 + 0.08x = $15,000
0.08x = $12,500
x = $156,250. Choice C is correct.

To hone your skills on these concepts, try the following word problems. Complete solutions are presented at the end of the chapter.

Word Problems: Investments & Interest: EASY - MODERATE

1. Over the summer, Bill borrowed $6,500 from the bank at 8% simple interest. If he pays the money back over three years, what total amount of interest will Bill pay on the loan?

    a. $156
    b. $520
    c. $1040
    d. $1560
    e. $2080

2. Ronda borrowed $15,000 from the bank at 9% simple interest. If she pays the money back over four years, how much will she pay each month in interest?

    a. $37.50
    b. $112.50
    c. $375.00
    d. $450.00
    e. $5,400.00

3. Stephanie has a certain amount of money invested at 4% and three times that amount invested at 7% If the total annual interest from her two investments is $17,500, how much does Stephanie have invested at 7%?

    a. $35,000
    b. $70,000
    c. $135,000
    d. $170,000
    e. $210,000

4. Walter put $150,000 into an investment account, which he left untouched for eleven years and three months. At that time, he withdrew the entire amount, plus all of the simple annual interest he had earned. If the total balance in Walter's account was $272,514, what simple rate of annual interest did the account earn?

    a.   5.64%
    b.   6.14%
    c.   7.26%
    d.   8.88%
    e.   16.14%

5. A retiree needs to earn $25,000 in interest per year from her three investments to make ends meet. She already has $200,000 invested at 8% interest and $80,000 invested at 3% interest. How much additional money must she invest at 5% interest to reach her $25,000 total?

    a. $32,000
    b. $66,000
    c. $96,000
    d. $112,000
    e. $132,000

6. Jade placed a large sum of money in a bank CD that pays 8% simple interest per year. Then, she deposited the same amount, plus an additional $5000, in a real estate investment trust (REIT) that paid 12% simple annual interest. If her total annual return from both investments is $26,000, how much money did Jade place into the bank CD?

    a. 72,000
    b. 96,000
    c. 110,000
    d. 127,000
    e. 132,000

7. Pam plans to invest $35,000 in an account that pays 7.5% annually. How many additional dollars much she invest for the same amount of time at 4% annual interest so that her total income for the first year is 5% of her total investment?

    a. $4375
    b. $8,750
    c. $43,750
    d. $65,000
    e. $87,500

8. Ken deposited a total of $50,000 in a bank CD and a money market account. The bank CD offers a 4.5% annual return, while the money market account offers a 3.25% annual return. If Ken earns $800 more per year from the CD than the money market account, how much did he invest in the money market account?

    a. $18,710
    b. $20,967
    c. $29,032
    d. $29,832
    e. $31,290

Word Problems: Investments & Interest: AS HARD AS IT GETS

9. Investments A, B, and C yield $22,000 in total annual interest. Investment B. which earns 7% interest, is $25,000 larger than investment A, which earns 5% interest. In contrast, Investment C, which earns 9% interest, is $7,500 less than three times Investment A. How much is Investment A?

    a. $50,192.31
    b. $53,653.85
    c. $93,214.29
    d. $99,642.86
    e. $100,384.62

10. Gina invested an unknown amount of money in an account that pays 10% annually. Later, she invested an additional $87,500 for the same amount of time at 3% interest. If Gina's two investments earn a total of 6% annual interest, how much was her original investment?

    a. $32,825
    b. $55,500
    c. $65,625
    d. $262,500
    e. $525,000

Answer Key: Word Problems - Interest

(*Note*: Some of these problems can also be solved by using two equations – and two variables. Please see Chapter 19 for techniques and strategies)

1. This is a straightforward problem that we can solve using the formula, Interest = Principal x Rate x Time. In this case, the Principal = $6500, the Rate = 0.08 and the Time = 3 years.

Hence, Interest = ($6500)(0.08)(3) = **$1,560** in total interest. Choice D is correct.

2. To solve this problem, we must first calculate the total interest that Ronda will pay on the loan. To do so, we use the basic formula, Interest = Principal x Rate x Time. In this case, the Principal = $15000, the Rate = 0.09 and the Time = 4 years.

Hence, Interest = ($15000)(0.09)(4) = $5,400 in total interest over 4 years.

Now, we must convert this number to a monthly basis. If Ronda pays $5,400 in total interest over 4 years, then she pays $5,400/48 = **$112.50** in interest per month. Choice B is correct.

3. To solve, we must first determine how much interest Stephanie earns on each investment separately. For simplicity, we will x = the amount she has invested at 4%. Therefore, 3x = the amount that she has invested at 7%.

The interest on the account that pays 4% = 0.04x
The interest on the account that pays 7% = (0.07)3x = 0.21x

According to the problem, 0.04x + 0.21x = $17,500.

Therefore, 0.25x = $17,500, so x = $70,000 = amount invested at 4%.
3x = **$210,000** = the amount invested at 7%. Choice E is correct.

4. In this problem, we know the beginning and ending amounts and are being asked to calculate the rate of simple annual interest that was earned over 11.25 years. To solve, we will use the basic equation:

Interest = Principal x Rate x Time. The trick is to work backwards from our final total to determine the rate of interest that was paid. In this case, our total of $272,514 represents the initial deposit of $150,000 plus the interest that was earned.

Mathematically, $272,514 = $150,000 + PRT = $150,000 + ($150,000)(X)(11.25), so
$272,514 = $150,000 + (1,687,500)X, or X = 122514/1,687,500 = 0.0726 = **7.26%**. Choice C is correct.

5. In this problem, the interest payments from all three investments must equal $25,000 per year. To solve, we will let x = the amount of money that the retiree must invest at 5%. Our equation becomes:

8%($200,000) + 3%($80,000) + 5%(x) = $25,000
(0.08)($200,000) + (0.03)($80,000) + (0.05)(x) = $25,000
16,000 + 2,400 + 0.05x = $25,000
0.05x = $6,600
x = **$132,000**. Choice E is correct.

6. Let x = the amount in the bank CD; x + 5000 = the amount in the REIT

Interest = Principal x Rate x Time. In this case, we know the total amount that Jade earned per year, which is the sum of the two individual investments. So,

X(0.08)(1) + (x + 5000)(0.12)(1) = 26,000
8x + 12(x + 5000) = 2,600,000

20x = 2540000
x = **$127,000** in bank CD. Choice D is correct.

7. Let x = the additional dollars that Pam must invest at 4%. Her total investment is therefore 35,000 + x. By definition, the sum of both interest payments will be Pam's total interest:

0.075(35,000) + 0.04(x) = 0.05(35,000 + x). Solving for x,
2625 + 0.04x = 1750 + 0.05x
875 = 0.01x, so x = **$87,500**. Choice E is correct.

8. Here, we are asked to calculate how much of the $50,000 Ken placed into one of two investments. Let x = the amount in the money market and 50000 − x = the amount in the bank CD.

In this case, we know the interest rates on the two products and the difference between them. So, we can use this information to set up an equation to solve for the initial amount of money invested. The trick is to include the additional $800 in earnings on the correct side of the equation (since the CD earns him $800 more, we must add it to the OTHER side of the equation to make the quantities equal).

Principal x Rate x Time of Money Market = Principal x Rate x Time of CD
x(0.0325)(1) + 800 = (50000 − x)(0.0450)(1)
0.0325x + 800 = 2250 − 0.0450x
0.0775x = 1450
x =**$18,709.68** in the money market.   Choice A is correct.

9. To solve this problem, we must first define our variables:

Investment A = x
Investment B = x + $25,000
Investment C = 3x - $7,500

Next, we must write expressions to define the amount of interest that each investment earns:

Investment A = (0.05)x
Investment B = (0.07)(x + $25,000)
Investment C = (0.09)(3x − $7,500)

Finally, we must add these amounts, which − by definition − are equal to $22,000.

(0.05)x + (0.07)(x + $25,000) + (0.09)(3x − $7,500) = $22,000
(0.05)x + (0.07)x + $1,750 + (0.27)x - $675 = $22,000
(0.39)x = $20,925
x = **$53,653.85**. Choice B is correct.

10. To solve, we must first define our variables. In this case, we will let x = Gina's initial investment.
Her second investment is $87,500, which makes her total investment = x + $87,500.
Next, we must write expressions to describe the interest that each investment earns:

The first investment earns (0.10)x
The second investment earns (0.03)($87,500)
The total investment earns (0.06)(x + $87,500)

Therefore, our equation becomes:

(0.10)x + (0.03)($87,500) = (0.06)(x + $87,500)
(0.10)x + $2625 = (0.06)x + $5250
(0.04)x = $2625
x = **$65,625**. Choice C is correct.

Chapter 9: Coin Problems….and Other "Counting" Scenarios

When you encounter a coin problem on a standardized test, try to consider it in practical terms. Most coin problems are no more – or less- difficult that counting a pile of change in various denominations.

The easiest way to deal with them is to work with **cents,** rather than dollars. In your calculations, you should present each denomination as follows:

One penny = 1 cent
One nickel = 5 cents
One dime = 10 cents
One quarter = 25 cents
One half dollar = 50 cents
One dollar = 100 cents

Then, simply use the information that is given to:

1. Define your variables
2. Set up an equation that allows you to solve for the unknown quantity

The following examples show typical coin problems on the SAT, GRE, and GMAT – and the best way to approach them.

Example 1: Determining the Number of a Certain Type of Coin

Zoe has 30 coins, a combination of nickels and dimes, which are worth a total of $2.65. How many of Zoe's coins are dimes?

    a. 20
    b. 21
    c. 22
    d. 23
    e. 24

Solution: We must set up an equation to solve this problem, in which we add the number of nickels and dimes to reach the $2.65 total. First, let's define our variables. If x = # nickels, then $(30 - x)$ = # dimes.

Therefore, $5x$ = the value of the nickels and $(10)(30 - x) = (300 - 10x)$ = the value of the dimes.

If the total value of the coins is $2.65, then our equation becomes: $5x + (300 - 10x) = 265$.
Solving for x, there are $x = 7$ nickels and $30 - x = 23$ dimes. Choice D is correct.

Example 2: Three Different Types of Coins

At the end of her shift, Barb has 5 times as many dimes as she has nickels and 7 more pennies than nickels. If the total amount of these coins is $7.89, how many of them are nickels?

    a. 5
    b. 12
    c. 14
    d. 21
    e. 60

Solution: In this problem, students often become confused because there are three types of coins, rather than two. Don't be. Simply let x be the value that you are solving for – in this case the number of nickels. Then, define the other variables in terms of x.

If x = the number of nickels, then $5x$ = the number of dimes, and $x + 7$ = the number of pennies.

Therefore, the value of the nickels is 5x. The value of the dimes is (10)5x = 50x. The value of the pennies is (1)(x + 5) = (x + 5). Since the total of these amounts is $7.89, our equation becomes:

5x + 50x + (x + 5) = 789
56x + 5 = 789
56x = 784
x = 14 nickels. Choice C is correct.

This example illustrates a key point. If possible, when you choose your variables, let x equal the type of coin that you are solving for. If you do, you can stop working once you calculate its value, which will save you time and (possible) mistakes.

Example 3: Items Costing Different Amounts

Jane bought a total of twenty souvenir t-shirts during her vacation in Florida. Some were a tropical theme, which cost $15.00 each, while others were a cartoon theme, which cost $20.00 each. If Jane paid a total of $360.00 for the twenty t-shirts, how many cartoon theme shirts did she buy?

     a.   6
     b.   8
     c.   10
     d.   12
     e.   16

Solution: We can solve this problem using the same strategy that we used for coin problems. First, let's define our variables. We will let x = the number of cartoon shirts, while (20 – x) = the number of tropical shirts.

Therefore, the value of the cartoon shirts is ($20.00)(x), while the value of the tropical shirts is ($15.00)(20 – x). Since the total cost for the shirts is $360.00, our equation becomes:

($20.00)(x) + ($15.00)(20 – x) = 360.00
20x + 300 – 15x = 360
5x = 60
x = 12 cartoon shirts. Choice D is correct.

Example 4: Extending the Concept to Wages and Salaries

Patrice earns twice per hour as Jenny. Jenny earns $3 more per hour than Courtney. Together, they earn $57 per hour. How much is Patrice's hourly wage?

     a.   12
     b.   15
     c.   18
     d.   21
     e.   30

Solution: We can solve this problem using the same strategy that we used for coin problems. First, let's define our variables. Normally, we would let Patrice's wage = x, because this is the value we have been asked to find. However, doing so would require us to work with fractions, which are tedious and time consuming. So, we will let Courtney's wage = x to save time. We will, however, have to make sure that we complete the additional calculations after we solve for x to determine Patrice's wage.

First things first – let's make x = Courtney's hourly wage. Therefore, Jenny's wage = x + 3. Since Patrice earns twice as much as Jenny, her hourly wage is 2 (x + 3).

Therefore: x + (x + 3) + 2 (x + 3) = 57. Solving for x, we find that x = 12, which means Courtney earns $12 per hour, Jenny earns 12 + 3 = $15 per hour and Patrice earns 2(15 + 2) = $30 per hour. Choice E is correct.

Example 5: Two Ticket Prices: How Many of Each Were Sold?

An adult ticket to the Brooklyn Zoo costs $11.00, while a child's ticket costs $6.00. If a total of 750 people visited the zoo on Sunday and the total ticket sales were $5,000, how many children's tickets were sold that day?

    a. 100
    b. 150
    c. 600
    d. 650
    e. 700

Solution: This is another "combination" scenario in which the sum of two different types of tickets equals the total sales volume. We can answer the question by using the same strategy that we used for coin problems.

First, we must define our variables. We will let x = the number of children's tickets. Therefore, the number of adult tickets = (750 − x).

Next, we must define the sales revenue from each type of ticket:

For children's tickets, the sales = $6.00x
For adult tickets, the sales = $11.00(750 − x)

Since the total sales = the sum of adult and children's tickets, our equation becomes:

$6.00x + $11.00(750 − x) = $5000
$6.00x +$8250 - $11.00x = $5000
-$5.00x = -$3250
x = 650 children's tickets sold.   Choice D is correct.

Now that you've seen several types of coin and counting problems – try the following examples. Detailed solutions are presented at the end of the chapter.

Word Problems: Coins & Counting: EASY - MODERATE

1. Grace had $124.50 in her cookie jar, which consisted of nickels, dimes, and quarters. If Grace had 50 more nickels than quarters and 30 more dimes than nickels, how many quarters did Grace have?

    a. 285
    b. 315
    c. 335
    d. 345
    e. 365

2. Ben found a jar with 320 coins, all dimes and quarters, which were worth $77.90. How many of the coins were dimes?

    a. 14
    b. 15
    c. 32
    d. 210
    e. 306

3. In a jar containing dimes and nickels, the ratio of nickels to dimes is 3:5. If there are 80 coins, what is value of the nickels (in dollars)?

    a. $0.10
    b. $0.50
    c. $1.00
    d. $1.50
    e. $2.50

4. Colin has 75 coins that are worth $16.50. If the coins are all quarters and dimes, how many fewer dimes than quarters does Colin have?

    a.   15
    b.   30
    c.   45
    d.   60
    e.   75

5. Tracy collected money from 200 people to benefit a local charity. If the total amount of the donations Tracy collected was $6,500 and each person gave her either $20 or $50, how many fewer people donated $50 than $20?

    a.   40
    b.   60
    c.   80
    d.   120
    e.   160

6. If the value of x quarters is equal to the value of x + 32 nickels, x =

    a.   8
    b.   14
    c.   18
    d.   20
    e.   25

7. David has 20 pennies, 12 quarters and 27 dimes. How many nickels does this amount of money equal?

    a.   27
    b.   54
    c.   60
    d.   114
    e.   118

8. If the value of P quarters is equal to the value of P + 45 dimes, what is the value of P?

    a.   10
    b.   15
    c.   25
    d.   30
    e.   45

9. A store sells both videos and DVDs. The average price of a video is $12.00, while the average price of a DVD is $15.00. If, last month, the store sold 40 more DVDs than videos, and the total receipts were $6000, how many DVDs did the store sell?

    a. 200
    b. 205
    c. 220
    d. 240
    e. 245

10. Beth's Bridal Shop sells two designer gowns online: Victorian Lady and Summer Delight. Selling just these two products, the company makes $44,995 in profits each year on the sale of 450 gowns. If the profit per gown is $75 and $140 for Victorian Lady and Summer Delight, respectively, how many Victorian Lace gowns does the shop sell per year?

    a. 173
    b. 177
    c. 273
    d. 277
    e. 303

11. An online store sells two products: a hardcover and soft cover book of sonnets. Altogether, the company earned $65,000 in profits last year on the sale of 5000 units. If their profit on the hardcover book is $5 and their profit on the soft cover version is $15, how many soft cover books did they sell?

    a. 1000
    b. 1500
    c. 2000
    d. 3500
    e. 4000

12. Adam earns twice as much per hour as Josh. Josh earns $5 more per hour than Connie. Together, they earn $75 per hour. What is Adam's hourly wage?

    a. $15
    b. $20
    c. $25
    d. $30
    e. $40

Word Problems: Coins & Counting: AS HARD AS IT GETS

13. Three students – Nina, Tina, and Gina – are gathering change to do their weekly laundry. Nina has 7 more quarters than Tina, but one third as many as Gina. If girls have a total of 88 quarters, how many quarters does Gina have?

    a. 12
    b. 19
    c. 26
    d. 57
    e. 64

14. Netflix sells individual DVDs for $20 and packages of three DVDs for $50. Last month, Netflix sold 1000 DVDs for an average price of $18.00. How many individual DVDs did Netflix sell?

    a.   100
    b.   200
    c.   300
    d.   400
    e.   500

15. At a Van Halen concert with $2,275,000 in total ticket sales, the number of tickets sold in Section A was 100 less than three times the number of tickets sold for Section B, and the number of tickets sold in Section C was half the number of tickets sold in Section B. If Section B tickets cost $300, Section A tickets cost $250 and Section C ticket cost $200, how many tickets were sold in Section C?

    a.   500
    b.   1000
    c.   1500
    d.   2000
    e.   3000

16. Grace had six coins in her purse that totaled 63 cents. When she got off the bus, Grace lost one of the six coins. What are the odds that the lost coin was a penny?

    a.   1:6
    b.   1:5
    c.   1:4
    d.   1:3
    e.   1:2

17. At the end of an evening, a cashier adds the coins in her cash register. If she has A nickels, B dimes and C quarters, how many pennies does this equal?

    a.   5A + 10B + 25C
    b.   ABC/100
    c.   100(A +B + C)
    d.   (5A + 10B + 25C)/100
    e.   25A + 10B + 5C

Answer Key Word Problems: Coins & Counting

(*Note*: Some of these problems can also be solved by using two equations – and two variables. Please see Chapter 19 for techniques and strategies)

1. To solve, we must first define our variables. In this case, x = the number of quarters, x + 50 = the number of nickels, and x + 80 = the number of dimes. Since the sum of the coins = $124.50, our equation becomes:

Quarters + Dimes + Nickels = Total
25x + 10(x + 80) + 5(x + 50) = 12450
25x + 10x + 800 + 5x + 250 = 12450
40x = 11400
x = **285** quarters. Choice A is correct.

2. First, we must define our variables. In this case, x = the number of dimes. Therefore, 320 − x = the number of quarters. Since the value of these two coins is $77.90, our equation becomes:

$10x + 25(320 − x) = 7790$
$10x + 8000 − 25x = 7790$
$--15x = -210$
$x = $ **14** dimes. Choice A is correct.

3. In this case, the test writers have thrown us a curveball by presenting the number of nickels to dimes as a ratio. Don't be intimidated by it – just use the information to define the variables.

In this case, since the ratio of nickels to dimes is 3:5, we will let 3x = the number of nickels and 5x = the number of dimes. Since their total is 80, our equation becomes:

$3x + 5x = 80$
$8x = 80$
$x = 10$
Therefore, the number of nickels is 3(10) = 30; their value is 5(30) = **$1.50**. Choice D is correct.

4. First, we must define our variables. In this case, x = the number of quarters. Therefore, 75 − x = the number of dimes. Since the total value of these two coins is $16.50, our equation becomes:

$25x + 10(75 − x) = 1650$
$25x + 750 − 10x = 1650$
$15x = 900$
$x = 60$ quarters, 75 − 60 = 15 dimes. There are 60 − 15 = **45** fewer dimes than quarters. Choice C is correct.

5. First, we must define our variables. In this case, we will let x = the number of $50 donations. Therefore, 200 − x = the number of $20 donations. Since the total value of these two types of donations is $6,400 our equation becomes:

$\$50x + \$20(200 − x) = \$6,400$
$\$50x + \$4000 − \$20x = \$6,400$
$\$30x = \$2,400$
$x = 80$ $50 donations. Therefore, the number of $20 donations is 200 − 80 = 120.

The question asks us to find the *difference* between these values, which is 120 − 80 = **40**. Choice A is correct.

6. This problem puts a new spin on the traditional coin problem. We must simply convert the information in the problem to a mathematical formula and solve. If we have x quarters, then their value is 25x. From the problem, we know that 25x is equal to that of (x + 32) nickels, which can be represented as 5(x + 32). Hence, 25x = 5(x + 32). Solving for x, we find x = **8**. Choice A is correct.

7. To solve, we must determine the number of nickels that each type of coins represented. Then, we must add the amounts together:

20 pennies = 4 nickels
12 quarters = 60 nickels
27 dimes = 54 nickels. Therefore, the total number of nickels = 4 + 60 + 54 = **118**. Choice E is correct.

8. Once again, we can solve this problem by converting the words to an algebraic equation. If we have P quarters, their value is 25P. By definition, 25P = 10(P + 45). If we solve for P, we find 15P = 450, or P = **30**. Choice D is correct.

9. Let x be the number of videos sold and (x + 40) = the number of DVDs sold. Therefore, the value of the videos sold is 12x, while the value of the DVDs sold is 15(x + 40). Since the total sales figure is the sum of these two amounts, out equation becomes:

12x + 15(x+ 40) = 6000
27x + 600 = 6000
27x = 5400
x = 200 = # of videos sold
x + 40 = **240** = number of DVDs sold. Choice D is correct.

10, Let x = the # of Victorian Lady gowns sold and 450 – x = the # of Summer Delight gowns sold. The total profit ($44,995) is the sum of the two gowns, which makes our equation:

75x + 140 (450 –x) = 44,995
75x + 63,000 – 140x = 44,995
-65x = -18005
x = 277 Victorian Lady Gowns; 450 –277 = **173** Summer Delight Gowns. Choice D is correct.

11. Let x = # of soft cover books and 5000 – x = the # of hardcover books

The sum of their individual profits equals the total annual profit, or:
15x + 5(5000 – x) = 65000
15x + 25000 –5x = 65000
10x = 40000
x = **4000** soft cover books. Choice E is correct.

12. Let x = Connie's hourly wage. Josh's wage = x + 5. Since Adam earns twice as much as Josh, his hourly wage is 2 (x + 5). Therefore:

 x + (x + 5) + 2 (x + 5) = 75
4x + 15 = 75
4x = 60
x = Connie's wage = $15, Josh's wage = $20. Adam's wage = $40.
As a check, we can verify that $15 + $20 + $40 = **$75**. Choice E is correct.

13. To solve this problem, we must combine the three relationships into a single equation. First, we must define our variables:

Tina = x; Nina = x + 7; Gina = 3(x + 7). Hence, our equation is Tina + Nina + Gina = 88, or
x + (x + 7) + 3(x + 7) = 88
5x + 7 + 21 = 88
5x = 60
x = 12. Tina has 12 quarters. Nina has x + 7 = 19 quarters. Gina has 3(x + 7) = 3(12 + 7) = **57.** Choice D is correct.

14. The key to this question is the word *average*. If Netflix sold 1000 DVDs for an *average price* of $18.00, then the total amount of money they received was (1000)($18) = $18,000. We can now use this figure to calculate the number of individual DVDs vs. the number of 3-packs.

First, let's define our variables. X = the number of 3-packs of DVDs that were sold. Therefore, the sales from those DVDs = 50x. The number of individual DVDs sold is (1000 – 3x); their sales = 20(1000 – 3x). Therefore, our equation becomes:

50x + 20(1000 – 3x) = $18,000
50x + 20,000 – 60x = $18,000
-10x = -2000
x = 200 three--packs sold

Therefore, the number of *individual* DVDs sold = 1000 – (3)(200) = 1000 – 600 = **400**. Choice D is correct.

15. Although the verbiage in this question is confusing, it is actually just a simple problem in which concert tickets were sold at three different prices. Knowing the total sales, we must determine how many were sold at one of the three price points.

To solve, we must first define our variables.

For simplicity, we will let X = the number of tickets sold in Section B. Their value is 300x.
Therefore, the number of tickets in Section A = 3x – 100. Their value is 250(3x – 100).
Finally, the number of tickets in Section C = 1/2x. Their value is 200(1/2x) or 100x.

Our equation is simply:

Section A + Section B + Section C = Total Sales
250(3x – 100) + 300x + 100x = $2,275,000
750x - 25,000 + 400x = $2,275,000
1150x = $2,300,000
x = 2000 tickets sold in Section B

The number of tickets sold in Section C = 2000/2 = **1000**. Choice B is correct.

16. The hardest part of this question is determining the composition of the coins. The only way 6 coins can add up to 63 cents is if two of them were quarters, one was a dime, and the other three were pennies: 25 + 25 + 10 + 1 + 1 + 1. Hence, the probability that one of the coins is a penny is 3/6 or **1:2**. Choice E is correct.

17. To solve, we must convert all of the terms to pennies and add them together. Let's start with what we know.

There are 5 pennies in 1 nickel.   Hence, our coefficient for A is 5.
There are 10 pennies in 1 dime.   Hence, our coefficient for B is 10.
There are 25 pennies in 1 quarter. Hence, our coefficient for C is 25.

The number of pennies in A nickels, B dimes and C quarters is therefore **5A + 10B + 25C**. Choice A is correct

Chapter 10: Age & Weight Problems

One of the most common types of algebraic word problems on the SAT, GRE and GMAT is a comparison of people's ages:

Theresa is 10 years older than Cindy. However, 5 years ago Theresa was twice as old as Cindy. How old is Cindy?
Sue is three times as old as Grace. Lee is 5 years older than Grace. If their combined age is 58, how old is Grace?

Silly? Yes. Contrived? Definitely. But these problems – however impractical - are a staple on standardized tests because they evaluate your reasoning ability. Consequently, we would be remiss if we did not devote a chapter to them.

Regardless of the scenario, the problems are solved in the same way:

1. Define your variables
2. Write an equation to represent their relationship
3. Solve for the unknown

For many students, the hardest part of these questions is transcribing the verbiage into mathematical terms. A few rules of thumb:

1. Let x = a person's current age. Then, you can represent his/her age 5 years ago as $x - 5$ and his/her age 5 years from now as $x + 5$.

2. Draw a quick chart that defines the variables; this will greatly enhance your ability to write the equation correctly.

As always, the best way to explain the approach is by relevant examples:

Example 1: When No Exact Ages are Given

Kate is eight years older than her brother Jake. Four years ago, Kate was twice as old as Jake. How old is Jake now?

    a.   4
    b.   6
    c.   8
    d.   10
    e.   12

Solution: The problem describes a relationship between the ages of two siblings – Kate and Jake – at two points in time. Our first step will be to draw a quick chart for the information we are given:

Name	Current Age	Age 4 years ago
Kate		
Jake		

Since the question asks us to determine Jake's current age, we will let that value = x. Once we do, we know that Kate's current age = $x + 8$.

Four years ago, Jake's age was $x - 4$. Kate's age was $(x + 8) - 4$

Name	Current Age	Age 4 years ago
Kate	$x + 8$	$(x + 8) - 4$
Jake	x	$x - 4$

Now, we must write our equation to solve for x. Since we are being asked to solve for Jake's age, we will establish our equation using *Kate's data from four years ago.*

From the table, we know that Kate's age 4 years ago = (x + 8) – 4.
From the problem, we ALSO know that Kate's age 4 years ago was twice Jake's age, or 2(x - 4)

Therefore, (x + 8) – 4 = 2(x - 4)
x + 4 = 2x – 8
x = 12 = Jake's current age. Choice E is correct

When you are first learning how to solve these problems, it helps to check your work. If Jake is currently 12, then Kate = 8 + 12 = 20.

Four years ago, Kate was (12 + 8) – 4 = 16.   Jake was 12 – 4 = 8. (Kate's age 4 years ago was indeed twice Jake's age)

Example 2: When an Exact Age is Given

The sum of Adam's age and Eve's age is 54. Six years ago, Adam was 4 years older than Eve. How old is Eve now?

      a.   23
      b.   25
      c.   26
      d.   28
      e.   29

Solution: The problem gives us the sum of the current ages of Adam and Eve. We also know that Adam was 4 years older than Eve six years ago. Our task is to find Eve's current age.

Our first step will be to draw a quick chart for the information we are given:

Name	Current Age	Age 6 years ago
Adam		
Eve		

Since the question asks us to determine Eve's current age, we will let that value = x. Once we do, we know that Adam's current age = 54 - x.

Six years ago, Adam's age was (54 –x) – 6. Eve's age was x – 6

Name	Current Age	Age 6 years ago
Adam	54 - x	(54 – x) – 6
Eve	x	x - 6

 Now, we must write our equation to solve for x. Since we are being asked to solve for Eve's age, we will establish our equation using Adam's *data from six years ago*.

From the table, we know that Adam's age 6 years ago = (54 - x) – 6.
From the problem, we ALSO know that Adam was 4 years older than Eve 6 years ago, or (x – 6) + 4

Therefore, (54 -x) – 6 = (x – 6) + 4
48 – x = x – 2
2x = 50
x =25 = Eve's current age. Choice B is correct.

Now, let's check our work. If Eve is currently 25, then Adam = 54 – 25 = 29.
Six years ago, Adam was 29 – 6 = 23 and Eve was 25 – 6 =19.
Eve's age six years ago was indeed 4 less than Adam's age.

Example 3. Problems with Three Timeframes

Wayne is three times as old as his granddaughter Sharon. In twelve years, Wayne will be six times as old as Sharon was four year ago. How old is Sharon now?

        a.   4
        b.   6
        c.   12
        d.   24
        e.   36

Solution: This problem has an additional level of difficulty because it adds a third timeframe. Don't let that throw you. Instead, follow the same approach you would use for any other type of problem.

Our first step will be to draw a quick chart for the information we are given:

Name	Current Age	Age 12 years from now	Age 4 years ago
Wayne			
Sharon			

Now, let's fill in what we know. Since the question asks us to determine Sharon's current age, we will let that value = x. Once we do, we know that Wayne's current age = 3x.

Twelve years from now, Sharon's age will be x + 12, while Wayne's age will be 3x + 12
Four years ago, Sharon's age was x – 4, while Wayne's age was 3x – 4.

Name	Current Age	Age 12 years from now	Age 4 years ago
Wayne	3x	3x + 12	3x - 4
Sharon	x	x + 12	x – 4

Since we are looking for Sharon's age, we must use the *Wayne's data twelve years from now*.

From the table, we know that Wayne's age twelve years from now = 3x + 12.

From the problem itself, we ALSO know that Wayne's age twelve years from now is "six times as old as Sharon was four year ago," which can be written mathematically as 6(x – 4).

Our equation, therefore, is:

3x + 12 = 6(x – 4)
3x + 12 = 6x - 24
3x = 36
x = 12 = Sharon's current age. Choice C is correct.

Example 4: One Person's Age at Various Points in Time

If Melanie's age three years from now plus her age two years ago plus five times her age three years ago is equal to 84 years. How old is Melanie now?

        a.   14
        b.   15
        c.   16
        d.   17
        e.   18

Solution: For age problems with a single person, our chart is much simpler:

Melanie Now	Melanie plus 3	Melanie minus 2	Melanie minus 3

Now, let's fill in our values. As always, we will let Melanie's current age = x.
Her age a year from now will be x + 3

Her age two years ago was x – 2
Her age five years ago was x - 3

Melanie Now	Melanie plus 3	Melanie minus 2	Melanie minus 3
x	x + 3	x – 2	x – 3

By definition, our equation is:

(x +3) + (x – 2) + 5(x – 3) = 84
x + 3 + x – 2 + 5x – 15 = 84
7x = 98
x = 14 = Melanie's current age. Choice A is correct.

Example 5: Weight Problems: Different Measurement – Same Approach

Valerie weighs three times as much as Tiffany. Brittany weighs six pounds more than Valerie. If their combined weights are 356, how much does Brittany weigh?

     a.   134
     b.   140
     c.   146
     d.   150
     e.   156

Solution: When a problem gives us the exact weights for the subjects – or their total weight – we can solve it by using the information we have to build an equation to solve for the unknown (in this case, Brittany's weight).

Let Tiffany's weight = T. Therefore, Valerie's weight = 3T and Brittany's weight = 3T + 6.

Since the sum of the three weights is 356, our equation becomes:

T + 3T + (3T + 6) = 356
7T + 6 = 356
T = 50. Tiffany weights 50, Valerie weighs 150, Brittany weighs 156. Choice E is correct.

Once you are comfortable with the various types of age/weight problems, try your hand at these examples. Detailed solutions can be found at the end of the chapter.

Word Problems: Age / Weight : EASY – MODERATE

1. Theresa is 10 years older than Cindy. However, 5 years ago Theresa was twice as old as Cindy. How old is Cindy?

     a.   5
     b.   10
     c.   12
     d.   15
     e.   20

2. Nathan is seven years older than his sister Claire, who is three years younger than Jayne, who is 28 years old. How old is Nathan?

     a.   22
     b.   25
     c.   28
     d.   29
     e.   32

3. Jocelyn weighs 60% as much as Connie. If Jocelyn gains 8 pounds, she will weigh 75% as much as Connie. What is Jocelyn's weight (in pounds)?

    a.   32.0
    b.   35.5
    c.   40.0
    d.   43.3
    e.   53.3

4. Sue is twice as old as Grace. Lee is 5 years older than Grace. If their combined age is 65, how old is Grace?

    a.   12
    b.   15
    c.   16
    d.   18
    e.   24

5. Three sisters, Hannah, Juliet and Patricia, have weights that are consecutive even numbers. Eighteen less than Juliet's weight equals 50 less than the sum of Hannah and Patricia's weights. What is Juliet's weight?

    a.   26
    b.   28
    c.   30
    d.   32
    e.   34

6. Liz is 42 years old and Amelia is 24. How many years ago was Liz three times as old as Amelia?

    a.   9
    b.   10
    c.   15
    d.   18
    e.   20

7. Rafe is four times as old as Monica. In ten years, Rafe will be 10 times as old as Monica was 5 years ago. How old will Rafe be in five years?

    a.   19
    b.   24
    c.   25
    d.   29
    e.   34

8. If Candy's age ten years from now minus her age eight years ago plus six times her age four years ago is equal to 120 years, how old will Candy be in eleven years?

    a.   20
    b.   21
    c.   30
    d.   32
    e.   41

9. Dave is 36 years older than his triplet daughters. If the sum of their four ages is 15 greater than Dave's age, how old is Dave?

     a.   38
     b.   39
     c.   40
     d.   41
     e.   42

Word Problems: Age / Weight : AS HARD AS IT GETS

10. A family has four children: a set of triplets and an older son. Five years ago, the sum of the ages of the triplets and their older brother was 122. If the brother is six years older than his siblings, then how old are the triplets today?

     a.   32
     b.   34
     c.   35
     d.   36
     e.   40

11. Two sisters, Candy and Jessie, joined Weight Watchers to prepare for bikini season. Initially, their combined weight was 200 pounds. During their month in Weight Watchers, Candy lost 20% of her original weight, while Jessie gained 10% of her original weight. If the sum of the sisters' weights after Weight Watchers is 180 pounds, what was Candy's original weight (in pounds)?

     a.   67
     b.   80
     c.   100
     d.   120
     e.   133

12. Chelsea is three times as old as Bob. In twelve years, she will be two years less than twice Bob's age. How old was Chelsea when Bob was born?

     a.   10
     b.   15
     c.   20
     d.   24
     e.   It cannot be determined from the information given.

13. Bea is three times as old as Genie was two years ago. Four years from now, Bea will be 50% of Genie's age. What is their current combined age?

     a.   3.2
     b.   3.4
     c.   6.8
     d.   8.6
     e.   It cannot be determined from the information given.

Answer Key: Age / Weight Problems

(*Note*: Some of these problems can also be solved by using two equations – and two variables. Please see Chapter 19 for techniques and strategies)

1. First, we must summarize our data in a table:

Name	Current Age	Age 5 years ago
Theresa	x + 10	(x + 10) − 5
Cindy	x	x - 5

Next, we must write our equation. Five years ago, Theresa was twice as old as Cindy, which gives us the following equation:

$x + 5 = 2 (x - 5)$
$x + 5 = 2x − 10$
$x = $ **15.** Choice D is correct.

2. In this case, we can start with Jayne, whose actual age we are given. Then, we can work backwards to determine Nathan's age.

Jane = 28
Claire = 28 − 3 = 25
Nathan = 25 + 7 = **32**. Choice E is correct.

3. First, we must summarize our data in a table:

Name	Current Weight	Hypothetical Weight
Connie	x	-
Jocelyn	0.6x	0.6x + 8

In this case, Connie's weight does not change. Our equation is simply the relationship between the two weights if Jocelyn gains eight pounds: $0.6x + 8 = 0.75x$

Solving for x, Connie's weight = 53.3 lbs and Jocelyn's weight = **32** lb. Choice A is correct.

4. In this problem, we know the relationship among the ages of Sue, Grace, and Lee – and their combined age. We can use this information to build an equation to solve for Grace's age.

For simplicity, we will let Grace's age = x. Thus, Sue's age is 2x, while Lee's age is x + 5.
Since the sum of their ages is 65, our equation becomes:

$x + 2x + (x + 5) = 65$
$4x + 5 = 65$
$4x = 60$
$X = $ **15** = Grace's age. Choice B is correct.

5. We will use the information we have to build an equation to solve for Juliet's weight. Since the weights are consecutive even numbers, we can let Hannah's weight =x, Juliet's weight = (x + 2) and Patricia's weight = (x + 4).

By definition, Juliet's weight less 18 equals the sum of Hannah and Patricia's weights minus 50. Mathematically, our equation becomes:

$(x+2) − 18 = \{x + (x+4)\} − 50$
$x − 16 = 2x − 46$
$x = 30, x + 2 = 32, x + 4 = 34.$ Since Juliet's weight (x+2) = **32,** Choice D is correct.

6 .Here, we are given the current ages of two women and asked to calculate a time when those numbers met a specified set of criteria. Currently, Liz = 42 and Amelia = 24. Therefore, X years ago, Liz = 42 − x and Amelia = 24 − x.

The correct equation to express the relationship between their ages x years ago is therefore:

42 − x = 3 (24 − x)
42 − x = 72 − 3x
2x = 30. x = **15** Choice C is correct.

7. Our first step will be to draw a quick chart for the information we are given:

Name	Current Age	Age 10 years from now	Age 5 years ago
Rafe			
Monica			

To avoid working with fractions, we will Let Monica's current age = x. Once we do, we know that Rafe's current age = 4x.

Ten years from now, Monica's age will be x + 10, while Rafe's age will be 4x + 10
Five years ago, Monica's age was x − 5, while Rafe's age was 4x − 5.

Name	Current Age	Age 10 years from now	Age 5 years ago
Rafe	4x	4x + 10	4x - 5
Monica	x	x + 10	x − 5

From the table, we know that Rafe's age ten years from now = 4x + 10

From the problem itself, we ALSO know that Rafe's age ten years from now is "ten times as old as Monica was 5 years ago," which can be written mathematically as 10 (x − 5).

Our equation, therefore, is:

4x + 10 = 10(x − 5)
4x + 10 = 10x - 50
6x = 60
x = 6 – Monica's current age.

Rafe's current age is 4(6) = 24. Five years from now, Rafe will be 24 + 5 = **29**. Choice D is correct.

8. For age problems with a single person, our chart is:

Candy Now	Candy plus 10	Candy minus 8	Candy minus 4

Now, let's fill in our values. As always, we will let Candy's current age = x.
Her age 10 years from now will be x + 10
Her age 8 years ago was x − 8
Her age 4 years ago was x - 4

Candy Now	Candy plus 10	Candy minus 8	Candy minus 4
X	x + 10	x − 8	x − 4

By definition, our equation is:

 (x +10) - (x − 8) + 6(x − 4) = 120
x + 10 - x + 8 + 6x − 24 = 120
6x = 126
x = 21 = Candy's current age. In 11 years, Candy will be **32.** Choice D correct

9. The triplets' age = x, which makes Dave's age = x + 36.

Thus, X + X + X +(X + 36) = (X + 36) + 15
3x = 15
X = 5
X + 36 = **41**. Choice D is correct.

10. First, let's summarize what we know in a chart:

	Today	Five Years Ago
Triplets	x	x − 5
Brother	x + 6	(x + 6) − 5 = x + 1

First, let's assign our variables. We will let x = the current age of the triplets, which makes the brother's age = x + 6. Five years ago, their ages can be represented by x − 5 (triplets) and (X + 6) - 5 = x + 1 (brother). According to the problem, five years ago, the sum of the ages was 122:

3 (x − 5) + (x + 1) = 122
3x − 15 + x + 1 = 122
4x = 136
X = **34** = age of triplets. Choice B is correct.
X + 6 = 40 = brother's age

11. First, let's summarize what we know in a chart.

Candy	C pounds	0.20 loss
Jessie	J pounds	0.10 gain

Thus, we can write the following two equations to define the relationship between the variables:

C + J = 200
0.80C + 1.10J = 180

If we combine the equations, we can solve for C:

C + J = 200, so J = 200 − C
80C + 110(200 − C) = 18,000
80C + 22,000 − 110C = 18,000
-30C = -4,000

C = **133.33** pounds. Choice E is correct.
J = 66.67 pounds

12. Our first step will be to draw a quick chart for the information we are given:

Name	Current Age	Age 12 years from now	Age x years ago (at Bob's birth)
Chelsea	3x	3x + 12	3x − x
Bob	x	x + 12	0

Twelve years from now, Chelsea's age will be 3x + 12, while Bob's age will be x + 12

From the problem, we ALSO know that Chelsea's age twelve years from now will be "two less than twice Bob's age," 2(x + 12) - 2.

Our equation, therefore, is:

3x + 12 = 2(x + 12) − 2
3x + 12 = 2x + 24 − 2 = 2x + 22
x = 10 = Bob's current age.

But we weren't asked Bob's age; we were asked how old Chelsea was when Bob was born, which will be 3x − x, or 3(10) − 10 = 30 − 10 = **20.** Choice C is correct.

As a check, we can run through these numbers and confirm that they make sense. Currently, Bob is 10 and Chelsea is 30 (3 times 10). Therefore, when Bob was born 10 years ago, Chelsea was 30 − 10 = 20.

13. This problem is tough because it requires the use of two equations to solve. First, let's define our variables. In this case, we will let B = Bea's current age and G = Genie's current age.

From the problem we know that $B = 3(G - 2) = 3G - 6$. (Their relationship 2 years ago)
We also know that $B = 0.5(G + 4) = 0.5G + 2$ (Their relationship 4 years from now)

To solve for Genie's age, we simply combine these equations:

$3G - 6 = 0.5G + 2$
$2.5G = 8$
$G = 3.2$ years old
Therefore, $B = 3(3.2 - 2) = 3(1.2) = 3.6$ years old

Their combined ages are 3.2 years and 3.6 years = **6.8 years**. Choice C is correct.

To check this answer, let's see if it holds for the other time periods that are mentioned in the problem.

If Bea is currently 3.6 years old and Genie is 3.2 years old, then 2 years ago, Bea was 1.6 years old and Genie was 1.2 years old. Bea's current age (3.6) is indeed 3 times Genie's age 2 years ago (1.2).

Chapter 11: Rate & Distance Problems

The SAT, GRE and GMAT often include at least one word problem that uses the rate formula:

Distance = Rate X Time

The underlying concept is simple, as illustrated by the following examples:

Example: If Joe drove for 5 hours at 50 miles per hour, how far did he travel?
Distance = Rate x Time = (5 hours)(50 miles/hour) = **250 miles**

Example: If Joe travels at an average rate of 70 miles per hour, how long will it take him to travel 560 miles?
Distance = Rate x Time, so **Time = Distance/Rate** = (560 miles/70miles per hour) = **8 hours**

Example: If Joe travelled from Miami to Atlanta, which is 640 miles, in 8 hours, how fast was he driving?
Distance = Rate x Time, so **Rate = Distance/Time** = (640 miles)/8 hours = **80 miles per hour**

Unfortunately, the SAT, GRE and GMAT rarely test these concepts in such a straightforward manner. Instead, they include pesky word problems in which you must apply your knowledge of the rate equation to some fairly contrived situations, with TWO vehicles moving at different speeds (and for different amounts of time).

Here are the most common types of problems – and the fastest way to solve them.

Example 1: Two Cars on the Move – Find the Speed

Paul and Regina got into their cars in the school parking lot and drove in opposite directions. If Paul drove 20 miles per hour faster than Regina, and they were 360 miles apart after driving for 4 hours, how fast was Regina driving (in miles per hour)?

    a. 20
    b. 25
    c. 35
    d. 40
    e. 45

Solution: The first step for this type of problem is to draw a quick chart of what we know.

Driver	Distance	Rate	Time
Paul	4(x + 20)	x + 20	4
Regina	4x	x	4

In this case, we will let x = Regina's rate (or speed), which is what we are asked to find. Paul's speed is therefore x + 20.

Since they both travel for 4 hours, we can complete the Distance entry for both Paul and Regina, which will be 4(x + 20) and 4x, respectively. But how do we USE the information on the chart?

Well, Paul and Regina might have started in the same place and driven for the same amount of time, but they drove at different speeds, which meant that Paul *travelled farther* than Regina did.

Therefore, the 360 miles is the TOTAL distance that the two of them drove. Mathematically, it can be represented by the SUM of Paul's distance, 4(x + 20), and Regina's distance, 4x. Hence, our equation becomes:

4x + 4(x + 20) = 360
8x +80 = 360
8x = 280
x =35 miles per hour = Regina's speed. Choice C is correct.

Example 2: Two Trains on Opposite Tracks - Finding the Time

Train A and Train B left the Kansas City Station at the same time and travelled in opposite directions. If Train A travelled at an average rate of 115 miles per hour and Train B travelled at an average rate of 85 miles per hour, how many hours will it take Train A and Train B to be 1,800 miles apart?

      a.   6
      b.   7
      c.   8
      d.   9
      e.   11

Solution: The first step for this type of problem is to draw a quick chart of what we know.

Driver	Distance	Rate	Time
Train A	115x	115	x
Train B	85x	85	x

In this case, we will let x = the time it takes for Train A and Train B to travel 1,800 miles.

We can also enter the rates for each train and write an expression for their respective distances. Next, we must use this information to solve for x.

Train A and Train B each travelled *a portion* of the total distance, which is 1,800 miles. Our equation, therefore, is:

Train A's Distance + Train B's Distance = Total Distance
115 x + 85X = 1,800
200x = 1800
X = 9 hours Choice D is correct

Example 3: One Person, Different Speeds - Finding the Distance

A bus carried 60 students from their school to an amusement park at a speed of 40 miles per hour. On the trip back, the bus travelled at a rate that was 10 miles per hour less. As a result, it took the bus an additional 90 minutes to get back to the school. How many miles was the amusement park from the school?

      a.   90
      b.   120
      c.   180
      d.   360
      e.   1080

Solution: The first step for this type of problem is to draw a quick chart of what we know.

Route	Distance	Rate	Time
To Park	40x	40	x
From Park	30(x + 1.5)	30	x + 1.5

In this case, we will let the amount of time the bus travels to the amusement park = x. Its return time (in hours) is therefore x + 1.5.

Once we have the expressions for the distance travelled to – and from – the amusement park, we can use them to write an equation to solve for the distance.

Distance to Park = Distance from Park
40x = 30(x + 1.5)
40x = 30x + 45
10x = 45
x = 4.5 hours = amount of time required for the bus to reach the amusement park from the school

Therefore, we can use the information in our table to calculate the distance between the school and the park: 40x = (40)(4.5) = 180 miles. Choice C is correct.

Example 4: Vehicles Starting at Different Times

Grace raced to the hospital at 80 miles per hour to visit her ailing mother. An hour later, her twin brother Glen raced along the same road in the same direction at 100 miles per hour. How many hours will it take Glen to catch up to Grace?

    a. 2
    b. 3
    c. 4
    d. 5
    e. 6

Solution: The first step for this type of problem is to draw a quick chart of what we know.

Driver	Distance	Rate	Time
Grace	80(x + 1)	80	x + 1
Glen	100x	100	x

In this case, the vehicles travel the same distance at different speeds. Our equation is:

$80(x + 1) = 100x$
$80x + 80 = 100x$
$80 = 20x$
$X = 4$ hours = amount of time it will take Glen to catch up to Grace

Example 5: An SAT, GRE and GMAT Staple: Finding the Average Rate

On Valentine's Day, a busy florist drove his delivery truck from Palm Beach to Miami at an average rate of 45 miles per hour. On his return trip to Palm Beach, he encountered rush hour traffic, which slowed him to an average speed of 25 miles per hour. What was the driver's average speed for the trip, in miles per hour?

    a. 30
    b. 32
    c. 35
    d. 36
    e. 38

Solution: As you probably suspect, the seemingly obvious answer of 35 mph, which is Choice C, is incorrect. When cars travel at different speeds, they take different lengths of time to cover the same distance. Consequently, we cannot simply average the two speeds to get the correct answer. Instead, we must use the following formula to determine the average rate:

Average Rate = Total Distance / Total Time

In this case, the test writers did not give us any specific numbers, so we are free to pick any value for the total distance. In this case, we will use 100 miles for the total distance, which makes each leg of the trip (the distance from Palm Beach to Miami) equal to one-half of 100, or 50 miles.

For the trip from Palm Beach to Miami,
Average Rate = 50 miles/ 45 miles per hour = 1.11 hours

For the return trip from Miami to Palm Beach,
Average rate = 50 miles / 25 miles per hour = 2 hours

Hence, the total time was 3.11 hours

Going back to the original equation, for the total trip,

Average Rate = Total Distance / Total Time = 100 miles/3.11 hours = 32 miles per hour

The correct answer is Choice B.

Word Problems: Rate & Distance: EASY - MODERATE

1. Kayla and Ali are 12 miles apart. If Kayla starts walking toward Ali at 6 miles per hour and at the same time Ali starts walking toward Kayla at 4 miles per hour, how much time will pass before they meet?

        a.   48 minutes
        b.   62 minutes
        c.   68 minutes
        d.   70 minutes
        e.   72 minutes

2. The distance between Annapolis and Charlotte is 150 miles. A car travels from Annapolis to Charlotte at 75 miles per hour and returns from Charlotte to Annapolis along the same route at 50 miles per hour. What is the average speed for the round trip?

        a.   60.0
        b.   62.5
        c.   65.0
        d.   67.5
        e.   70.0

3. Jake has to get home from the prom by 2 am. If he leaves the prom at 11:30 pm and his house is 96 miles away, how fast does Jake have to drive to get home by 2 am (in miles per hour)?

        a.   36.0
        b.   38.4
        c.   48.0
        d.   76.8
        e.   96.0

4.Two motorcyclists are 540 miles apart. At 10:00 am they start traveling toward each other at rates of 65 and 70 miles per hour. At what time will they pass each other?

        a.   1:00 pm
        b.   1:30 pm
        c.   2:00 pm
        d.   3:30 pm
        e.   4:00 pm

5. The Big Red Boat and the Carnival Cruise Ship left Port Canaveral at the same time and sailed in opposite directions. If the Big Red Boat traveled 35 miles per hour slower than the Carnival Cruise Ship, and they were 490 miles apart after sailing for 10 hours, how fast was the Carnival Cruise Ship sailing (in miles per hour)?

        a.   7
        b.   15
        c.   40
        d.   42
        e.   50

6. A US Air commercial jet and a Sea Hawk helicopter left the Chicago airport at the same time and headed in opposite directions. If the US Air jet flew at an average rate of 500 miles per hour and the Sea Hawk helicopter flew at an average rate of 100 miles per hour, how many hours would it take the two flights to be 4,200 miles apart (assuming no stops to re-fuel)?

     a.   7
     b.   8
     c.   10
     d.   12
     e.   20

7. A Greyhound bus drove down the highway at 60 miles per hour. Three hours later, a second Greyhound bus traveled the same route at 40 miles per hour. How many hours will it take the second bus to reach the first?

     a.   4
     b.   5
     c.   6
     d.   8
     e.   9

8. Ben drove his car from Chicago to Philadelphia at an average rate of 75 miles per hour. On his return trip to Chicago, he encountered bad weather, which forced him to reduce his speed to 40 miles per hour. What was the Ben's average speed for the trip (in miles per hour?

     a.   52
     b.   55
     c.   60
     d.   62
     e.   65

9. Julie drives to her grandmother's house every week at an average speed of 50 miles per hour. On the way home, she takes the same route, but averages 75 miles per hour. If Julie's total round trip is 10 hours, how far away is her grandmother's house?

     a.   30
     b.   60
     c.   150
     d.   300
     e.   600

10. Jill and Kim leave school at the same time and drive in opposite directions. After two hours, they are 100 miles apart. How fast is Jill driving, if Kim is driving 10 miles per hour faster?

     a.   20
     b.   30
     c.   35
     d.   40
     e.   50

11. Wendy drove the 700 miles between New York and Chicago in 12 hours. Before the 5 pm dinner rush, she averaged 70 miles per hour. Afterward 5 pm, Wendy averaged only 50 miles per hour. At what time did Wendy begin her trip?

    a. 9 am
    b. 11 am
    c. 12 noon
    d. 1 pm
    e. It cannot be determined from the information given

12. Jack and Jill left home at the same time and travelled to the airport using the same route. Jack drove at an average speed of 75 miles per hour, while Jill drove an average speed of 45 miles per hour. In how many hours will Jack's car be 45 miles ahead of Jill's?

    a. ½
    b. 1
    c. 3/2
    d. 2
    e. 5/2

Word Problems: Rate & Distance: AS HARD AS IT GETS

13. An American Airlines jet leaves Logan Airport at 8 am and travels directly south at a speed of 650 mph. A Delta Airlines jet leaves the same airport at 1 pm and travels due east. At 2 pm, the two jets are exactly 4,000 miles apart. What is the speed of the Delta Airlines jet (in mph)?

    a. 675
    b. 750
    c. 775
    d. 850
    e. 889

Answer Key: Rate & Distance Problems

(*Note*: Some of these problems can also be solved by using two equations – and two variables. Please see Chapter 19 for techniques and strategies)

1. The first step for this type of problem is to draw a quick chart of what we know:

Girl	Distance	Rate	Time
Kayla	x		6
Ali	12 - x		4

Next, we must define our variables. The distance Kayla walks is x. The distance Ali walks is 12 - x. When they meet, each girl will have walked an equal amount of time.

Using the rate equation, we know that Time = Distance/Rate. Since Kayla's time = Ali's time, our equation becomes:
Kayla's Distance / Kayla's Rate = Ali's Distance / Ali's Rate
$x / 6 = (12 - x) / 4$. To simply, we will multiply both sides of the equation by 12 (the LCD)
$2x = 3(12 - x)$
$2x = 36 - 3x$
$5x = 36$
$X = 36/5 = 7.2$ miles = the total distance the girls walked.

Plugging this number back into the rate equation yields: T = D/R = (7.2 miles per hour) / 6 hours = 1.2 hours, or 72 minutes. Choice E is correct.

2. The first step for this type of problem is to draw a quick chart of what we know:

Route	Distance	Rate	Time
To Charlotte	150	75	2
From Charlotte	150	50	3

A car traveling at 75 mph will cover 150 miles in 2 hours. A car traveling at 50 mph covers the same 150 miles in 3 hours. The total travel time is therefore 5 hours.

Average speed = Total distance / Total time.
For the entire round trip, the average speed = (150 + 150) / 5 = **60** mph. Choice A is correct.

3. This is the rare problem in which we can simply plug our numbers into the basic rate equation. Jake needs to travel 96 miles in 2.5 hours. How fast does he have to drive? Rate = Distance/Time = 96/2.5 = **38.4** miles per hour. Choice B is correct.

4. The first step for this type of problem is to draw a quick chart of what we know:

Motorcycle	Distance	Rate	Time
A	65x	65	x
B	70x	70	x

Here, we can use the rate equation to determine the time at which the two motorcyclists will pass each other. By definition, they are traveling the same distance, which is 540 miles. Also by definition, that distance equals the SUM of the quantities (Rate x Time) for each motorcycle. Hence, our equation becomes:
65x + 70x = 540
135x = 540
x = 4. They will pass after 4 hours, which will be **2:00 pm**. Choice C is correct.

5. The first step for this type of problem is to draw a quick chart of what we know:

Driver	Distance	Rate	Time
Big Red Boat	10(x - 35)	x - 35	10
Carnival Cruise	10x	x	10

In this case, we will let x = the rate (or speed) of the Carnival Cruise ship, which is what we are asked to find. The speed of the Big Red Boat is therefore x - 35.

Since they both travel for 10 hours, we can complete the Distance entry for the Big Red Boat and the Carnival Cruise ship as 10(x - 35) and 10x, respectively.

Next, we must write our equation to solve for the speed of the Carnival Cruise ship. Although both ships started in the same place and sailed for the same amount of time, they travelled at different speeds. The 490 miles distance is the TOTAL distance that the two of them sailed.

Mathematically, it can be represented by the SUM of the Big Red Boat's distance, 10(x - 35), and the Carnival Cruise ship's distance, 10x. Hence, our equation becomes:

10x + 10(x - 35) = 490
20x – 350 = 490
20x = 840
X = **42** miles per hour = speed of the Carnival Cruise ship. Choice D is correct.

6.The first step for this type of problem is to draw a quick chart of what we know.

Driver	Distance	Rate	Time
US Air	500x	500	x

| Sea Hawk | 100x | 100 | x |

In this case, we will let x = the time it takes for the jet and the helicopter to travel 4,200 miles.

We can also enter the rates for each plane and write an expression for their respective distances. Next, we must use this information to solve for x.

The US Air jet and the Sea Hawk helicopter each travelled *a portion* of the total distance, which is 4,200 miles. Our equation, therefore, is:

Jet's Distance + Helicopter's Distance = Total Distance
500 x + 100X = 4,200
600x = 4,200
X = **7** hours. Choice A is correct

7: The first step for this type of problem is to draw a quick chart of what we know.

Bus	Distance	Rate	Time
One	60(x + 3)	60	x + 3
Two	40x	40	x

In this case, the buses travel the same distance at different speeds. Our equation is:

60(x + 3) = 40x
60x + 180 = 40x
-180 = 20x
x = **9** hours = amount of time it will take the second bus to reach the first bus. Choice E is correct.

8. Because Ben is traveling at different speeds on each leg of his trip, he takes a different amount of time to cover the same distance. Consequently, we cannot simply average the two speeds to get the correct answer. Instead, we must use the following formula to determine the average rate:

Average Rate = Total Distance / Total Time

In this case, the test writers did not give us any specific numbers, so we are free to pick any value for the total distance. In this case, we will use 100 miles for the total distance, which makes each leg of the trip (the distance from Chicago to Philadelphia) equal to one-half of 100, or 50 miles.

For the trip from Chicago to Philadelphia,
Average Rate = 50 miles/ 75 miles per hour = 0.67 hours

For the return trip from Philadelphia to Chicago,
Average rate = 50 miles / 40 miles per hour = 1.25 hours

Hence, the total time was 0.67 + 1.25 = 1.92 hours

Going back to the original equation, for the total trip,
Average Rate = Total Distance / Total Time = 100 miles/1.92 hours = **52** miles per hour. Choice A is correct.

9. The first step for this type of problem is to draw a quick chart of what we know.

Route	Distance	Rate	Time
To Grandma's	50x	50	x
From Grandma's	75(10 − x)	75	10 - x

In this case, we will let the amount of time Julie travels to her grandmother's house = x. Her return time is therefore 10 − x.

Once we have the expressions for the distance travelled to – and from – grandma's house, we can use them to write an equation to solve for the distance.

Distance to Grandma's = Distance from Grandma's
$50x = 75(10 – x)$
$50x = 750 – 75x$
$125x = 750$
$x = 6$
$50x =$ **300 miles**. Choice D is correct.

10. The first step is to draw a quick chart of what we know:

Girl	Distance	Rate	Time
Jill	2x	x	2
Kim	2 (x + 10)	x + 10	2

Next, we must define our variables. In this case, we will let Jill's speed = x. Therefore, Kim's speed = x + 10. We also know that both girls drive for the same amount of time, which is 2 hours.

We can now write an equation to solve for Jill's time based on the distance they travelled:

Jill's Distance + Kim's Distance = Total Distance

$2x + 2(x + 10) = 100$
$2x + 2x + 20 = 100$
$4x + 20 = 100$
$4x = 80$
$X =$ **20** = Jill's speed. Choice A is correct.

11. The first step is to draw a quick chart of what we know:

Timeframe	Distance	Rate	Time
Before the dinner rush	70x	70	x
After the dinner rush	50(12 – x)	50	12 – x

Wendy's 12 hour trip is divided into two parts: before and after the dinner rush. If we let her time travelling before the dinner rush = x, then the time she travelled after dinner = 12 – x.

We can now write an equation to solve for Wendy's time based on the total distance she travelled:

Distance Before Dinner + Distance After Dinner = Total Distance

$70x + 50(12 – x) = 700$
$70x + 600 – 50x = 700$
$20x = 100$
$x = 5$ hours = time Wendy travelled before 5 pm. Hence, Wendy left at **12 noon**. Choice C is correct.

12. The first step is to draw a quick chart of what we know:

Driver	Distance	Rate	Time
Jack	75x	75	x
Jill	45x	45	x

In this case, Jack and Jill will drive the same amount of time at different speeds. We want to know the amount of time it will take for Jack to be 45 miles ahead of Jill, which can be represented by:

$75x – 45x = 45$
$30x = 45$

X = **3/2** hours.   Choice B is correct.

Because this is a relatively simple scenario, it is easier for some students to think it through without the chart.   If Jack drives 75 miles per hour while Jill drives 45 miles per hour, then he travels 76 – 45 = 30 additional miles each hour.

The time required for Jack to be 45 miles ahead of Jill is therefore 1.5 times 30 = 1.5 hours.

13. The scenario can be depicted as a right triangle in which the hypotenuse = 4,000 miles. The American Airlines jet flew south for 6 hours. Since Distance = Rate x Time, Distance = 650 x 6 = 3,900 miles.

In contrast, the jet that flew east flew for only one hour, so its Distance = Rate x Time = Rate X 1, or Distance = Rate.

To find this distance, which is the same as the rate, we must solve the following equation:

Distance (American Flight) + Distance (Delta Flight) = Total Distance

$3,900^2 + d^2 = 4,000^2$
$d^2 = 4,000^2 - 3,900^2 = 16,000,000 - 15,210,000 = 790,000$
D = **889** mph. Choice E is correct.

Chapter 12: Work Problems

Work problems usually present a scenario in which two people (or machines) are working together to complete a job or task. Inevitably, the people or machines will work at a different rate of speed, which means that they will accomplish different amounts of the job.

Alternatively, work problems may involve pipes of different diameters that fill (or drain) a pool, tank, or other container. Since the sizes of the pipes are different, they will fill the containers at different rates.

Regardless of the premise, the general principles of most work problems are the same:

1. The amount of work done by one person, machine, or pipe plus the amount of work done by the second person, machine, or pipe equals *the total amount of work done* in a specific period of time.

2. For each person, machine, or pipe, the amount of work accomplished is equal to their rate of speed times the amount of time that they work (**Work = Rate X Time**).

Thankfully, work problems are easy to understand if we work through a few examples. The following problems show the types of work problems and the level of difficulty (from easy to complex) that you can expect to see on the SAT, GRE, and GMAT.

Work Problem Example 1: Working Together

Gayle, Roger, and Ben agree to wallpaper a large apartment building that their father owns in San Diego. Gayle can wallpaper the entire building alone in 5 days, while it would take Roger only 4 days to wallpaper the entire building if he worked alone. If Ben could complete the job by himself in 3 days, how many days will it take the three siblings to wallpaper the building if they all work together?

      a.   0.75
      b.   1.28
      c.   1.75
      d.   2.25
      e.   2.75

Solution: Let x represent the amount of time that the three siblings will need to wallpaper the entire building. If we do, then Gayle will complete $x/5$ of the job, while Roger will complete $x/4$ of the job and Ben will complete $x/3$ of the job. Mathematically, our equation becomes:

Gayle + Roger + Ben = 1
$x/5 + x/4 + x/3 = 1$

To simplify, we must multiply each side of the equation by our least common denominator, which is 60: $12x + 15x + 20x = 60$
$47x = 60$
$x = 60/47 = 1.28$ days. Thus, if all three siblings work together, it will take them 1.28 days to wallpaper the apartment building. Choice B is correct.

Work Problem Example 2: Determining a Single Participant's Speed

Mary can clean her apartment in 60 minutes. If she works with Sue, they can complete the job in 20 minutes. How long would it take Sue to clean the apartment alone?

      a.   15
      b.   20
      c.   30
      d.   35
      e.   45

Solution: To solve, we will use the same equation as in the previous example, Work = Rate x Time. However, in this case, our unknown is Sue's individual rate for cleaning the apartment.

We will write an equation to solve for this unknown X, which is the number of minutes it would take Sue to clean the apartment alone.

Mary + Sue = 1
20/60 + 20/X = 1
1/3 + 20/x = 1

To simplify, we must multiply each side of the equation by our least common denominator, which is 3x:
1x + 60 = 3x
60 = 2x
30 = x. Sue would require 30 minutes to clean the apartment alone. Choice C is correct.

Work Problem Example 3:   Someone Arrives Late….. or Leaves Early

Gina can design a web site for a client in 8 hours. Hillary can design the same site in 12 hours. If Hillary arrives three hours late to help Gina with the site, how much total time (in hours) will it take to design the web site?

      a.   3.0
      b.   4.5
      c.   5.0
      d.   6.0
      e.   6.5

Solution: By definition, the total time is the sum of the two workers, or Gina + Hillary = 1. To solve, we must first determine the amount of work done by each girl. Then, we must make a small adjustment in the work formula to account for the additional work done by Gina:

Gina   Work = Rate x Time = 1/8 x X = X/8
Hillary   Work =Rate x Time = 1/12 x X = X/12

If both girls had worked the same amount of time, our equation would have been X/8 + X/12 = 1. But, Hillary started three hours late. During that time, Gina had already completed (3)(1/8), or 3/8 of the work. Hence, our new equation is: 3/8 + X/8 + X/12 = 1

To solve, we must multiply both sides of the equation by 24, which is our least common denominator:
9 + 3X + 2X = 24
5X = 15
X = 3 hours

Thus, we know that Gina and Hillary can complete the job *together* in 3 hours. Since Gina had already worked for 3 hours before Hillary arrived, the *total time to complete the site that day* (which is what the question asks) is 3 + 3 = 6 hours, or answer Choice D.

Work Problem Example 4:   Pipes Filling a Container

Pipe D can fill a bathtub in 30 minutes. Pipe R can fill the same bathtub in 45 minutes. Pipe Q can fill it in 25 minutes. If someone opens all three pipes at the same time, how long (in minutes) will it take to fill the bathtub?

      a.   10.5
      b.   12.0
      c.   15.0
      d.   17.5
      e.   18.0

Solution: In this case, we will use the basic rate equation to solve for the total amount of time required to fill a bathtub. Our equation is:

x/30 + x/45 + x/25 = 1

To solve, we must multiply both sides of the equation by 450, which is our least common denominator:
15x + 10x +18x =450
43x = 450
x = 10.47 = 10.5 minutes. Choice A is correct.

Work Problem Example 5: Filling and Draining at the Same Time

A tank of sugar syrup can be filled in 3 hours and drained in 6 hours. How long will it take to fill the tank if an employee forgets to close the drain valve?

    a.   1.5
    b.   3.0
    c.   4.5
    d.   6.0
    e.   9.0

Solution: In this case, the rate to fill the tank is x/3, while the rate to drain it is x/6. Since the drain is emptying the tank, our equation becomes x/3 – x/6 = 1.

To solve, we must multiple both sides by the least common denominator, which is 6:
2x - 1x = 6, or x = 6 hours to fill the tank. Choice D is correct.

To gain experience – and build your confidence – try the following work problems.

Word Problems: Work: EASY - MODERATE

1. Olivia can transcribe three times as fast as Karen. If they both spend an equal amount of time transcribing 1200 pages of notes, how many pages will Olivia have transcribed?

    a.   300
    b.   450
    c.   800
    d.   900
    e.   1000

2. Gina and Hillary have a small web design business. Gina can design a web site for Client A in 2 hours. Hillary can design the same site in 3 hours. How long will it take them in minutes to design the site if they both work at the same time?

    a.   60
    b.   66
    c.   72
    d.   90
    e.   100

3. A Quick Print Copy Center owns two high-speed copiers for large jobs. Photocopier A can print 100 books in five hours, while photocopier B will take seven hours to print 50 books. How long will it take to print 100 books if photocopiers A and B work together?

    a.   1.84
    b.   3.36
    c.   3.68
    d.   4.36
    e.   7.36

4. Ryan and Jake can paint a house in 4 days if they work together. Alone, it takes Ryan 6 days to paint the house. How many days would it take Jake to paint the house if he worked alone?

    a. 5
    b. 6
    c. 8
    d. 10
    e. 12

5. If Kyle works alone, he can wash the night shift dishes in 55 minutes. It will only take him 40 minutes if he works together with Harry. How long will it take Harry to wash the night shift dishes by himself?

    a. 65
    b. 87
    c. 95
    d. 147
    e. 165

6. A faucet can fill a tank in 60 minutes, while the drain takes 80 minutes to empty it. If the drain is left open when the faucet is turned on, how many minutes will it take to fill the tank?

    a. 100
    b. 120
    c. 140
    d. 180
    e. 240

7. A research lab has a new hand pump, which can fill a bucket in 32 seconds. It also has an older pump that can fill the same bucket in 48 seconds. If both pumps are used at the same time, how many seconds will it take to fill the bucket?

    a. 18.0
    b. 19.2
    c. 28.5
    d. 36.4
    e. 40.0

8. Pipe A can fill a tank in 40 hours. Pipe B can fill the same tank in 72 hours. Pipe C can empty the tank in 96 hours. If all three pipes are open at the same time, how many hours will it take to fill the tank?

    a. 20
    b. 35
    c. 40
    d. 56
    e. 60

9. Professor Davis can write a book manuscript in 5 days. His graduate student Miguel can write the same manuscript in 10 days. After working alone for 3 days, Professor Davis was called away on urgent business, which left Miguel alone to finish the manuscript. How many days did it take Miguel to finish it?

    a. 2
    b. 3
    c. 4
    d. 5
    e. 6

Word Problems: Work: AS HARD AS IT GETS

10. Cement truck 1 can pour 600 gallons of concrete mix in 2.1 hours. Cement truck 2 can pour the same amount in 2.9 hours. How many minutes longer than cement truck 1 would it take cement truck 2 to pour 130,000 quarts of concrete mix?

    a.   48
    b.   126
    c.   432
    d.   2600
    e.   6825

11. Two separate pipes are used to fill a 2000-gallon swimming pool. If Pipe A fills the pool at a rate of 15 gallons of water per minute and Pipe B fills the pool at a rate of 45 gallons per minute, how many minutes will it take to fill the pool to the top, if it already has 500-gallons of water in it?

    a.   17.5
    b.   21
    c.   25
    d.   30
    e.   32.5

12. Three surgeons – Anna, Claire, and Diane – are asked to perform an emergency appendectomy. Working alone, Anna could complete the operation in 8 hours. Claire could do the job in 10 hours, while it would take Diane 12 hours by herself. On this particular shift, all three of the surgeons worked together on the appendectomy for two hours. At that point, Diane left to answer a page and never returned. An hour later, Claire left to handle another emergency – she also never returned. How long (in minutes) did it take Anna to complete the appendectomy, after Claire and Diane both left?

    a.   56
    b.   60
    c.   66
    d.   70
    e.   76

Answer Key for Word Problems: Work

(*Note*: Some of these problems can also be solved by using two equations – and two variables. Please see Chapter 19 for techniques and strategies)

1. Let x = # of pages that Karen transcribes. 3x = # pages that Olivia transcribes. x + 3x = 1200, so 4x = 1200, or x = 300. Olivia transcribed 3x, or **900** pages. Choice D is correct.

2. The problem asks us to determine the total amount of time that is needed for both girls to complete the job. First, we must figure the amount of work that each girl does as a percentage of the total amount:

Gina   Work = Rate x Time   (1/2) x T = ½ T
Hillary Work = Rate x Time   (1/3) x T = 1/3T

Now, we must add them together to figure the total time for the job:

½ T + 1/3 T = 1
3/6T + 2/6T =1
3T + 2T = 6
5T = 6
T = 6/5 hours, or 1.2 hours

Solving for T, we find that they can complete the job in 1.2 hours if they work together, or **72** minutes. Choice C is correct.

3. Here, we can use the basic equation for work problems, in which 1/Time A + 1/Time B = 1/Total Time to complete the job. In this case, machine A takes 5 hours to copy 100 books, while machine B takes 7 hours to print 50 books, or 14 hours to print 100.

1/5 + 1/14 = 1/Total Time
0.2714 = 1/Total Time
Total Time = **3.68** hours. Choice C is correct.

4. Here, we must use the basic work equation to solve for Jake's time:

1/Time A + 1/Time B = 1/ Total Time
1/6 + 1/X = ¼. We will multiply both sides by 12x, which is the LCD
2x + 12 = 3x
1X = **12**. Choice E is correct.

5. In this case, our variable x is the amount of time that Harry needs to complete the dishes alone. Thus, our equation becomes 40/55 + 40/x = 1

To solve, we must multiply both sides of the equation by 55x, which is our least common denominator:

40x + 2200 = 55x
2200 = 15x
x = 146.67 = **147** minutes. Choice D is correct.

6. In this case, our variable x is the amount of time it will take to fill the tank. Thus, our equation becomes x/60 - x/80 = 1. To solve, we must multiply both sides of the equation by 240, which is our least common denominator:

4x – 3x = 240, or x = **240** minutes to fill the tank. Choice E is correct.

7. For this problem, our unknown x is the total time required to fill the bucket if both pumps are used. Hence, our equation becomes 1/32 + 1/48 = 1/x

To solve, we must multiply both sides of the equation by 96x, which is our least common denominator:

3x + 2x = 96
5x = 96
x = **19.2** seconds. Choice B is correct.

8. Our unknown is the total amount of time needed to fill the tank, which is the sum of the intake pipes, minus the drain pipe. Hence, our equation is 1/40 + 1/72 – 1/96 = 1/x

To solve, we must multiply both sides of the equation by 4320x, which is our least common denominator:

108x + 60x – 45x = 4320
123x = 4320
x = **35.12** hours. Choice B is correct.

9. To solve, we must first calculate the amount of work that Professor Davis did in 3 days, which is (1/5)(3) = 3/5. Miguel, therefore, only had to complete 2/5 of the book. Since Miguel's rate is 1/10, our equation becomes 1/10 = (1/x)(2/5), or 1/10 = 2/5x

1/10 = 2/5x
x = **4** days. Choice C is correct

10. Although the original information is given in hours and gallons, the answer choices are presented in terms of minutes and quarts. This means that both values must be converted:

Truck 1   2.1 hours/600 gallons = 126 min/600 gallons = 126 min / 2400 qt
Truck 2   2.9 hours/600 gallons = 174 min/600 gallons = 174 min / 2400 qt

In this case, we are asked to calculate the *difference in times* that the trucks would take to pour 130,000 quarts of concrete. To solve, we must determine the time required by each truck and compare the numbers.

Truck 1   126 min / 2400 qt = 6825 min / 130,000 qt
Truck 2   174 min / 2400 qt = 9425 min / 130,000 qt

9425 – 6825 = **2600**, which is Choice D.

11. Here, we must use the basic work equation to solve for the total time. The trick is to use the correct amount of water needed, considering that the 2000-gallon pool already contains 500 gallons of water. Hence, our equation becomes:

1/Time A + 1/Time B = 1/ Total Time
15/1500 + 45/1500 = 1/X
60/1500 = 1/X
Thus, X = **25** minutes. Choice C is correct.

12. This work problem is as tedious and time-consuming as you are likely to see on a standardized test. Nevertheless, it is relatively easy to solve if you keep track of what you are calculating in each step.

First, we must calculate how much of the surgery was completed during the first two hours, when Anna, Claire and Diane were working together. If Anna can do the operation alone in 8 hours, then she did 2(1/8) = 2/8 = ¼ of the work in the first two hours. If Claire can do the operation alone in 10 hours, then she did 2(1/10) = 2/10 = 1/5 of the job during the first two hours. Finally, if Diane can do the operation alone in 12 hours, then she did 2(1/12) = 2/12 = 1/6 of the job during the first two hours.

The total of those three fractions is the amount of the surgery that was done in the first two hours: ¼ + 1/5 + 1/6 = 15/60 + 12/60 + 10/60 = 37/60.

Next, we must determine how much of the job that Anna and Claire completed during the third hour, when they worked together. That amount is 1/8 + 1/10 = 5/40 + 4/40 = 9/40.

Thus, by the time Anna was alone in the operating room, the amount of work completed was 37/60 + 9/40 = 74/120 + 27/120 = 101/120. To determine how much time Anna will need to finish the job, we must subtract that number from 1, which is: 120/120 – 101/120 = 19/120.

By definition, based on Anna's individual rate (8 hours to complete the job alone), 19/120 = x/8. If we solve this equation for x, we find that it will take Anna 19/15, or **76/60** hours to complete the appendectomy, which is 1 hour and 16 minutes. Choice E is correct.

Chapter 13: Mixture Problems

The SAT, GRE, and GMAT present two types of mixture problems.

1. A business sells items or tickets at two different prices. Students must determine how many were sold at each price. We have already covered this type of problem in the Chapter 9. Please review the sample problems if you require additional practice.

2. Someone mixes two ingredients to produce a blend with a different concentration than the original components. Students must derive – and solve - an original equation to determine the amount or concentration of one of the items.

This chapter focuses on the second type of mixture problem. Although the details for each problem will differ, they all require the same basic approach:

1. Draw a simple chart that summarizes the information you are given for each ingredient and for the final mixture

2. Write and solve an equation for the unknown

Note: Many of these problems can ALSO be solved by writing equations with TWO variables. To see examples of this method, please see Chapter 19.

Here are the most common types of mixture problems on standardized tests, along with the most efficient ways to tackle them.

Example 1. Blending Ingredients w/ Different Costs

Jenny wants to blend a gourmet hot fudge sauce that costs 75 cents per pound with a caramel sauce that costs 95 cents per pound to make 500 pounds of a mixture that costs 80 cents per pound. How many pounds of the caramel sauce must Jenny use?

     a.   20
     b.   25
     c.   125
     d.   375
     e.   480

Solution: First, we must draw a table with the information that we know.

Ingredient	Quantity	Price/pound	Total Cost
Hot fudge	$500 - x$	75	$75(500 - x)$
Caramel	x	95	95x
Mixture	500	80	40,000

Since the problem asks us to calculate the amount of caramel that Jenny needs, we will let that value = x. Therefore, the amount of hot fudge = 500 – x. Once we label our variables, we can write the expression for the total cost of each ingredient. We can also calculate the cost of the final mixture.

Since the cost of the hot fudge plus the cost of the caramel equals the total cost of the blend, our equation becomes:

Cost of Caramel + Cost of Hot Fudge = Total Cost
$95x + 75(500 - x) = 40,000$
$95x + 37,500 - 75x = 40,000$
$20x = 2500$
$X = 125$ pounds of caramel needed. Choice C is correct.

Example 2. Strengthening or Diluting the Concentration of a Liquid

How many quarts of alcohol must be added to a 50 quart solution that is 35% alcohol to yield a solution that is 45% alcohol?

    a.   5
    b.   9
    c.   10
    d.   12
    e.   15

Solution: First, we must draw a table with the information that we know.

Ingredient	Quantity (Quarts)	%Alcohol	Amount Alcohol
Diluted	50	35	(50)(35) =1750
Pure	x	100	100x
Mixture	50 + x	45	45(50 + x)

In this case, we are being asked to calculate the amount of pure (100%) alcohol that is needed to increase the percentage of alcohol in a mixture from 35% to 45%.   Hence, we will let that value = x, which makes the quantity of the total mixture = 50 + x.

When we complete our table, we can solve for the unknown quantity by writing an equation for the AMOUNT of alcohol in the three solutions:

The amount of alcohol in both ingredients = the total amount in the mixture.

Diluted + Pure = Mixture
1750 + 100x = 45(50 + x)
1750 + 100x = 2250 + 45x
55x = 500
x = 9.09 = 9 quarts of 100% alcohol should be added. Choice B is correct.

Example 3. Evaporating a Solution

A lab assistant made a mistake when she was mixing a new cough syrup. She unintentionally added too much water, which yielded 600 pounds of cough syrup that was 5% alcohol. How many pounds of water will the lab assistant need to evaporate from the batch to increase the alcohol concentration to 15%?

    a.   30
    b.   40
    c.   150
    d.   300
    e.   400

Solution: Many students are confused by this question, because it requires them to evaporate the initial solution in order to strength it. Don't be thrown by this change. It simply means that our final solution will weigh LESS than the original. Let's take it one step at a time. First, we must draw a table with the information that we know.

Weight of Solution (lbs)	% of Alcohol	Amount of Alcohol
600	5	3000
x	0	0
600 – x	15	15(600 – x)

In this case, we will let x = the amount of water to be removed. Therefore, the weight of the final solution (in which the water has been evaporated off) will equal 600 – x.

Once we have these variables, we can complete the rest of the chart, and derive our expressions for the AMOUNT of alcohol in each solution. We can then use the information to write an equation to solve for our unknown.

Since our only change is to remove water – and to concentrate the amount of alcohol – our equation is:

$3000 = 15(600 - x)$
$3000 = 9000 - 15x$
$15x = 6000$
$x = 400$ pounds of water must be removed. Choice E is correct.

Example 4: Mixtures of Financial Products

A financial manager buys two types of bonds for his client. He buys $20,000 worth of Bond A and $15,000 worth of Bond B, which pays an annual interest rate 2% higher than Bond A. If the total return on the client's bonds is $3000, what was the interest rate for Bond B?

       a. 5.71%
       b. 7.71%
       c. 8.51%
       d. 9.71%
       e. 10.51%

Solution: Sometimes, the "mixtures" in word problems are financial products, rather than ingredients or alcohol solutions. Despite this difference, we must use a similar approach to solve them. First, we must draw a table with the information that we know.

Type of Bond	Amount	Interest Rate	Total Return
Bond A	$20,000	x	20,000x
Bond B	$15,000	x + 2	15,000(x + 2)
Total	$35,000		3,000

Here, we are asked to determine the interest rate for Bond B, based on the initial investment in each bond and the total rate of return. We can do this by writing an equation that represents the sum of the interest from both bonds.

First, let's assign our variables. We will let x = the Rate for Bond A. Therefore the rate for Bond B = x + 2. Next, we can use these variables to write expressions for the total return for each bond.

Return from Bond A + Return from Bond B = Total Return
$20,000x + 15,000 (x +0.02) = 3,000$
$20,000x + 15,000X + 300 = 3,000$
$35000x = 2700$
$x = 0.0771 = 7.71\% =$ Interest Rate for Bond A

Therefore, the interest rate for Bond B = 7.71 + 2 = 9.71%.   Choice D is correct.

Now that we have reviewed the most common types of problems, test your skills – and reinforce relevant strategies – by solving the following examples.

Word Problems: Mixtures: EASY - MODERATE

1. A bartender creates a new drink by mixing 12 ounces of gin with 24 ounces of vodka. If gin costs $1.20 per ounce and vodka costs $1.80 per ounce, how much should a 16 ounce batch of the new drink cost?

       a. $13.60
       b. $14.40
       c. $16.00
       d. $25.60
       e. $43.20

2. A vineyard wants to blend Wine A, which is 10% alcohol, with Wine B, which is 18% alcohol, to yield Wine C, which is 15% alcohol. To make a batch of Wine C that weighs 3,200 ounces, how many ounces of Wine A must be used?

    a.   600
    b.   1,200
    c.   1,800
    d.   2,000
    e.   2,400

3. A chef must blend a gourmet cheese that costs $25 per pound with processed cheese spread that costs $10 per pound to make a 2000-pound batch that costs $20 per pound. How many pounds of the gourmet cheese can the chef use?

    a.   333
    b.   1,000
    c.   1,333
    d.   1,500
    e.   4,000

4. How many gallons of pure gin must be added to a 100 gallon solution that is 15% gin to yield a solution that is 20% gin?

    a.   5.00
    b.   6.25
    c.   15.0
    d.   50.0
    e.   62.5

5. At the end of a shift, a cosmetics factory salvages its leftover shampoo by evaporating the extra water and using the resulting solution in a different formulation. If they end the shift with 1,000 pounds of shampoo that is 20% alcohol, how many pounds of water must the factory evaporate from the batch to increase the alcohol concentration to 30%?

    a.   300.00
    b.   333.33
    c.   450.00
    d.   600.00
    e.   666.67

6. A retiree places $50,000 in a CD that pays an attractive rate of interest. She also places $75,000 in a second CD that pays an annual interest rate that is 3% lower than the first CD. If the total return on the retiree's CDs is $10,000, what was the interest rate on the $50,000 CD?

    a.   6.8%
    b.   7.8%
    c.   9.8%
    d.   10.8%
    e.   11.8%

7. A scientist has a 10-ounce solution that is 15% acid. If 5 ounces of pure acid are added to the solution, what percent of the resulting mixture is acid?

    a.   6.5
    b.   37.5
    c.   43.3
    d.   65.0
    e.   75.0

8. To dilute 300 quarts of a 25% solution of garlic to a 20% solution, how much water should a chef add?

    a.   15
    b.   60
    c.   75
    d. 120
    e. 125

Word Problems: Mixtures: AS HARD AS IT GETS

9. Rory gets 20 miles per gallon with regular gas that costs $3.85 per gallon and 25 miles per gallon with premium gas that costs $4.50 per gallon. Rory paid $226.00 for gas on a trip of 1,200 miles. How many gallons of premium gas did she buy (to the nearest gallon)?

    a. 12
    b. 16
    c. 24
    d. 32
    e. 40

10. A caterer is preparing a cookie platter with oatmeal, chocolate chip, and peanut butter cookies. The customer wants twice as many oatmeal cookies as chocolate chip cookies and cannot spend more than $30.00 for the entire platter. If oatmeal cookies cost 25 cents each, chocolate chip cookies are 75 cents each and peanut butter cookies are 50 cents each, and the total number of cookies is 50, how many chocolate chip cookies can be included in the platter without exceeding the $30.00 price limit?

    a. 7
    b. 8
    c. 14
    d. 16
    e. 28

11. Connie has two investments, A and B. Her income from A, which pays 6%, is $10,000 more than her income from B, which pays 4%. If Connie has $750 more invested in A than B, what is the TOTAL amount of Connie's two investments?

    a. $497,750
    b. $498,500
    c. $996,250
    d. $1,006,250
    e. $1,026,160

12. A bartender wants to blend Drink A, which is D% alcohol, with Drink B, which is E% alcohol, to yield Drink C, which is F% alcohol. To make a batch of Drink C that weighs 1,000 ounces, how many ounces of Drink A must be used?

    a. $1000(F - E)/(D + E)$
    b. $1000(F - E)/(D - E)$
    c. $1000(F + E)/(D - E)$
    d. $(F - E)/1000(D - E)$
    e. $(F - E)(D - E)/1000$

Answer Key: Word Problems – Mixtures

(*Note*: Some of these problems can also be solved by using two equations – and two variables. Please see Chapter 19 for techniques and strategies)

1. First, we must draw a table with the information that we know.

Ingredient	Quantity	Price/ounce	Total Cost
Gin	12	$1.20	(12)($1.20)
Vodka	24	$1.80	(24)($1.80)
Mixture	36	x	36x

The problem asks us to calculate the amount that a 16-ounce batch of the drink mix should cost. Hence, we will let the cost of one ounce of the mixture = x.

Since we know the amounts and costs of both ingredients, we can write an equation to solve for the cost per ounce of the mixture:

Cost of Gin + Cost of Vodka = Total Cost
$12(1.2) + 24 (1.8) = 36x$
$14.4 + 43.2 = 36x$
$36x = 57.6$
$x = 1.6$ = the cost of one ounce of the mixed drink
Therefore, the cost of a 16-ounce batch of the drink = $(16)(1.6) = 25.60. Choice D is correct.

2. First, we must draw a table with the information that we know.

Ingredient	% Alcohol	Amount (oz)	Total Amount of Alcohol
Wine A	10	x	10x
Wine B	18	3200 – x	18(3200 – x)
Wine C	15	3200	15(3200)

The problem asks us to calculate the amount of Wine A that is needed to create a blend with 15% alcohol. We will let x = the oz of Wine A needed. Therefore, the amount of wine B needed = 3200 – x.

Since the total alcohol in Wine C is the sum of the amounts in Wines A and B, we can write an equation to solve for x:

Alcohol in Wine A + Alcohol in Wine B = Total Alcohol in Wine C

$10x + 18(3,200 - x) = 15(3,200)$
$10x + 57,600 - 18x = 48,000$
$-8x = -9,600$
$x = 1,200$ oz of Wine A. Choice B is correct.

3. First, we must draw a table with the information that we know.

Ingredient	Quantity	Price/pound	Total Cost
Gourmet cheese	x	$25	$25x
Processed cheese	2,000 – x	$10	$10(2,000 – x)
Blend	2,000	$20	$40,000

Since the problem asks us to calculate the amount of gourmet cheese the chef can use, we will let that value = x. Therefore, the amount of processed cheese = 2000 – x. Once we label our variables, we can write the expression for the total cost of each ingredient. From the problem, we can also calculate the cost of the final blend.

Since the cost of the gourmet cheese plus the cost of the processed cheese equals the total cost of the blend, then our equation becomes:

Cost of Gourmet Cheese + Cost of Processed Cheese = Total Cost
25x + 10(2,000 − x) = 40,000
25x + 20,000 − 10x = 40,000
15x = 20,000
x = **1,333** pounds of gourmet cheese. Choice C is correct.

4. First, we must draw a table with the information we know.

Ingredient	Quantity (Gallons)	Percent Gin	Amount Gin
Diluted	100	15	1,500
Pure	x	100	100x
Mixture	100 + x	20	20(100 + x)

In this case, we are being asked to calculate the amount of pure (100%) gin that is needed to increase the percentage of gin in a mixture from 15% to 20%. Hence, we will let that value = x, which makes the quantity of the total mixture = 100 + x.

When we complete our table, we can solve for the unknown quantity by writing an equation for the AMOUNT of gin in the three solutions:

The amount of gin in both ingredients = the total amount in the mixture.

Diluted + Pure = Mixture
1,500 + 100x = 20(100 + x)
1,500 + 100x = 2,000 + 20x
80x = 500
x = **6.25** gallons of pure gin should be added. Choice B is correct.

5. First, we must draw a table with the information that we know.

Weight of Solution (lbs)	% Alcohol	Amount of Alcohol (lbs)
1000	20	20(1,000)
x	0	0
1000 − x	30	30(1000 − x)

In this case, we will let x = the amount of water to be removed. Therefore, the weight of the final solution (in which the water has been evaporated off) will equal 1000 − x.

Once we have these variables, we can complete the rest of the chart, and derive our expressions for the AMOUNT of alcohol in each solution. We can then use the information to write an equation to solve for our unknown.

Since our only change is to remove water – and to concentrate the amount of alcohol – our equation is:

20(1,000) = 30(1000 − x)
20,000 = 30,000 − 30x
30x = 10,000
x = **333.33** pounds of water must be removed. Choice B is correct.

6. First, we must draw a table with the information that we know.

CD	Amount	Interest Rate	Total Return
First	$50,000	x	50,000x
Second	$75,000	x − 3	75,000(x − 3)
Total	125,000		10,000

Here, we are asked to determine the interest rate for one CD, based on the initial investment in each CD and the total rate of return. We can do this by writing an equation that represents the sum of the interest from both CDs.

First, let's assign our variables. We will let x = the rate for the $50,000 CD. Therefore, the rate for the $75,000 CD = x - 3. Next, we can use these variables to write expressions for the total return for each CD. Finally, we can use these expressions to write an equation for the total return:

Return from $50,000 CD + Return from $75,000 CD = Total Return
$50,000x + 75,000 (x - 0.03) = 10,000$
$50000x + 75000X - 2,250 = 10,000$
$125,000x = 12,250$
$x = 0.098 = $ **9.8%** = Interest Rate for $50,000 CD. Choice C is correct.

7. First, we must draw a table with the information we know.

Solution	Quantity (oz)	Percent Acid	Amount Acid (oz)
Original	10	15	10(0.15) = 1.5
Added	5	100	5(1.0) = 5
Final	15		1.5 + 5 = 6.5

In this case, the tabulated data tells us the entire story. The final 15-ounce solution contains 6.5 ounces of acid. 6.5/15 = **43.3**% acid. Choice C is correct.

8. First, we must draw a table with the information that we know.

Quantity of Solution (qt)	% Garlic	Amount of Garlic (qt)
300	25	300(0.25)
x	0	0
x + 300	20	0.20(x + 300)

In this case, we will let x = the amount of water to be added. Therefore, the weight of the final solution (in which the water has been added) will equal x + 300.

Once we have these variables, we can complete the rest of the chart, and derive our expressions for the AMOUNT of garlic in each solution. We can then use the information to write an equation to solve for our unknown.

Since our only change is to add water – and to dilute the amount of garlic – our equation is:

$300(0.25) + 0 = 0.20(x + 300)$
$75 = 0.20x + 60$
$0.20x = 15$
$x = $ **75** quarts of water. Choice C is correct.

9. From the information in the problem, we can write the following equations:

Cost of Gas: $226.00 = $3.85 (Amount of Regular) + $4.50 (Amount of Premium)
Amount of Gas: 1200 miles = 20 (Regular) + 25(Premium)

First, we will solve the mileage equation for r in terms of p:

1200 miles = 20 (Regular) + 25(Premium)
$20r = 1200 - 25p$
$R = 60 - 1.25p$

Now, we will plug this value for r into the second equation:

$3.85(60 - 1.25p) + 4.50p = 226.00
$231 - 4.8125p + 4.50 = 226.00
$231 - 0.3125p = 226.00
$-0.3215p = -5$

$P = 15.56$ gallons = **16** gallons. Choice B is correct.
$R = 60 - 1.25(16) = 40$ gallons

10. To solve this problem, we must write three different equations: one with the total number of cookies, another with the total cost for the platter, and a third equation with the number of chocolate chip and oatmeal cookies.

For simplicity, we will let A = the number of oatmeal cookies, C = the number of chocolate chip cookies and D = the number of peanut butter cookies. Thus, our three equations are:

Number of cookies: $A + C + D = 50$
Cost of the platter: $0.25A + 0.75C + 0.50D = \$30.00$
Chocolate chip vs. oatmeal cookies: $A = 2C$

We can easily eliminate the final equation by substituting 2C for A in the other two equations. Then, we have:

$2C + C + D = 50$
$0.25 (2C) + 0.75C + 0.50D = \$30.00$

Which simplify to:

$3C + D = 50$
$1.25C + 0.50D = \$30.00$

Next, we can re-write the first equation as $D = 50 - 3C$ and this value into the final equation:

$1.25C + 0.50D = \$30.00$
$1.25C + 0.50(50 - 3C) = \$30.00$
$1.25C + 25 - 0.9C = \$30.00$
$0.35C = \$5.00$

C = **14**. Choice D is correct.
$A = 2C = 28$
$D = 50 - 14 - 28 = 8$

11. First, we must draw a table with the information that we know.

Investment	Amount	Interest Rate	Total Return
A	x + $7506		6(x + 750)
B	x	4	4x

Here, we are asked to determine the total amount of money invested in A + B. First, we will solve for B.

We will therefore let x = the amount of money invested in B, which means that the amount of money invested in A = x + 750.

From the problem, we know that Connie's income from A is $10,000 more than her income from B. Therefore, our equation is:

Income from A – Income from B = 10,000
$0.06(x + 750) - 0.04x = 10,000$
$0.06x + 45 - 0.04x = 10,000$
$0.02x = 9955$
x = $497,750 = amount of investment B
x + 750 = $498,500 = amount of investment A
A + B = $497,750 +$ 498,500 = **$996,250.** Choice C is correct.

To check our answer, we can simply plug in the amount of interest that each investment earns to see if it matches the stipulations in the question stem.

The total return for A is 0.06($498,500) = $29,910.
The total return for B is 0.04($497,750) = $19,910.
Connie's income from A is indeed $10,000 more than her income from B.

12. First, we must draw a table with the information that we know.

Ingredient	% Alcohol	Amount (oz)	Total Amount of Alcohol
Drink A	D	x	Dx
Drink B	E	$1000 - x$	$E(1000 - x)$
Drink C	F	1000	$F(1000)$

The problem asks us to calculate the amount of Drink A that is needed to create a blend with F% alcohol. We will let x = the oz of Drink A needed. Therefore, the amount of Drink B needed = $1000 - x$.

Since the total alcohol in Drink C is the sum of the amounts in Drinks A and B, we can write an equation to solve for x:

Alcohol in Drink A + Alcohol in Drink B = Total Alcohol in Drink C
$Dx + E(1000 - x) = 1000F$
$Dx + 1000E - Ex = 1000F$
$Dx - Ex = 1000F - 1000E$
$(D - E) x = 1000(F - E)$
$X = \mathbf{1000(F - E)/(D - E)}$. Choice B is correct.

Chapter 14: Groupings

There are three different types of grouping problems on the SAT, GRE and GMAT. Thankfully, they are easy to solve if you know the correct strategies. As always, we will illustrate the problems with actual examples:

Example 1: Either / Or / Both

Every diner at a local restaurant either ordered soup, salad or both. 35% of the diners ordered both soup and salad, while 45% ordered only salad. What percentage ordered only soup?

        a.   10%
        b.   15%
        c.   20%
        d.   25%
        e.   30%

Solution: This is the easiest - and most straightforward – type of grouping problem on the SAT, GRE and GMAT. We have three distinct groups, which must add up to 100%.

Since the original two groups are 45% and 35%, the remaining group must be 100% - 45% - 35% = 20% of the total. Choice C is correct.

Example 2: Either / Or / Both / Neither

One hundred vacationers on a cruise ship have signed up for the ship's activities. Sixty sign up for ballroom dancing lessons. Thirty-five sign up for aerobics class. Twenty sign up for neither ballroom dancing nor aerobics class. How many have signed up for BOTH ballroom dancing and aerobics class?

        a.   5
        b.   10
        c.   12
        d.   15
        e.   18

Solution: In Either/Or/Both/Neither problems, the premise might be customers at a restaurant choosing soup and salad or high school student studying Spanish or French. Regardless of the scenario, the approach is the same. You simply need to create an equation to identify and quantify each group. The trick is that the total number of people (in this case 100) includes FOUR groups:

Ballroom dancers
Aerobics students
Those doing both
Those doing neither

Their relationship is defined as follows:

Group 1 + Group 2 + Neither – Both = 100

Why must we divide them into 4 groups, rather than 3? Because we don't want to count the people who are doing both activities twice.

Once we establish this simple equation, we can plug in numbers to solve for the unknown, which in this case is the group defined as Both.

Group 1 + Group 2 + Neither – Both = 100
60 + 35 + 20 – Both = 100
Both = 15, which is Choice D.

Example 3: Distinct Either/Or Categories

A pet shop has an inventory of 150 animals - 105 of the animals are cats and the rest are dogs. If 85 of the animals are female and 80% of the dogs are female, how many of the pets are male cats?

   a.   9
   b.   36
   c.   45
   d.   49
   e.   56

Solution: The most important thing to notice about an either/or problem is that the categories are distinct, with no possibility of overlap. Second, you should note that the test writers have given you enough data to solve the problem, but they have presented it in the most convoluted way possible.

The best way to attack this type of problem is to summarize the data you are given in a simple table. Once you do, the answer will either be obvious – or surprisingly easy to calculate.

In this case, we have cats and dogs in a pet shop; some are male, while others are female. When we put the information into our chart, we get:

	Cats	Dogs	Total
Male	56	9	65
Female	49	36	85
Total	105	45	150

From the table, we can answer the question; the number of male cats is 56. Choice E is correct.

To hone your skills on these concepts, try the following word problems. Complete solutions are presented at the end of the chapter.

Word Problems: Groupings: EASY TO MODERATE

1. Fifty students in a local conservatory either studied voice, piano or both. 40% of the students studied voice, while 25% studied both voice and piano. What percentage of the students studied only piano?

   a.   20%
   b.   25%
   c.   30%
   d.   35%
   e.   40%

2. Seventy-five freshmen have signed up for extracurricular activities. Fifty sign up for cheerleading. Thirty sign up for the yearbook staff. Eleven sign up for both cheerleading and the yearbook staff. How many of the seventy-five freshman have signed up for NEITHER cheerleading nor the yearbook staff?

   a.   3
   b.   6
   c.   8
   d.   16
   e.   18

3. At a local hospice with 200 patients, 120 have HIV and the rest have cancer. If 70 of the patients are under 18 and one quarter of the cancer patients are over 18, how many of the patients are under 18 with HIV?

      a. 10
      b. 20
      c. 60
      d. 70
      e. 80

4. Students at St. Agnes Academy either study French, Spanish or both. Sixty percent of the students study French, while fifteen percent study both Spanish and French. What percentage of the students only study Spanish?

      a. 10%
      b. 15%
      c. 20%
      d. 25%
      e. 30%

5. Six hundred and fifty employees at a software company have registered for classes at the corporate health center. Two hundred and seventy five have signed up for karate. Five hundred and eighty have signed up for low calorie cooking. Three hundred employees have signed up for both karate and low calorie cooking. How many employees have signed up for NEITHER karate and low calorie cooking?

      a. 95
      b. 105
      c. 125
      d. 150
      e. 200

6. At a local modeling agency with 500 models, 300 have green eyes and the rest have blue eyes. If 400 of the models are over six feet tall and ten percent of the blue eyed models are less than six feet tall, how many of the green eyed models are over six feet tall?

      a. 20
      b. 80
      c. 100
      d. 180
      e. 220

Word Problems: Groupings: AS HARD AS IT GETS

7. X students are attending summer courses at Harvard University. Y have registered for History, Z have registered for Science, and Q have registered for neither History nor Science. How many have signed up for BOTH History and Science?

      a. $(Y + Z)/X$
      b. $(Y + Z - Q)/X$
      c. $X/(Y + Z + Q)$
      d. $Y + Z + Q - X$
      e. $Y + Z - Q - X$

Answer Key: Word Problems - Groupings

1. In this case, we have three distinct groups, which must add up to 100%. Since the original two groups are 40% and 25%, the remaining group must be 100% - 40% - 25% = **35%** of the total. Choice D is correct.

In case you are wondering, it doesn't matter how many students are enrolled in the conservatory, because we are dealing with percentages. The number 50 is extraneous information that is included strictly to confuse you.

2. In this case, we have four groups of students:

Cheerleaders
Yearbook Staff
Both cheerleading and yearbook staff
Neither activity

Hence, our equation is: Cheerleaders + Yearbook Staff + Neither – Both = 75.
50 + 30 + Neither - 11 = 75
Neither = **6.** Choice B is correct.

3. The best way to attack this type of problem is to summarize our data in a simple table.

In this case, the hospice patients either have HIV or cancer. Some of the patients are under 18, while others are over 18. When we put the information into our chart, we get:

	HIV	Cancer	Total
Under 18	10	60	70
Over 18	110	20	130
Total	120	80	200

From the table, we can answer the question; the number of HIV patients under 18 is **10.** Choice A is correct.

4. In this case, we have three distinct groups, which must add up to 100%. Since the original two groups are 60% and 15%, the remaining group must be 100 – 60 – 15 = **25%** of the total. Choice D is correct.

5. In this case, we have four groups of employees (650 total):

Taking Karate: 275
Taking a cooking class: 580
Taking karate AND a cooking class: 300
Taking neither activity: ?

Hence, our equation is Karate + Cooking + Neither – Both = 650.
275 + 580 + Neither - 300 = 650
Neither = **95**. Choice A is correct.

6. The best way to attack this type of problem is to summarize our data in a simple table.

In this case, the models have either green eyes or blue eyes. Some are over 6 feet tall, while others are less than 6 feet tall. When we put the information into our chart, we get:

	Green Eyes	Blue Eyes	Total
Under 6 ft.	80	20	100
Over 6 ft.	220	180	400
Total	300	200	500

From the table, we can answer the question; the number of green eyed models over six feet tall is **220**. Choice E is correct.

7. To solve this problem, we must simply plug the variables back into our formula:

Group 1 + Group 2 + Neither – Both = Total

In our case,

Group 1 = Y
Group 2 = Z
Neither = Q
Both = unknown
Total = X

Hence: Y + Z + Q – Both = X
Both = **Y + Z + Q – X**. Choice D is correct.

Chapter 15: Probability, Possibility, Combinations & Permutations

The newest versions of the SAT, GRE, and GMAT include several topics related to possibility, probability, combinations, and permutations. This chapter presents the underlying concepts and the most typical kinds of word problems you are likely to see.

Probability

Probability = Favorable outcomes /Total possible outcomes

<u>Example</u>: For a six-sided die, the probability of rolling a 6 is 1/6.

<u>Example</u>: If you have 12 jelly beans in a jar and 8 of them are blue, the probability of picking a blue jelly bean at random is 8/12 = 2/3. This probability can also be expressed as .67 or 67 percent.

Conditional Probability

A conditional probability is the probability that one event occurs given that a second event occurred.

For example, suppose that we randomly select one of the first 10 positive integers. The conditional probability of choosing a 4 - given that an *even integer* was chosen - is 1 out of 5 (1/5) because there are 5 even integers between 1 and 10 and 4 is one of them.

The probability of two separate events occurring is the *product* of the probability of the first event occurring and the conditional probability of the second event occurring (given that the first event occurred).

<u>Example</u>: If you have 3 red candies and 4 orange candies in a bag, the probability of withdrawing an orange candy is 4/7 (since we have 4 orange candies out of a total of 7 candies).

If an orange candy is withdrawn and not replaced, then the probability of withdrawing another orange candy is 3/6 (since we now have 3 orange candies and a total of 6 candies left).

So the probability of withdrawing *two orange candies in a row* is: 4/7 x 3/6 = 12/42 = 2/7.

Number of Possibilities

The fundamental counting principle: If there are **a** ways one event can happen and **b** ways a second event can happen, there are **a x b** ways for the two events to happen.

<u>Example</u>: With five sweaters and six skirts, you can put together 5 X 6 = 30 different outfits.

<u>Example</u>: With three different kinds of bread and two types of cheese, we can create 3 X 2 = 6 different types of sandwiches.

Permutations

Sometimes, a word problem will ask us to determine the number of ways we can arrange elements sequentially, such as people in a line or items on a shelf. The solution is simply a **factorial**: the number of possibilities for the first item times the number of possibilities for the second times the number of possibilities for the third item, etc.

<u>Example</u>: How many different ways can we arrange six different books on a shelf?

Solution: The number of possibilities will be 6! = 6 x 5 x 4 x 3 x 2 x 1 = **720 possible ways**.

Other times, we will be asked to determine the number of ways to arrange a smaller group that is being drawn from a larger group. In this case, we must use the mathematical formula for permutations:

$$P(n,r) = \frac{n!}{(n-r)!}.$$

Where **n** = the number of items in the larger group and **r** = the number of items we are choosing

Example: Six artists submit their paintings in a competitive art show. The artists who win the first, second and third place prizes will each receive a cash award. How many possible outcomes are there for the first, second, and third place prizes?

Solution: 6! / (6-3)! = 6! / 3! = 6 x 5 x 4 = **120 possible outcomes**.

An important point about permutations – the order MATTERS. In the example above, it matters which artist won first, second, and third place; we cannot simply move their positions within the group. Hence, *every time we move an artist to a new position, it constitutes a new arrangement.*

Combinations

Sometimes, a word problem will ask us to consider different combinations of items within a larger group. If the order or arrangement of the items in the smaller group does NOT matter, then we can simply calculate the number of *possible* combinations. Our formula is:

$$^nC_k = \binom{n}{k} = \frac{n!}{k!(n-k)!}.$$

Where **n** = the number of items in the larger group and **k** = the number of items we are choosing

Example: How many different ways can we choose five ice cream toppings from a selection of eight?

Solution: In this case, the order of the toppings does not matter. Thus, we can use the formula for combinations to solve it:

8C5 = 8! / [5!(8 − 5)!] = 8! / 5! x 3! = (8 x 7 x 6 x 5!) / (8 x 7 x 6 x 5!) / (5! x 3 x 2 x 1) = **56 different ways**

A Final Tip about Combinations & Permutations

If you find yourself becoming confused about combinations and permutations, consider this final example.

For the three letters x, y, and z, there is only ONE combination (x, y, z) but SIX possible permutations: (x,y,z), (x,z,y), (y,x,z), (y,z,x), (z,y,x), and (z,x,y).

In permutations, order matters. In combinations, it does not.

Here are the most common ways the SAT, GRE, and GMAT will test your knowledge of these topics.

Example 1. Convoluted Wording and Extraneous Information

At the company picnic, each of the firm's 20 employees placed a raffle ticket into a bowl. At the end of the night, the company president picked one ticket randomly from the bowl and awarded the first prize to Greg. He then picked another ticket randomly from the bowl and awarded the second prize to Pete. Finally, after awarding two more prizes in the same manner, the president picked a fifth random ticket from the bowl and awarded the fifth prize to Jim. Assuming that the first four tickets were not placed back into the bowl after the first four prizes were awarded, what was the probability of Jim winning the fifth prize?

    a.   1.25%
    b.   2.50%
    c.   5.00%
    d.   5.25%
    e.   6.25%

Solution: Sometimes the test writers ask questions that are simple and direct. More often, however, they raise the level of difficulty by presenting a scenario in which multiple events occur, which may (or may not) impact the subsequent ones.   Your job is to decide which information is relevant to the question that is being asked, and which is simply a distraction.

This problem is embarrassingly easy to answer. The challenge is to cut through the non-essential details and get to the relevant facts. None of the information about Greg, Pete and the first four drawings relates to Jim's drawing, EXCEPT that the first four winning tickets were removed from the bowl (and not replaced) before drawing number five.

Hence, Jim's ticket was one of 16 tickets left in the bowl during the fifth drawing. His probability of winning the prize was 1/16, or 0.0625, which is 6.25%. Choice E is correct.

Example 2: Probability of Consecutive Events Occurring

What is the probability that a coin with one side heads and the other side tails will turn up heads on three consecutive tosses?

    a.   1/32
    b.   1/16
    c.   1/8
    d.   ¼
    e.   ½

Solution: For any given toss, the probability of getting heads is ½. For three tosses, we just multiply the three probabilities: ½ x ½ x ½ = 1/8. Choice C is correct.

Example 3. Probability of Picking A Particular Type

What is the probability of getting a red jelly bean from a dispenser that contains 80 red jelly beans, 48 green ones, 36 purple ones, 26 pink ones and 210 white ones?

    a.   1/8
    b.   1/6
    c.   1/5
    d.   1/4
    e.   1/3

Solution: First, we must determine the total number of jelly beans in the dispenser, which is 80 + 48 + 36 + 26 + 210 = 400.   Then, we must calculate the probability of getting a red jelly bean, which is 80/400 = 1/5. Choice C is correct.

Example 4. Determine the Number of Possible Combinations

There are five possible electives for Julie to take at her local community college this summer: English, Math, Statistics, History and Social Studies. Her counselor has advised Julie to choose two of them. How many possible combinations of the two courses are there?

      a.   30
      b.   25
      c.   15
      d.   12
      e.   10

Solution: For 5 items, there are 10 possible combinations of any 2 of them (5 x 2 = 10).

In this case, they are: English/Math, English/Statistics, English/History, English/Social Studies, Math/Statistics, Math/History, Math/Social Studies, Statistics/History, Statistics/Social Studies, and History/Social Studies. Choice E is correct.

Example 5. Order Doesn't Matter

Pizza Hut offers six possible toppings for their personal pan pizzas: pepperoni, sausage, onion, cheese, mushrooms and peppers. If you choose four of these toppings, how many possible combinations are there?

      a.   4
      b.   16
      c.   24
      d.   30
      e.   36

Solution: Use the factorial formula to solve: 6! / 4! = (6 x 5 x 4 x 3 x 2 x 1) / (4 x 3 x 2 x 1) = 30. Choice D is correct.

Example 6. Order Matters

There are twelve runners competing in a road race. Only the first five to cross the finish line will be ranked. How many possible ways are there to order the first five racers?

      a.   792
      b.   5,040
      c.   11,880
      d.   95,040
      e.   665,280

Solution: For situations in which the *order matters*, the correct formula is 12!/(12- 5)! = 12! / 7! =

(12 x 11 x 10 x 9 x 8 x 7 x 6 x 5 x 4 x 3 x 2 x 1) / (7 x 6 x 5 x 4 x 3 x 2 x 1) = 95,040. Choice D is correct.

Word Problems: Probability: EASY - MODERATE

1. What is the probability of getting a white jelly bean from a dispenser that contains 28 red jelly beans, 48 green ones, 36 purple ones, 26 pink ones, 30 blue ones and 28 white ones?

      a.   1/8
      b.   1/7
      c.   1/6
      d.   1/5
      e.   ¼

2. If you roll a 6-sided die, which sides are numbered 1 through 6, what is the probability that you will roll a 3?

      a.   1/6
      b.   1/5
      c.   1/4
      d.   1/3
      e.   ½

3. For a graduation gift, Sally's mother offered to buy her three CDs from her list of seven favorites. How many different combinations does Sally have to choose from?

      a.   21
      b.   42
      c.   840
      d.   1,764
      e.   2,520

4. What is the probability that a card chosen at random from a standard deck of 52 cards is a King?

      a.   1/52
      b.   1/26
      c.   1/13
      d.   1/12
      e.   4/12

5. You are arranging four brightly colored decorative tiles on the bathroom wall: they are red, green, pink and purple. How many possible ways are there to arrange them on the wall (assuming that no tile is repeated)?

      a.   4
      b.   8
      c.   16
      d.   24
      e.   64

6. A bookstore is preparing a display with five different novels by a best-selling author. How many possible arrangements are there in the display (assume no title is repeated)?

      a.   25
      b.   120
      c.   125
      d.   500
      e.   600

7. A candy dish contains only Snickers bars, Mars bars, and Hershey bars. The probability of choosing a Snickers bar at random is 1/5 and the probability of choosing a Mars bar at random is 3/10. If there are 200 candy bars in the dish, how many are Hershey bars?

      a.   50
      b.   75
      c.   100
      d.   125
      e.   150

8. The ratio of Democrats to Republicans at a particular polling center is 5 to 7. What is the probability that a person chosen at random from the center is a Democrat?

     a. 1/7
     b. 5/12
     c. 1/2
     d. 5/7
     e. It cannot be determined from the information given.

9. Two dozen musicians auditioned for an orchestra. Fifteen played the piano, while nine played the harp. If one pianist and one harpist are chosen from the group of twenty-four, how many different pairs of musicians are possible?

     a. 24
     b. 48
     c. 96
     d. 112
     e. 135

10. American Idol invited the top ten finalists to perform on their national tour. Only the top three would be offered a chance to sing solos. How many possible ways are there to order the top three finalists?

     a.   30
     b.   720
     c.   5,040
     d. 604,800
     e. 3,628,800

Word Problems: Probability: AS HARD AS IT GETS

11. Two concentric circles exist in a plane. If the larger circle has a diameter of 72 and the small circle has a diameter of 48, what is the probability that any point chosen at random from the large circle will also be in the small circle?

     a. 22.22%
     b. 33.33%
     c. 44.44%
     d. 55.56%
     e. 66.67%

12. Jenny is flying to Memphis on a jet that seats 480 passengers. The plane has 80 rows with six seats across – three seats on each side of the center aisle. What is the probability that Jenny will get a seat that is either a window seat or in the last ten rows?

     a. 3/12
     b. 5/12
     c. 1/3
     d. 3/8
     e. 2/5

13. According to the bookies in Las Vegas, the odds that Contestant X will lose American Idol are 44 to 6. What is the probability that Contestant X will win American Idol?

    a.   6%
    b.   12%
    c.   18%
    d.   88%
    e.   94%

14. A candy dish contains only chocolates and caramels. There are three times as many chocolates as caramels. The chocolates are either vanilla-filled or nut-filled, and four times as many chocolates are nut-filled as vanilla-filled. If one piece of candy is selected randomly from the dish, what is the probability that it will be a nut-filled chocolate?

    a.   3/20
    b.   1/5
    c.   1/4
    d.   9/20
    e.   3/5

Answer Key: Probability, Possibility, Combinations & Permutations

1. First, we must determine the total number of jelly beans: 28 + 48 + 36 + 26 + 30 + 28 = 196. Then, we can determine the probability of choosing one of a specific color: 28/196 = **1/7**. Choice B is correct.

2. The probability is **1/6**, or Choice A.

3. In this case, order does not matter. We can use the factorial formula to solve: 7! / 3! = (7 x 6 x 5 x 4 x 3 x 2 x 1) / (3 x 2 x 1) = **840**. Choice C is correct.

4. There are four kings in a deck of 52 cards. Thus, the probability of choosing a king is 4/52, or **1/13**. Choice C is correct.

5. For permutations, the correct formula is 4!/(4- 4)! = (4 x 3 x 2 x 1) / 1 = **24**. Choice D is correct.

6. For permutations, the correct formula is 5!/(5- 5)! = (5 x 4 x 3 x 2 x 1) / 1 = **120**. Choice B is correct.

7. If the probability of choosing a Snickers bar is 1/5 (or 2/10) and the probability of choosing a Mars bar is 3/10, then the probability of choosing EITHER a Snickers bar or a Mars bar is 2/10 + 3/10 = 5/10.

Therefore, the probability of choosing a Hershey bar is 1 – 5/10 = 5/10 = 1/2.
If there are 200 candy bars in the dish, then there are 1/2 x 200 = **100** Hershey bars. Choice C is correct.

8. To solve this problem, we must remember the basic rules for working with ratios. If the ratio of Democrats to Republicans is 5 to 7, then our whole is twelve. On a practical basis, it means that 5 out of every 12 voters are Democrats. Choice B is correct.

9. The orchestra will fill two positions – one pianist and one harpist. The possible combinations are 15 X 9 = **135**. Choice E is correct.

10. For situations in which the *order matters*, the correct formula is $10!/(10-3)! = 10!/7! =$

$(10 \times 9 \times 8 \times 7 \times 6 \times 5 \times 4 \times 3 \times 2 \times 1) / (7 \times 6 \times 5 \times 4 \times 3 \times 2 \times 1) = \textbf{720}$. Choice B is correct.

11. The area of the large circle is $(36)(36)\,\pi$, or $1{,}296\,\pi$, while the area of the small circle is $(24)(24)\,\pi$, or $576\,\pi$. To determine the probability of any given point being in both circles, we simply divide the two quantities and convert to a percentage: Area of the small circle / Area of the large circle = $576\,\pi /1{,}296\,\pi$, or 0.444, or **44.44%**. Choice C is correct.

12. For this question, we must determine the individual probability that Jenny will get a window seat OR be seated in the last ten rows. Then, we must subtract the number of seats that fall into both categories.

The probability of Jenny getting a window seat is $(2)(80)/480 = 160/480$
The probability of Jenny getting a seat in the last ten rows is $(10)(6)/480 = 60/480$

However, the last ten rows include 20 window seats, which we must subtract from the total probability. Hence, our answer is: $160/480 + 60/480 - 20/480 = 200/480 = \textbf{5/12}$. Choice B is correct.

13. If the odds of a contestant losing the contest are 44 to 6, then her odds of winning are 6 to 44. To answer the question, we must convert this to a fraction: $6/(6 + 44) = 6/50 = 0.12 = \textbf{12}\%$. Choice B is correct.

14. Immediately, we can divide the total into fourths:

Chocolates ¾ (or 15/20)
Caramels ¼ (or 5/20)

For the chocolates, we can further divide the 3/4 figure into two amounts, which reflect the number of vanilla-filled and nut-filled:

Vanilla-filled $(3/4)(2/10) = 6/40 = 3/20$
Nut filled $(3/4)(8/10) = 24/40 = 3/5$

Therefore, the probability of getting a nut-filled chocolate is **3/5**. Choice E is correct.

Chapter 16: Series, Sequences, and Repeating Decimals

In recent years, the SAT, GRE, and GMAT have become notorious for including tricky questions regarding series or sequences of numbers. Here are the most common areas to review.

Series

A series is a progression of numbers that are arranged according to a specific design.

The easiest ones are *arithmetic progressions*, such as 3, 5, 7, 9,..... in which each number is two digits greater than the previous one in the series. Likewise, series can include examples such as 2, 4, 16, 256, etc., in which the each number is the perfect square of the preceding number.

Arithmetic Sequence

Standardized tests often ask students to calculate the *nth* term in an arithmetic sequence – or the sum of a particular set of consecutive integers. For these questions, it's extremely helpful to use the relevant algebraic formulas:

Sum = Number of Items (First Item + Last or Desired Item) / 2

Example: What is the sum of the first 15 positive integers?

   Sum = 15(1 + 15)/2 = (15)(16)/2 = 120

For an arithmetic sequence in which the first term is **A** and the difference between the terms is **D**, the *nth* term is:
$$A_n = A_1 + (n - 1)D$$

Example: What is the eighth even positive integer?

   A8 = 2 + (8 – 1)2 = 2 + 14 = 16.

This chapter includes several problems that use these formulas correctly.

Items in a Consecutive Series

Another popular question requires students to determine the number of items in a consecutive set, when simply the endpoints are given. The scenario might be:

The number of raffle tickets on a roll.
The number of checks in a checkbook.
The volumes of encyclopedia on a shelf at the library.

Whatever the scenario, the student must determine the total number of items in a consecutive series. To do so, **subtract the endpoints and add 1.**

Example 1: Series

If the following series continues in the same pattern, what will the next term be?

   45, 47, 37, 39, 29, 31, 21....

   a.   11
   b.   19
   c.   23
   d.   25
   e.   It cannot be determined from the information given.

Solution: The terms increase by 2, then decrease by 10. If the same pattern continues, the next term will be 23. Choice C is correct.

Example 2. Arithmetic Sequence

What is the sum of the first 80 integers?

    a. 1,600
    b. 1,620
    c. 3,200
    d. 3,240
    e. 6,480

Solution: There are actually two ways to solve this problem. The first is to add the numbers between 1 and 80 on your calculator. But what if the question asked you to find the sum of the first 300 even or odd integers? Would you really want to take the time to add them manually?

Here's where it's helpful to use the formula for the sum of the numbers in an arithmetic series:

Sum = {(Number of Items) (First Item + Last or Desired Item)} / 2

Sum = 80(1 + 80)/2 = (80)(81)/2 = 3,240. Choice D is correct.

Example 3: Geometric Progression

If the population of Smithfield, which is currently 500,000, grows by 2,500 people each year, in how many years will the population double?

    a.   100
    b.   200
    c.   250
    d.   500
    e. 1,000

Solution: This problem can easily be solved using an algebraic formula. First, let's define our variables.

We will let x = the # of years until the population doubles. Mathematically, this can be expressed as:

2(500,000) = 500,000 + 2,500x
1,000,000 = 500,000 + 2,500x
500,000 = 2,500x
x = 200 years. Choice B is correct.

Example 4. Repeating Decimals

For the repeating decimal 0.015689015689015689……, what is the 37th digit to the right of the decimal point?

    a. 0
    b. 1
    c. 5
    d. 6
    e. 8

Solution: For repeating decimals, you must first determine the actual string of numbers that repeat. Then, you can simply count the number of decimal places to determine the identity of a specific digit in the string. In this case, the repeating pattern is 015689, which is a string of 6 digits. Hence, 37th digit to the right of the decimal point will be the *first* number in the series, which is 0. Choice A is correct.

Example 5. Consecutive Integers in a Set

When an accountant requested her client's sales records for tax season, she received a stack of invoices numbered 00236 through 00435. How many invoices were in the stack?

    a. 198
    b. 199
    c. 200
    d. 201
    e. 202

Solution: To count the number of consecutive integers in a set, **subtract the endpoints and add 1.** In this case, 00435 - 00236 + 1 = 200. There were 200 invoices in the stack. Choice C is correct.

Word Problems: Series & Sequences: EASY - MODERATE

1. A vending machine contains 300 jelly beans in four different colors, which are dispensed in the following order: red first, blue second, white third and green fourth. Assuming that they are dispensed in this same order every time, what will be the color of the last jelly bean in the vending machine?

    a. red
    b. blue
    c. white
    d. green
    e. it cannot be determined from the information given

2. Robin's wedding anniversary is 100 days after her birthday. If her birthday is on a Wednesday this year, on what day of the week will Robin's anniversary fall?

    a. Monday
    b. Tuesday
    c. Wednesday
    d. Thursday
    e. Friday

3. For the repeating decimal 0.98763219876321987632l...... , what is the 54th digit to the right of the decimal point?

    a. 1
    b. 2
    c. 3
    d. 6
    e. 7

4. What is the sum of the first 150 positive integers?

    a. 10,500
    b. 11,250
    c. 11,325
    d. 11,400
    e. 15,000

5. If the population of Walnut Grove is 300,000 and grows by 5,000 people each year, in how many years will the population triple?

     a.   60
     b.   90
     c.   120
     d.   240
     e.   300

6. When a store owner compiled her weekly sales records, she had a stack of invoices numbered 014567 through 019876. Upon further examination, however, the store owner realized that invoice numbers 014876 and 018999 were missing. How many invoices did the store owner have available for her weekly calculations?

     a.   5307
     b.   5308
     c.   5309
     d.   5310
     e.   5311

7. What is the next term in the following series: 11, 12, 13, 24, 15, 48…….

     a.   14
     b.   17
     c.   36
     d.   96
     e.   None of the above.

8. What is the next term in the following series? 1, 7, 13, 19…….

     a.   13
     b.   21
     c.   25
     d.   27
     e.   29

9. If the following series continues in the same pattern, what will the next term be?

          3, 5, 4, 7, 5, 9, 6, 11………

     a.   3
     b.   5
     c.   6
     d.   7
     e.   13

10. When an accountant requested her client's sales records for tax season, she received a stack of invoices numbered 001313 through 003131 and a second stack numbered 8929 through 9892. How many invoices were in the two stacks?

     a.   964
     b.   1,819
     c.   2,871
     d.   2,872
     e.   2,873

11. What is the sum of the positive integers between 80 and 180?

    a. 5,000
    b. 9,090
    c. 13,000
    d. 13,130
    e. 18,180

12. If the following series continues in the same pattern, what will the next term be?

        2, 6, 3, 9, 6, 18, 15......

    a. 6
    b. 9
    c. 12
    d. 21
    e. 45

13. What is the next term in the following series?

        100, 90, 105, 95, 110, 100, 115......

    a. 90
    b. 95
    c. 100
    d. 105
    e. 110

14. What is the next term in the following series?

        85, 84, 82, 79, 75.......

    a. 71
    b. 70
    c. 69
    d. 68
    e. 64

15. The population of Walnut Grove is currently 453,788. If the population increased by 4343 people per year for the preceding 8 years, what was the population in Walnut Grove 8 years ago?

    a. 41,904
    b. 56,723
    c. 91,467
    d. 419,044
    e. 434,744

16. What is the thirteenth even positive integer minus the twelfth odd even positive integer?

    a. 1
    b. 2
    c. 3
    d. 12
    e. 13

17. A sequence of terms begins with 11 and each term has a difference of 12. What is the thirteenth term in the sequence?

     a. 143
     b. 154
     c. 155
     d. 157
     e. 167

18. If the first term in an arithmetic sequence is 15 and the 132th term is 3,290, what is the common difference between the terms?

     a. 10
     b. 15
     c. 25
     d. 30
     e. 35

19. Find the sum of the 35 terms in a sequence that start with 2 and ends with 70.

     a.   600
     b.   930
     c. 1,200
     d. 1,260
     e. 2,520

Word Problems: Series & Sequences: AS HARD AS IT GETS

20. Jane and Harry wanted to create a memorable combination for their home safe. For the first three digits, Jane used the sum of the first 40 even integers. For the second three numbers, Harry used the sum of the first 20 odd integers. For the final three numbers, they used the difference between the first two quantities. What was the nine-digit combination for the safe?

     a. 800200600
     b. 800210590
     c. 840200600
     d. 840210590
     e. 840210630

21. W, which is a positive integer, is the first term in a sequence. After W, each term in the sequence is 2 greater than one-half the preceding term. What is the ratio of the second term to W?

     a. 1/2W/(W + 2)
     b. (W + 4)2W
     c. (W + 2)/2
     d. W/2
     e. 4(W + 1)/2

22. The first term in a sequence is -20. Every consecutive term is 15 greater than the term that immediately preceded it. What is the value of the 120st term in the sequence?

     a. 1,765
     b. 1,770
     c. 1,775
     d. 1,780
     e. 1,785

23. The first term of a sequence of integers is 100,000. Every term after the first is equal to one-half of the preceding term if that term is even, or is equal to four-fifths of the preceding term if that term is odd. What is the eighth term of the sequence?

    a.   781
    b.   1,000
    c.   1,250
    d.   1,563
    e.   2,500

24. The following number is formed by writing the integers from 150 to 200 in consecutive order. What is the 63th digit?   150,151.............199, 200

    a.   0
    b.   1
    c.   2
    d.   3
    e.   6

25. A concert hall has seats arranged in 50 consecutive rows. The first row has 300 seats, and each successive row has 5 fewer seats. How many seats are in the entire hall?

    a.   7,500
    b.   8,625
    c.   8,875
    d.   17,250
    e.   17,750

Answer Key: Series, Sequences, and Repeating Decimals

1. 300/4 = 75. The final jelly bean in the vending machine will be the fourth color in the rotation, which is green. Choice D is correct.

2. 100/7 = 14 + 2 remainder. Hence, Robin's anniversary will fall two days after Wednesday, which is Friday. Choice E is correct.

3. In this decimal, the repeating pattern is 9876321, which is a string of 7 digits. The first 49 digits will be 7 repetitions of this pattern. Then, in the eight repetition of the pattern, the 54th digit to the right of the decimal point will be the *fifth* number in the series, which is 3. Choice C is correct.

4. The fastest way to solve this problem is by using the formula for the sum of the numbers in an arithmetic series:

Sum = Number of Items (First Item + Last or Desired Item) / 2
Sum = 150(1 + 150)/2 = (150)(151)/2 = **11,325**. Choice C is correct.

5. This problem can easily be solved using an algebraic formula. First, let's define our variables. We will let x = the # of years until the population triples. Mathematically, this can be expressed as:

3(300,000) = 300,000 + 5,000x
900,000 = 300,000 + 5,000x
600,000 = 5,000x
x = **120** years. Choice C is correct.

6. To find the original number of invoices in the series, we must subtract the endpoints and add one: 019876 – 014567 + 1 = 5310. Next, we must subtract the two missing invoices: 5310 - 2 = **5308**. Choice B is correct.

7. If you look carefully, you will see that this example is actually a combination of TWO sub-series. The odd numbers (11, 13, 15 ….) form an arithmetic series, in which each number increases by two. The even numbers (12, 24, 48, ….) form an arithmetic sequence, in which each number is twice the previous one. The next number in the series will be part of the arithmetic sequence. According to the design, it is 15 + 2, or **17**. Choice B is correct.

8. Each term in the series increases by 6. Hence, the next term will be 19 + 6 = **25**. Choice C is correct.

9. This problem is a combination of two sub-series. In the first one, each number increase by 1 (3,4,5,6); in the second, each number increases by 2 (5,7,9,11). The next number would be 6 + 1, or **7**. Choice D is correct.

10. To count the number of consecutive integers in a set, we must subtract the endpoints and add 1. In this case, we must complete the calculation for the two stacks separately, and then add the two amounts together.

Stack 1: 3,131 – 1,313 + 1 = 1,819
Stack 2: 9,892 – 8,929 + 1 = 964
1,819 + 964 = 2,783. Choice E is correct.
11. Solving this problem requires two steps. First, we must determine the number of consecutive integers in the set. To do so, we will subtract the endpoints and add 1. 180 – 80 + 1 = 101

Next, we must find the sum of these 101 numbers:

Sum = Number of Items (First Item + Last Item) / 2
Sum = 101(80 + 180)/2 = (101)(260)/2 = **13,130**. Choice D is correct.

12. The series goes according to these steps: multiply the term by 3, subtract 3, multiply the new term by 3, subtract 3, multiple the new term by 3, subtract 3, etc. The next term would be 15 x 3, or **45**. Choice E is correct.

13. The steps in these series are: subtract 10, then add 15, repeat. The next term would be 115 – 10, or **105**. Choice D is correct.

14. The first term decreases by 1, the second decreases by 2, the third decreases by 3, etc. The next term would be 75 – 5 = **70**. Choice B is correct.

15. This problem can easily be solved using an algebraic formula. First, let's define our variables.

We will let x = the population 8 years ago. Therefore,
453,788 = x + 4,343(8)
453,788 = x + 34,744
x = **419,044** residents 8 years ago. Choice D is correct.

16. We can solve this using the formulas for arithmetic sequences:

13th even: 2 + (13-1)(2) = 2 + 24 = 26
12th odd: 1 + (12 – 1)(2) = 1 + 22 = 23
13th even integer = 26; 13th odd integer = 23; 26 – 23 = **3**. Choice C is correct.

17. A13 = 11 + 12(13 – 1) = 11 + 144 = **155**. Choice C is correct.

18. 3290 = 15 + D (132 – 1)

3275 = 131D
D = **25**. Choice C is correct.

19. S35 = 35/2(2 + 70) = (35/2) (72) = **1,260.** Choice D is correct.

20. This problem is easy to solve, but tedious. First, we must determine the first three numbers in the combination, which are equal to the sum of the first 40 even integers.

Sum = (Number of Items) (First Item + Last Item) / 2
Sum = (40)(2 + 40)/2 = (40)(42)/2 = **840 = first three digits of the combination**

Next, we must determine the sum of the first 20 odd integers:
Sum = (Number of Items) (First Item + Last Item) / 2
Sum = (20)(1 + 20)/2 = (20)(21)/2 = **210 = second three digits of the combination**

The final three digits in the combination are 840 – 210 = **630.**
Therefore, the complete combination of the safe is **840210630.** Choice E is correct.

21. If W is the first term, then the second term is W/2 + 2. The ratio of these two values is (second term)/(first term) = (W/2 + 2)/W, which simplifies to **(W + 4)/2W.** To check our work, let's assume that the first term W = 100. The second term would be 2 greater than one-half of one hundred, or 52. The ratio of 52/100 = 26/50= 13/25. (W + 4)/2W = 104/200 = 52/100 = 26/50 = **13/25.** Choice B is correct.

22. For an arithmetic sequence in which the first term is A and the difference between the terms is D, the *nth* term is: $A_n = A_1 + (n – 1)D$. In this case, the first term in the sequence is -20. The difference in terms is 15 and n = 120. The 120th term = -20 + (120 – 1)15 = -20 + 1800 – 15 = **1,765.** Choice A is correct.

23. To solve, we must perform each operation in order:

First term 100,000:
Second term = 100,000(0.50)= 50,000
Third term = 50,000(0.50) = 25,000
Fourth term = 25,000(0.50) = 12,500
Fifth term = 12,500(0.50) = 6,250
Sixth term = 6,250(0.50) = 3,125   ODD
Seventh term = 3,125(0.80) = 2,500
Eighth term = 2,500 (0.50) = 1,250. Choice C is correct.

24. The easiest way to answer this question without making a careless mistake is to write out the 63 digits in order. When we do, we discover that that 63th digit is a 0. Choice A is correct.

First ten digits:	1	5	0	1	5	1	1	5	2	1
Second ten digits:	5	3	1	5	4	1	5	5	1	5
Third ten digits:	6	1	5	7	1	5	8	1	5	9
Fourth ten digits:	1	6	0	1	6	1	1	6	2	1
Fifth ten digits:	6	3	1	6	4	1	6	5	1	6
Sixth ten digits	6	1	6	7	1	6	8	1	6	9
Last three digits:	1	7	0							

25. First, we must determine the number of seats in the final row.
50th row: a - d(n – 1) = 300 - 5(50 – 1) = 300 - 5(49) = 300 – 245 = 55 seats in the final row

Next, we must determine the number of seats in the entire concert hall.
Total seats: 50/2 (300 + 55) = 25 (355) = 8,875 seats. Choice C is correct.

Chapter 17: Statistics

The latest versions of the SAT, GRE, and GMAT include basic statistical concepts, such as mean, median, mode, range and standard deviation. In this chapter, we will define these terms and test your knowledge of them in relevant word problems. First, a few definitions:

The Average (or Mean): To find the average of a set of numbers, add them together and divide by the number of numbers.

Average or Mean = Sum of the terms / Number of terms

Example: Find the average of 12, 15, 23, 40, and 40.

Solution: First, we must add the numbers: 12 + 15 + 23 + 40 + 40 = 130.
Then, we must divide the total by 5: 130 / 5 = 26.
The average or mean of these numbers is **26.**

Median: The median of a set of numbers is the value that falls in the *middle* of the set.

Example: What is the median of these five test scores? 88, 86, 57, 94, and 73

Solution: To find the median of a data set, we must first list the scores in increasing (or decreasing) order: 57, 73, 86, 88, 94. The median is the middle number, or 86.

Note: If there is an even number of values in a set (six test scores, for instance), simply take the average of the two middle numbers.

Mode: The mode of a set of numbers is the value that appears most often.

Example: What is the mode for the following set of test scores? 88, 57, 68, 85, 99, 93, 93, 84, and 81.

Solution: The mode of the scores would be 93 because it appears more often than any other score.

Note: Sets can have more than one mode; if a set has two modes, it is called bi-modal.

Range: The range of a data set is its spread.

Example: What is the range of this data set? 11, 53, 113, 26, 34, 68, 90.

Solution: the range of the data set is 11 to 113.

Standard Deviation: The Standard Deviation is a complex statistical measure, but for testing purposes, you mainly need to know that it is the measure of the spread of the data.

For example, the numbers {0, 10, 20} have a Standard Deviation of about 8.17 while the numbers {9, 10, 11} have a Standard Deviation of about 0.82. Both have an average of 10, but because the first group was more "spread out" it had a higher Standard Deviation.

Now that we've reviewed the basics, let's go through a few word problems that test your understanding of them.

Example 1:   Working with Averages: Finding a Missing Number

The Bluebird baseball team scored the following number of runs in their first eight games: 12, 9, 8, 15, 6, 9, 17, and 7. How many runs do they need to score in game 9 to have an average of 12 runs per game for the entire 9-game season?

       a.   21
       b.   22
       c.   23
       d.   24
       e.   25

Solution: For this equation, we can simply use the equation for simple averages to find the missing number.

Average = Sum of Terms/Number of Terms
$12 = (12 + 9 + 8 + 15 + 6 + 9 + 17 + 7 + x) / 9$.
$12 = (83 + x) / 9$
$108 = 83 + x$
$x = 25$. Choice E is correct.

Example 2: Changing a Member of the Data Set

The average (mean) of eight numbers is 8. If 2 is subtracted from each of four of the numbers, what is the new average?

       a.   5.5
       b.   6
       c.   6.5
       d.   7
       e.   7.5

Solution: To solve this problem, we simply need to remember what it means if a number is an average (or mean) of a particular data set. Here, if 8 numbers have an average of 8, their sum is 64.

If we subtract 2 from 4 of the numbers, it removes 2(4), or 8 from the sum.
The new sum is 56, which means that the new mean is 56/8 =7. Choice D is correct.

Example 3:   Simple Average vs. Weighted Average

3a. In a kennel with 28 dogs, of which half are neutered and half are intact, the average (mean) weight of the neutered dogs was 83 pounds. If the average weight of the 14 intact dogs in the kennel was 92 pounds, what was the average weight of the entire kennel?

       a.   86.5
       b.   87.0
       c.   87.5
       d.   88.0
       e.   88.5

Solution: In this case, the number of intact dogs (14) is equal to the number of neutered dogs (also 14), which means that we can simply take the average of 83 + 92 and apply it to the entire kennel.   The result is 87.5, or Choice C, which is the correct answer.

The next problem, though, shows what happens when the two groups under consideration are NOT the same size. The calculation becomes more difficult.

3b. In a kennel with 27 dogs, the average (mean) weight of the neutered dogs was 83 pounds. If the average weight of the 15 intact dogs in the kennel was 92 pounds, what was the average weight of the entire kennel?

    a. 86.5
    b. 87.0
    c. 87.5
    d. 88.0
    e. 88.5

Solution: In this case, the number of neutered and intact dogs in the kennel is not the same, which means that we must take a *weighted average* for each of the two groups.

Here's how to approach a problem with weighted averages:

Total kennel average = (Sum of intact weights + Sum of neutered weights) / Total # of dogs

Now, we must weigh the averages properly in the equation:

Total kennel average = {(15)(92) + (12)(83)} / 27 = 88
Total kennel average = (1,380 + 996)/27
Total kennel average = 2,376/27= 88
The correct answer is Choice D.

Note: If these explanations confuse you, it helps to put the answer to the **first** example in the same format as the second one. In the first example, in which there were 14 neutered dogs and 14 intact dogs, we can still use the formula for weighted averages to solve the problem:

Total kennel average =(Sum of intact weights + Sum of neutered weights) / Total # of dogs
Total kennel average = {(14)(92) + (14)(83)} / 28 = 87.5
Hence, the correct answer is Choice C, 87.5.

Example 4: Average Problems with Consecutive Integers

If the average of seven consecutive odd numbers is 21, what is the largest of the seven numbers?

    a. 15
    b. 19
    c. 23
    d. 27
    e. 29

Solution: To solve this problem, we must write an equation that conveys the information in the following form:
Average = Sum of Terms / Number of Terms

We will let the first unknown odd number = x. The next six consecutive odd numbers can therefore be represented as $(x + 2),(x + 4)$, $(x + 6)$, $(x + 8)$, $(x + 10)$ and $(x + 12)$. If their average is equal to 21, then our equation becomes:

Average = Sum of Terms / Number of Terms
$21 = [x + (x + 2) + (x + 4) + (x + 6) + (x + 8) + (x + 10) + (x + 12)] / 7$
$21 = [7x + 42]/7$
$147 = 7x + 42$
$105 = 7x$
$x = 15$

But wait, we aren't done yet. From our calculations, we know that 15 is the smallest of the 7 numbers in the set. The largest number is $(x + 12) = 15 + 12 = 27$. Choice D is correct.

Example 5. Average Problems w/ Unknown Variables

The mean of two numbers is 5x – 12. If one of the numbers is x, what is the other number?

      a.   10n + 24/9
      b.   9n – 24
      c.   9n + 24/9
      d.   10n - 24
      e.   it cannot be determined from the information given

Solution: In this case, we know that there are two numbers being averaged, one of which is x. We do not know the value of the other number, so we must "assign" an arbitrary value. Since the answer choices all include a term with the variable n, let's use n to represent our unknown.

By definition, the sum of n + 2 divided by two = the average. According to the problem, in mathematical terms, (n + x) / 2 = 5x – 12. If we "solve" this equation, we find that x = 9n - 24, which is Choice B.

To test your skills on these concepts, try the following problems. Detailed solutions are at the end of the chapter.

Word Problems: Statistics: EASY - MODERATE

1. If the average of nine consecutive odd integers is 113, what is the smallest of the nine integers?

      a.   99
      b.   101
      c.   103
      d.   105
      e.   107

2. The Zippy Cheese Company has established a quality control program to minimize the number of underweight bars of cheese that leave their plant. During the first six weeks of the program, the number of bars that failed, by week, was 324, 119, 267, 219, 553, and 189. If management's goal is to have an overall average of 300 failing bars or less during the first seven weeks of the program, what is the highest number of bars that can fail during week seven?

      a.   297
      b.   307
      c.   359
      d.   429
      e.   548

3. Scientists recorded the daily temperature in a research aquarium. During a six-day period, the temperatures recorded (in °F) were 67, 73, 72, 56, 68, and 78. What was the median temperature (in °F)?

      a.   68.5
      b.   69
      c.   70
      d.   72.5
      e.   73

4. For marketing purposes, Ace Hamburgers is recording the number of customers who order hot dogs during the lunch rush. For the first half of January, these are their daily values: 43, 56, 42, 56, 47, 28, 36, 65, 67, 89, 81, 45, 54, 44, 34. What is the mode?

    a. 47
    b. 52.5
    c. 54
    d. 56
    e. 65

5. Office Depot has launched a new promotion to entice customers to buy ink cartridges. For the month of April, every customer who buys a printer gets a free ink cartridge, along with a coupon for future savings. At the end of the month, the store manager had recorded the following number of printers sold each day: 11, 23, 41, 23, 43, 12, 15, 13 45 32, 34, 12, 18, 34, 23, 23, 45, 13, 9, 25, 23, 43, 45, 12, 34, 12, 34, 54, 34, 30. The main office asks the manager to calculate the mode of this data set. What is it?

    a. 12
    b. 23
    c. 34
    d. 43
    e. 45

6. An IRS auditor has requested salary information for all board members of the SAG Corporation. A review of the files revealed that three members each earned $120,000 per year, while another four members each earned $90,000 per year, and an additional nine members each earned $50,000 per year. What is the mean salary of the board members?

    a. $73,125
    b. $86,000
    c. $86,625
    d. $93,125
    e. $106,000

7. The final exam for English Literature class is worth 1/3 of the overall grade. The average of 4 monthly exams counts for another third, while an oral presentation on sonnets is worth the final third. So far, Becky's exam scores are 68, 73, 80 and 95. She only scored a 70 on her oral presentation. What will Becky have to earn on the final exam to raise her average to 80?

    a. 87
    b. 88
    c. 89
    d. 91
    e. 92

8. In a family of eight children, half are girls and half are boys. If the average height of the girls is 56 inches and the average height of the boys is 42 inches, what is the average height of all eight children?

    a. 48
    b. 49
    c. 50
    d. 51
    e. 52

9. In a class of 55 students, the average waistline of the 30 girls was 24, while the average waistline of the 25 boys was 36. What was the average waistline for the entire class?

   a. 27.45
   b. 28.00
   c. 29.45
   d. 30.00
   e. 31.45

10. To get a grade of A in Spanish, Sara must achieve an average of 90 or above on six exams. Thus far, Sara's scores on the first five exams are 96, 81, 79, 87 and 100. What is the lowest possible score that Sara can get on the final exam to get an A grade in Spanish?

   a. 95
   b. 96
   c. 97
   d. 98
   e. 99

11. For the following data sat, what is the median minus the mode?

   7, 3, 15, 6, 7, 8, 9, 12, 5, 7, 6

   a. 0
   b. 0.7
   c. 1.0
   d. 1.7
   e. 2.0

12. The mean of two numbers is 11d + 5. If one of the numbers is d, what is the other number?

   a. (11g – 5)/d
   b. (g + 5)/d
   c. (g – 5)/10
   d. (g – 5) /(10 – d)
   e. it cannot be determined from the information given

13. The mean of seven numbers is 77. If 12 is subtracted from each of five of the numbers, what is the new mean?

   a. 65.00
   b. 66.66
   c. 68.43
   d. 70.15
   e. 72.00

14. In a hospital with 39 patients, the average (mean) temperature of the male patients was 101.7 F. If the average (mean) temperature of the 23 female patients was 98.5 F, what was the average temperature of all 39 patients (in degrees F)?

   a. 98.0
   b. 98.8
   c. 99.0
   d. 99.8
   e. 100.1

15. The Zippy Cheese Company monitors the number of bars that each employee can wrap per hour. The nine employees on the night shift wrapped the following number of bars: 234, 433, 239, 324, 333, 245, 343, 414, and 243. What is the median?

    a. 239
    b. 243
    c. 245
    d. 324
    e. 333

Word Problems: Statistics: AS HARD AS IT GETS

16. If the mean of integers E and F is G, what is the mean of E, F, and H, assuming that H is also a positive integer?

    a. $(G + H)/2$
    b. $(G + H)/3$
    c. $(E + F + H)/(G - 3)$
    d. $\frac{1}{2}G(E + F + H)$
    e. $(2G + H)/3$

17. If q, r, and s represent three numbers in which $r = q + 8$ and $s = r + 11$, what is the result when the median of the three numbers is subtracted from their mean?

    a. -1
    b. 0
    c. 1
    d. 2
    e. 3

18. The mean SAT score for a group of M students in Montana is 1400, while the mean SAT score for a group of V students in Virginia is 1650. When the scores of both groups are combined, the mean is 1600. What is the value of V/M?

    a. 1/4
    b. 1/2
    c. 1
    d. 2
    e. 4

Answer Key: Word Problems - Statistics

1. If 113 is the mean, then it is the fifth in the series of nine consecutive odd numbers. We can simply count back to get the first in the series, which will be 105 (113 – 111 – 109 – 107 - 105). Choice D is correct.

2. For this problem, we can simply use the equation for simple averages to find the missing number: 300 = (324 + 119 + 267 + 219 + 553 + 189 + x) / 7, So 300 = (1671 + x) / 7, so 2100 = 1671 + x, so x = 429. Choice D is correct.

3. To determine the median, we must first, arrange the numbers in ascending order: 56, 67, 68, 72, 73, 88. Since there is an even number of values, we must take the average of the middle two numbers as our median. Here, it is 68 + 72, which have an average of 70. Choice C is correct.

4. The mode is the value that occurs most frequently in the set of data. To find it, we must first arrange the values in ascending order: 28, 34, 36, 42, 43, 44, 45, 47, 54, 56, 56, 65, 67, 81, 89. Here, the mode is 56. Choice D is correct.

5. The mode is the value that occurs most frequently in the set of data. To find it, we must first arrange the values in ascending order: 9, 11, 12, 12, 12, 12, 13, 13, 15, 18, 23, 23, 23, 23, 23, 25, 30, 32, 34, 34, 34, 34, 34, 41, 43, 45, 45, 45, 54. The value that occurs most often is 34, or Choice C.

6. The mean equals the sum of all of the salaries divided by the number of salaries (in this case, 16). So, the mean = {3 (120,000) + 4 (90,000) + 9 (50,000)} /16 = (360,000 + 360,000 + 450,000)/16 = 1,170,000/16 = $73,125. Choice A is correct.

7. 17. Let's let x = the final exam grade. The average of Becky's four exams is (68 + 73 + 80 + 95)/4 = 79. Finally, her score for the oral presentation is 70. Since the final exam grade, oral presentation score and the average of her four exam grades all equal one-third of Becky's final grade, we simply need to solve the following equation for x: 1/3 (79) + 1/3 (70) + 1/3 (x) = 80. Hence, x = 91. Choice D is correct.

8. In this case, the number of girls (4) is equal to the number of boys (also 4), which means that we can simply take the average of 56 + 42 and apply it to the entire group of siblings. The result is (56 + 42)/2 = 49 inches. Choice B is correct.

9. Because the number of boys and girls is not the same, we must take a *weighted average* for each of the two groups.

Average for entire class =(Sum of Girls' Waistlines + Sum of Boys' Waistlines) / Total # Students
Average = {(30)(24) + (25)(36)} / 55
Average = (720 + 900)/55 = 1620/55 = 29.45. Choice C is correct.

10. To solve, we can use the following equation: 90 = (x + 96 + 81 + 79 + 87 + 100) / 6. When we solve the equation for x, we find that it is 97, which is Choice C.

11. First, we must arrange the numbers in ascending order: 3, 5, 6, 6, 7, 7, 7, 8, 9, 12, 15. Median = 7, Mode = 7. 7 – 7 = 0. Choice A is correct.

12. In this case, we know that there are two numbers being averaged, one of which is d. We do not know the value of the other number, so we must "assign" an arbitrary value. Since the answer choices all include a term with the variable g, let's use g to represent our unknown. By definition, their sum divided by two = the average.

Mathematically,
(d + g) / 2 = 11d + 5
2d + 2g = 22d + 10
2g -10 = 20d
g – 5 = 10d
d = (g - 5)/10. Choice C is correct.

13. For the original numbers, (7)(77) = 539 = sum. New sum= 539 – (12)(5) = 479. 479/7=68.43. Choice C is correct.

14. Because the number of male and female patients is not the same, we must take a *weighted average* for each of the two groups.

Average =(Sum of Males' Temperatures + Sum of Females' Temperatures/Total # Patients
Average = {(16)(101.7) + (23)(98.5)} / 39 = {1627.2 + 2265.5}/39 = 3892.7/39 = 99.8° F Choice D is correct.

15. To determine the median, we must first, arrange the numbers in ascending order: 234, 239, 243, 245, 324, 333, 343, 414, 433. The middle number, 324, is the median.   D

16. To solve, let's plug in a few values for the variables. Let's let E = 100 and F = 50. Their average or mean, which is G, is therefore 75.   (100 + 50)/2 = 150/2 = 75. (If we convert this to letters, we get (E + F)/2 = 2G/2 = G.)

Now, let's assume that H = 60. To average E, F, and H, we must perform the following calculation:

(100 + 50 + 60)3 = 210/3. Note: 210 = 150 + 60, which is 2G + H. (If we convert this to letters, we get (E + F + H)/3 = (2G + H)/3.)   Choice E is correct.

17. By definition, r = q + 8 and s = q + 8 + 11. The *median* of q, r, and s is simply the middle value, which is r, or (q + 8). The *mean* of the three numbers is their sum divided by three, or

{q + (q + 8) + (q + 8 + 11)} / 3 = (3q + 27)/3 = q + 9.

The difference between the mean and the median is (q + 8) – (q + 9) = -1. Choice A is correct.

18. From the data in the problem, we can write an equation to identify the value of V/M:

{1400M + 1650V} / (M + V) = 1600
1400M + 1650V = 1600M + 1600V
50V = 200M
V = 4M
V/M = 4. Choice E is correct.

Chapter 18: Problems Without Numbers (All Variables)

For many students, the most intimidating word problems are those that use letters – or other variables – in place of actual numbers. In extreme cases, students become so confused that they cannot identify simple mathematical operations that would normally be easy for them.

And that's why we have included this chapter – to give you a few basic tips that will increase your likelihood of solving "all variable" problems on the SAT, GRE, and GMAT quickly and correctly.

Our first tip is to read the problem slowly and carefully. Try to determine the mathematical operation that is being described. If you *can't*, substitute a few random numbers for the variables. In most cases, the scenario will be significantly easier to understand.

As always, here are a few examples:

Example 1. Basic Arithmetic

A local store employs X men and Y women. What portion of the staff is women?

    a. Y/X
    b. X/2Y
    c. Y/(XY)
    d. (X + Y)/Y
    e. Y/(X + Y)

Solution: If you were confused by this problem (and the answer choices), just plug in some random numbers to clarify the scenario. In this case, let's randomly let X = 10 and Y = 15. If the store employs 10 men and 15 women, then the portion of staff that is women is 15/25. In terms of the letters, this is Y/(X + Y). Choice E is correct.

Example 2. Different Units

How many seconds are there in A hours, B minutes and C seconds?

    a. ABC
    b. 60(ABC)
    c. 360AB/C
    d. 3600ABC
    e. 3,600A + 60B + C

Solution: To solve, we must convert all of the terms to seconds and add them together. Let's start with what we know.

The term for inches is represented by C, so we do not need to change it.
There are 60 seconds in 1 minute. Hence, our coefficient for B is 60.
There are 60 minutes in 1 hour. Hence, our coefficient for A is (60)(60) =3,600.

The number of inches in a distance of X yards, Y feet and Z inches is therefore 3,600A + 60B + C. Choice E is correct.

Example 3. Backwards Calculations

For her Halloween party, Janice went to a local candy store and bought X dozen candy bars at a price of Y per bar. When she left the store, Janice had Z cents left over. Assuming that she made no other purchases, how much money (in cents) did Janice have when she entered the candy store?

    a.   XYZ
    b.   XY + Z
    c.   (12X/Y) + Z
    d.   12XY – Z
    e.   12XY + Z

Solution: We can solve this problem by plugging in numbers or by doing a few simple "backwards" calculations. First, let's try Option 1, the plug- in approach.

Let's assume that Janice bought 10 dozen candy bars at a price of 50 cents per bar. Let's also assume that she had 20 cents left over. Hence, X = 10, Y = 50 and Z = 20.

Janice therefore spent (12)(10)(50 cents), which is 12XY. If she had 20 cents left over, then her original amount of money was 12XY + Z. Choice E is correct.

Option 2. If you don't want to plug in numbers, you can just reason the problem through. Janice bought X dozen candy bars, which = 12X. If they cost Y cents each, then she spent 12XY. Finally, she had Z cents left over, which we must add to her total amount of money. When we do, we get the same answer as we did with the plug-in method: 12XY + Z.

Example 4. Varying Cost Structures

During his vacation, Joe sent an urgent telegram to his family in Italy. Western Union charged him M cents for the first 10 words and N cents for each additional word. How much did Joe pay to send a telegram that was O words long (assuming O is greater than 10)?

    a.   M + NO
    b.   M + N(O – 10)
    c.   M + 1/MNO
    d.   MNO - N(O – 10)
    e.   M + O/10N

Solution: Once again, this is a simple problem is we substitute numbers for letters. Let's assume that Western Union charges 100 cents for the first 10 words and 5 cents for each additional word. Let's also assume that Joe's telegram was 30 words long. If we do, then M = 100, N = 5, and O = 30.

Joe's cost will be the basic charge for 10 words, plus the additional cost for every word over 10.
The basic cost = M = 100. The additional cost per word = N(O – 10).
Therefore, Joe's total cost = M + N(O – 10). Choice B is correct.

Example 5. Mixtures

What is the total cost (in cents) of A books, which cost B dollars each, and C books, which cost D cents each?

    a.   AB + CD
    b.   AB/CD
    c.   ABCD/100
    d.   100AB + CD
    e.   AB + CD/100

Solution: As always, let's substitute numbers for the variables and see what we get. Let's assume that we have 10 books that cost $2.00 each and 5 books that cost 75 cents each. Hence, A = 10, B = 2.00, C = 5 and D =0. 75.

The total cost of A books is 100(10)(2) = 100AB

The total cost of C books is (5)(0.75) = CD

Therefore, the total cost of all of the books is 100(10)(2) + (5)(0.75) = 100AB + CD. Choice D is correct.

Word Problems with Only Variables: AS HARD AS IT GETS

1. How many inches are there in X yards, Y feet and Z inches?

    a.   36X + 12Y + Z
    b.   3X + 12Y +12 Z
    c.   3X + 36Y +12 Z
    d.   (X + Y + Z)/12
    e.   (X +Y)/12 + Z

2. During an annual promotion, a department store buyer can purchase one I-Pod for Q dollars. Each additional unit costs X dollars less than the first one, or Q – X dollars. Which of the following represents the buyer's cost, in dollars, for G I-Pods bought during this promotion?

    a.   QGX
    b.   G (Q – X)
    c.   Q + (G – 1) (Q – X)
    d.   (Q – X) + (Q – X)/G
    e.   {Q + (Q – X)} / G

3. X roommates agree to split the cost of utilities for their apartment, which usually cost Y per month. At the end of the year, the monthly cost of utilities increased by $250. How much did each roommate have to contribute each month for his/her total share?

    a.   250/X
    b.   250Y/X
    c.   XY/250
    d.   (Y + 250)/X
    e.   X/Y + 250/X

4. Brianna receives a commission of H% on a sale of K dollars. What is her commission?

    a.   H/K
    b.   HK
    c.   1/HK
    d.   HK/100
    e.   100HK

5. If Q sandwiches will feed R children, how many sandwiches will be needed to feed S students?

    a.   RS/Q
    b.   QRS
    c.   1/QS
    d.   R/QS
    e.   QS/R

6. If D seamstresses can sew a wedding gown in E hours, how many hours will it take them to sew the gown if two of the seamstresses call in sick?

    a.   D – (E/2)
    b.   D/(E - 2)
    c.   E/(D – 2)
    d.   DE/(E – 2)
    e.   DE/2

7. Jake is a wholesale dealer of foreign and vintage cars. If he can buy J cars for G dollars, how much will M cars cost (in dollars)?

    a.   1/MGJ
    b.   (100/J)MG
    c.   MG/J
    d.   MJ/G
    e.   MGJ

8. There are P tenants in an apartment building, who agree to split the cost of utilities, N, in an equal manner. If the cost of utilities increases by $212 per month, how much must each tenant pay?

    a.   (P + 212)/N
    b.   (N + 212)/P
    c.   P(N – 212)/P
    d.   212/P
    e.   212P/N

9. Carol's sugar bowl was one-third full. When she added K cc of granulated sugar, the bowl was nine-tenths full. How much sugar (in cc) would Carol's sugar bowl hold if it was completely full?

    a.   13K/30
    b.   17K/30
    c.   9K/17
    d.   17K/9
    e.   30K/17

10. Heidi bought U wedding favors at a bridal shop at a price of V per favor. Afterwards, Heidi had W dollars left over. Assuming that she made no other purchases, how much money (in dollars) did Heidi bring to the bridal shop for favors?

    a.   UVW
    b.   UV + W
    c.   (U/V) + W
    d.   UV – W
    e.   It cannot be determined from the information given.

11. The cost to park at Yankee Stadium is J dollars for the first eight hours and P dollars for each additional hour. How much did Grace pay to park at the stadium for S hours (assuming that S is greater than eight)?

    a.   J + PS
    b.   J + 1/JPS
    c.   J + P(S – 8)
    d.   JPS - P(S – 8)
    e.   J +{(S – 8)/P}

12. What is the total cost (in cents) of W watermelons, which cost X dollars each, and Y apples, which cost Z cents each?

    a. WXYZ/100
    b. 100WX + YZ
    c. WX + 100YZ
    d. W + YZ/100
    e. 100WX/YZ

13. D students are enrolled in classes at the New York Art Institute. A are registered for painting, B have registered for ceramics, and C have registered for both painting and ceramics. How many have signed up for NEITHER painting nor ceramics?

    a. A + C − B − D
    b. D + A + B - C
    c. D + C − A + B
    d. D + C + A + B
    e. D − A − B + C

14. If M I-pods cost U dollars, what do N I-Pods cost?

    a. MU/N
    b. UN/M
    c. MUN
    d. 1/MUN
    e. MN/U

15. A vendor at a local flea market collects G dollars per day at her jewelry kiosk, but must spend one-quarter of her total sales each day on essential expenses. If the vendor saves the rest of her earnings, how many days will it take her to save $3,000 (in terms of G)?

    a. $1000/G
    b. G/$1000
    c. ($3000 − G)/G
    d. $4000/G
    e. $3000G

16. The Q members of the senior class agree to split the cleanup costs equally for their graduation dance, which will be P dollars. If R students fail to graduate and do not pay their share, but the cleanup costs remain the same, how many additional dollars will each of the remaining students have to contribute to pay the cleanup costs?

    a. P/(Q − R)
    b. (P/Q)(R - Q)
    c. PQ/(Q − R)
    d. PR/Q(Q − R)
    e. PQR/Q(Q − R)

17. Beth has 24 containers in two different sizes to store her homemade cookie dough. Twenty of the containers are the same size; their total capacity is F gallons. For the remaining four containers, which are all the same size, the total capacity is also F gallons. In terms of F, what is the capacity (in gallons) of each of the smaller containers?

    a. F/24
    b. F/20
    c. F/4
    d. F/24 + F/20
    e. F/24 + F/4

18. If Jennifer buys U dresses in addition to the number she already has in her closet, she will have V times as many as she originally owned. In terms of U and V, how many dresses did Jennifer originally own?

      a. $(V - U) / V$
      b. $(V + U) / (V - U)$
      c. $1/ (UV)$
      d. $U/(V - 1)$
      e. $(V - U) / (V - 1)$

19. The local mechanic pays s dollars for 20 gallons of antifreeze. Each gallon fills t radiators. In terms of t and s, what is the dollar cost of the antifreeze required to fill a single radiator?

      a. $st/20$
      b. $t/20s$
      c. $s/20t$
      d. $20st$
      e. $20/st$

20. Two landmarks in Rome that are R kilometers apart are T millimeters apart on a travel agency map that was drawn to scale. What is the distance in millimeters on the map between two landmarks that are R + 3 kilometers apart?

      a. $T + (3/R)$
      b. $T(R + 3)/R$
      c. $(T + 3)/R$
      d. $(R + 3)/T$
      e. $T + (R + 3)/R$

Answer Key: Word Problems with Only Variables

1. To solve, we must convert all of the terms to inches and add them together. Let's start with what we know.

The term for inches is represented by Z.
There are 12 inches in 1 foot. Hence, our coefficient for Y is 12.
There are 3 feet in one yard and 12 inches in one foot. Hence, our coefficient for X is 3 x 12 = 36.
The number of inches in a distance of X yards, Y feet and Z inches is therefore **36X + 12Y + Z**. Choice A is correct.

2. We want to find the total cost of a certain number of I-Pods. Let's randomly let Q = 100 and X = 30. This makes Q – X = 70. If G = 10 (also randomly selected), then the cost for the I-Pods would be 100 + (9)(70).

This corresponds to Choice C, which states the same relationship using the original variables:
Q + (G – 1) (Q – X).

3. Let's assume that 2 roommates split the cost of utilities, which are usually $500 per month. Therefore, X = 2 and Y = 500. Every month, each roommate pays 500/2, or Y/X for his/her share of the utilities. If the cost of utilities increases by 250, then Y increases by 250. Each roommate's cost is **(Y + 250)/X**. Choice D is correct.

4. Let's assume that H = 5% and K = $100. Brianna's commission would be ($100)(0.05) = $5.00. At first blush, this may seem like answer choice B, which is HK, but it is not. When we converted the 5% to 0.05 we divided the 5 by 100; hence, the solution was actually HK/100, which is Choice D.

For students who ARE comfortable working with variables, you can obtain the same answer by simply plugging the letters into the formula. If Brianna receives a H% commission, then: H% = H/100, or (H/100) (K) = HK/100

5. Don't be thrown by the use of letters instead of numbers – the problem is still a basic proportion, in which we must determine the value of an unknown x. The question asks us to determine the number of sandwiches needed for S students, knowing that Q sandwiches are needed to feed R students.

Our proportion, therefore, is Q/R = X/S.
X, therefore, equals QS/R, which is Choice E.

Alternatively, you can solve the problem by substituting numbers for the variables. Let Q = 10, R = 100, and S= 200.

10/100 = x/200
X = (200)(10)/100, which is QS/R.

6. The fewer seamstresses who participate, the longer it will take to sew the gown. Hence, this problem is one in which the variables vary inversely. Let x = the amount of time it will take to sew the gown with 2 fewer seamstresses. Our equation, therefore, is:

(D)(E) = (E – 2)(X)
X = **DE/(E – 2)** Choice D is correct.

7. To solve, let's plug in random numbers for each variable. In this case, let's assume that Jake bought 20 cars (J) for 100 dollars (G). The cost for a single car is therefore 100/20 or G/J or 5 dollars. The cost for any value of M will simply be that number times 5, which, in symbols, is **MG/J**. Choice C is correct.

8. Since we are not given exact numbers for P and N, we can use the plug-in technique to determine the relationship. Let's randomly let P = 10 and N = 100. If the N increases by $212, then each tenant owes 1/10 (100 + 212), or 1/P (N+212) = **(N + 212)/P**. Choice B is correct.

9. Most students overcomplicate this question and take too long to solve it. In this case, we can find the answer by doing a few quick calculations. First, we must determine how much of the bowl was filled by K cc. Mathematically, K cc = 9/10 – 1/3 = 27/30 - 10/30 = 17/30. To be totally filled, the bowl would require 30/30 of sugar, which is equal to K times its inverse, or **30/17K**. Choice E is correct.

10. We can solve this problem by plugging in numbers or by doing a few simple "backwards" calculations. First, let's plug- in numbers. Let's assume that Heidi bought 10 favors at a price of 2 dollars per favor. Let's also assume that she had 5 dollars left over. Hence, U = 10, V = 2 and W = 5.

Heidi therefore spent (10)(2), which is UV. If she had 5 dollars left over, then her original amount of money was **UV + W**. Choice B is correct.

Option 2. If you don't want to plug in numbers, you can just reason the problem through. If Heidi bought U wedding favors, which cost V dollars each, then she spent UV. Finally, she had W cents left over, which we must add to her total amount of money. When we do, we get the same answer as we did with the plug-in method: UV + W.

11. Once again, this is a simple problem if we substitute numbers for letters. Let's assume that Yankee Stadium charges $20 for the first 8 hours and $5 for each additional hour. Let's also assume that Grace parked for 12 hours. If we do, then J = 20, P = 5, and S = 12.

Grace's total cost will be the basic charge for 8 hours, plus the additional cost for every hour over 8. The basic cost = 20 = J. The additional cost per hour = 5(12 – 8) = P(S – 8). Therefore, Grace's total cost = 20 + 5(12 – 8) = **J + P(S – 8).** Choice C is correct.

12. As always, let's substitute numbers for the variables and see what we get. Let's assume that we have 10 watermelons that cost $3.00 each and 5 apples that cost 60 cents each. Hence, W = 10, X = 3.00, Y = 5 and Z = 0.60.

The total cost of W watermelons is 100(10)(3) = 100WX
The total cost of C apples is (5)(60) = YZ

Therefore, the total cost of the watermelons and apples is 100(10)(3) + (5)(6) = **100WX + YZ**. Choice B is correct.

13. To avoid counting students twice, we must divide them into four categories according to the following equation: Painting + Ceramics + Neither – Both = Total. Now, let's assign variables for each:

Painting = A, Ceramics = B, Both = C, Neither = Unknown, Total = D

Painting + Ceramics + Neither – Both = C
A + B + Neither - C = D
Thus, Neither = **D – A – B + C**. Choice E is correct

14. We can solve the problem using a simple proportion. U/M =?/N   ? = **NU/M**. Choice B is correct.
Alternatively, we can plug numbers into the equation for the variables and see what happens.   Let's let M = 10 and U = $100. The cost of a single I=Pod is therefore $100/10, or U/M. If N = 5, the cost of N I=Pods will be 5(U/M), or NU/M

15. First, let's substitute actual numbers for our variables. G = $100, or G/4 = $25. Thus,

Savings per day = G – G/4 = $100 – $25 = $75
The number of days needed to save $3,000 = $3,000/$75 = 40 days.
Mathematically, 40 = $3,000/0.75G = **$4000/G**. Choice D is correct

16. In this case, the easiest way to solve the problem is to substitute numbers for the variables. For the sake of simplicity, let's assume that Q = 100, P = 1000, and R = 20. Thus, the cost per person is P/ Q = 1000/100 = 10 dollars. If R = 20 students do not pay their share, then the additional cost for the 100 – 20 = 80 remaining students is (20 X 10) = 200. 200/80 = $2.5 dollars.

Now, we can solve the problem by converting this relationship from numbers to letters.   The cost per student is P/Q = 10 dollars. If R = 20 students do not pay their share, then the additional cost for the (Q - R) = 80 remaining students is: (P/Q) (R) / (Q – R) = 20 (1000/100) / (100 – 20) = 20 (10) / 80 = **$2.50**, which is Choice D.

17. Let's assume that F = 200 gallons. If the 20 smaller containers hold exactly 200 gallons, then they each hold 10 gallons.   In contrast, if the 4 larger containers can hold the same 200 gallons, they must each hold 50 gallons. The capacity of the smaller containers is therefore 200/20, or 10 gallons, which is **F/20**. Choice B is correct.

18. Let's assume that Jennifer originally had 7 dresses. Let's also assume that V = 4 and U = 21, which means that buying 21 dresses quadrupled the number than Jennifer owned.   Mathematically, this means that Jennifer's original number = 7 = 21/(4 – 1) or **U /(V – 1).** Choice D is correct

19. The easiest way to solve this problem is to set s and t equal to specific numbers. In this case, let's let s = $10 for 20 gallons and t = 2 radiators per gallon. The cost of the antifreeze needed to fill a single radiator is $10/20(2) = **s/20t**. Choice C is correct.

20. The easiest way to solve this problem is to substitute actual numbers for the variables. Let's assume that R = 100 kilometers and T = 2 millimeters. The distance between two landmarks that are 103 kilometers apart would be 2 (100 + 3)/100, which is **T(R + 3)/R**. Choice B is correct.

Chapter 19: Word Problems with Two Variables

Most word problems on the SAT, GRE and GMAT require students to find the value of a single unknown (x). Some situations, however, involve two unknowns (x and y) and two separate equations.

To solve, students must eliminate the same variable in both equations by addition, subtraction, multiplication, or substitution.

Example: Addition Method

Our two equations are:

x + y = 18
x − y = 6

Since the coefficients of the y terms are the same in both equations – and their signs are opposite - we can eliminate the y term from the equations by adding them together. When we do, we get 2x = 24. Therefore, x = 12.

Now, we can plug x = 12 into either equation to solve for y. y = 6

Example: Subtraction Method

Our equations are:

1x + 2y = 16
2x + 2y = 24

In this scenario, the y terms in both equations have the same coefficient, but their signs are the same. To eliminate the y variable, we can simply subtract the second equation from the first. When we do, we get -1x = -8, or x = 8.

Now, we can plug x = 8 into either equation to solve for y. y = 4

Example: Multiplication Method

Our equations are:

x + y = 100
0.25x + 0.05y = 10.00

In this scenario, the variables in one equation have integers as coefficients, while the variables in the other equation are decimals.

To combine the equations – and eliminate a variable – we must multiply the second equation by 100. When we do, our new set of equations is:

x + y = 100
25x + 5y = 1000

Next, we will multiply the first equation by 5, which will make our y coefficients the same:

5x + 5y = 500
25x + 5y = 1000

We can now subtract the second equation from the first, which will eliminate the y variable. When we do, we get -20x = - 500. X = 25.

Now, we can plug x = 25 into either equation to solve for y. y = 75.

Example: Substitution Method

Our equations are:

x + y = 100
3x + y = 150

In this scenario, we can easily rearrange the first equation to read y = 100 – x. We can then substitute this value for y in equation two, and solve for x. When we do, we get:

3x + (100 -x) = 150
3x + 100 - x = 150
2x = 50
x = 25

Now, we can plug x = 25 into either equation to solve for y. y = 75.

As you review the problems in this chapter, they will undoubtedly seem familiar to you. Why? In previous chapters, we tackled the SAME problems by writing and solving equations with a single variable. In *this* chapter, we offer you an alternative approach that may – or may not – save you time and energy. Our best advice is to experiment with both approaches – and choose the one that is right for *you*.

From our experience, the toughest part of solving word problems with two variables is to write – and combine – the equations correctly. The only way to master the technique is to practice. With that in mind, here are several types of word problems that can be easily solved by writing – and solving – equations with two variables.

Example 1: Mixtures (also covered in Chapter 13)

A chef must blend a type of oregano that costs $25 per pound with one that costs $10 per pound to make 2000 pounds that cost $20 per pound. How many pounds of the $50 oregano can the chef use?

   a.   668
   b.   998
   c.   1332
   d.   1332
   e.   1667

Solution: In this case, we can write two equations – one for the amount of each type of oregano and the other for their cost. As always, we must first define our variables. We will let = x the amount of $25 oregano and y = the amount of $10 oregano.

The first equation, which defines the *amount* of oregano, is simply x + y = 2000
The second equation, which defines their *cost*, is 25x + 10y = 20

To solve the problem for x, we must combine the equations in a way that eliminates y.

We can re-write equation 1 as y = 2000 – x and substitute this value for y into equation 2. When we do, we get:

25x + 10(2000 – x) = 20
25x + 20,000 – 10x = 20
15x = -19980
x = 1332 pounds of $25 oregano. Choice D is correct.

Example 2: Coins (also covered in Chapter 9)

Candy has 108 coins that are a combination of nickels and quarters. If the coins are worth $15.00, how many of them are nickels?

    a. 40
    b. 48
    c. 60
    d. 68
    e. 72

Solution: In this case, we can write two equations – one for the number of coins and the other for their value. As always, we must first define our variables. We will let = x the number of nickels and y = the number of quarters.

The first equation, which defines the *number* of coins, is simply x + y = 108
The second equation, which defines their *monetary worth*, is 0.05x + 0.25y = 15.00

To solve the problem for x, we must combine the equations in a way that eliminates y. First, we will multiply equation 2 by 100 to eliminate the decimals. When we do, we get:

x + y = 108
5x + 25y = 1500

Then, we can re-write equation 1 as y = 108 – x and substitute this value for y into equation 2. When we do, we get

5x + 25(108 – x) = 1500
5x + 2700 – 25x = 1500
-20x = -1200
x = 60 nickels. Choice C is correct.
y = 108 – 60 = 48 quarters

Example 3: Traveling (also covered in Chapter 11)

John and Kim leave the Pittsburgh Airport at the same time and head in opposite directions. John drives three times as fast as Kim. Two hours later, they are 120 miles apart. How fast is John driving (in miles per hour)?

    a. 15
    b. 20
    c. 24
    d. 45
    e. 72

Solution: In this case, we can write two equations – one for the speed of each car and the other for the distance they travel. As always, we must first define our variables. We will let x = Kim's speed and y = John's speed.

The first equation, which defines the *speed* of the cars, is simply y = 3x
The second equation, which defines the *distance* they travel, is 2x + 2y = 120

To solve the problem for x, we must combine the equations in a way that eliminates y. The fastest way is to substitute equation 1 into equation 2. When we do, we get:

2x + (2)3x = 120
8x = 120
x = 15 mph = Kim's speed
3x = (3)(15) = 45 mph = John's speed. Choice D is correct.

Example 4: Interest (also covered in Chapter 8)

Joe divided his $20,000 savings into two investments: a CD that pays 6% annual interest and a money market account that pays 9% annual interest. If Joe earns $1,600 per year from both investments, how much does he have in the CD?

    a. $6667
    b. $7250
    c. $12,250
    d. $13,333
    e. $16,667

Solution: In this case, we can write two equations – one for the amounts of Joe's two investments and the other for the interest that they earn. As always, we must first define our variables. We will let $= x$ the amount of money in the CD and $y =$ the amount in the money market account.

The first equation, which defines the *amount* of the investments, is simply $x + y = 20,000$
The second equation, which defines the *interest they earn*, is $0.06x + 0.09y = 1,600$

To solve the problem for x, we must combine the equations in a way that eliminates y. First, we will multiply equation 2 by 100 to eliminate the decimals. When we do, we get:

$x + y = 20,000$
$6x + 9y = 160,000$

Then, we can re-write equation 1 as $y = 20,000 - x$ and substitute this value for y into equation 2. When we do, we get:

$6x + 9(20,000 - x) = 160,000$
$6x + 180,000 - 9x = 160,000$
$-3x = -20,000$
$x = $6,666.67$ in the CD. Choice A is correct.
$y =$ money market account $= 20,000 - 6666.67 = $13,333.33$.

Example 5: Tickets at Different Prices (also covered in Chapter 9)

The senior class sold 600 tickets for the winter carnival, which brought in $10,000 in total revenue. If the cost of an adult ticket was $20 and the cost of a child's ticket was $12, how many children's tickets were sold?

    a. 200
    b. 250
    c. 300
    d. 350
    e. 400

Solution: In this case, we can write two equations – one for the number of tickets and the other for their cost. As always, we must first define our variables. We will let $= x$ the number of children's tickets and $y =$ the number of adult tickets.

The first equation, which defines the *number* of tickets sold, is $x + y = 600$
The second equation, which defines the *cost* of the tickets, is $12x + 20y = 10,000$

To solve the problem for x, we must combine the equations in a way that eliminates y. The fastest way is to re-write equation 1 as $y = 600 - x$ and substitute this value for y into equation 2. When we do, we get

$12x + 20(600 - x) = 10,000$
$12x + 12,000 - 20x = 10,000$
$-8x = -2000$
$x = 250$ children's tickets sold. Choice B is correct.
$y = 600 - 250 = 350$ adult tickets sold

Example 6: Algebra Word Problems (also covered in Chapter 7)

The sum of two numbers is 160 and their difference is 48. What is the smaller number?

   a. 56
   b. 58
   c. 62
   d. 102
   e. 104

Solution: In this case, we can write one equation for the first condition and a second equation for the second condition. As always, we must first define our variables. We will let = x the smaller number ad y = the larger number.

The first equation, which defines the first condition, is $x + y = 160$
The second equation, which defines the second condition, is $y - x = 48$

To solve the problem for x, we must combine the equations in a way that eliminates y. The fastest way is to re-write equation 1 as $y = 160 - x$ and substitute this value for y into equation 2. When we do, we get

$(160 - x) - x = 48$
$160 - 2x = 48$
$2x = 112$
$x = 56$. Choice A is correct.
$y = 160 - 56 = 104$.

Word Problems with Two Variables: EASY – MODERATE

1. Jessica has 275 coins that are a combination of dimes and quarters. If the coins are worth $50.00, how many of them are dimes?

   a. 75
   b. 100
   c. 125
   d. 150
   e. 175

2. Mr. & Mrs. Johnson have two investments with different rates of return. Their passbook savings account pays 3% annual interest, while their savings bonds pay 7.5% annual interest. If the total amount of the Johnson's two investments is $125,000 and they earn $7,500 per year from them, how much do they have invested in savings bonds?

   a. $33,333
   b. $41,667
   c. $66,667
   d. $83,333
   e. $86,667

3. The Boston Philharmonic charges $50 for adult tickets to their concerts and $20 for children's tickets. If they sold 800 tickets in a given weekend and received $25,000 in total ticket sales, how many adult tickets were sold?

   a. 300
   b. 400
   c. 500
   d. 600
   e. 700

4.Two airplanes leave the Orlando Airport at the same time and head in opposite directions. Plane A flies four times as fast as Plane B. Three hours later, they are 5,000 miles apart. How fast is Plane B flying (in miles per hour)?

    a.   300
    b.   333
    c.   500
    d.   667
    e.   900

5. The sum of two numbers is 24. Three times the larger number less two times the smaller number equals 17. What is the larger number?

    a.   9
    b.   11
    c.   13
    d.   15
    e.   17

6. A chemist must dilute a solution of 30% acid with a solution that is 10% acid to make 300 gallons of solution that is 25% acid. How many gallons of the 10% acid must the chemist use?

    a.   75
    b.   100
    c.   125
    d.   175
    e.   225

7. A clothing shop sells six pairs of shoes and eight pairs of socks for $995. The cost for four pairs of shoes and twelve pairs of socks is $750. How much would it cost to buy one pair of shoes?

    a. $58.12
    b. $69.75
    c. $77.50
    d. $139.50
    e. $148.50

8. A teenage actress set up a trust fund for her younger brother and sister. If she gave her sister $10,000 less than three times what she gave her brother, and the total amount in the trust fund was $500,000, how much did the actress give her brother?

    a. $125,000
    b. $127,500
    c. $170,000
    d. $375,000
    e. $372,500

9. At the end of the day, the clerk in a Laundromat has 3,500 coins that are a combination of nickels and quarters. If the coins are worth $750, how many of them are nickels?

    a.   625
    b.   750
    c.   1,350
    d.   2,750
    e.   2,875

Word Problems with Two Variables: AS HARD AS IT GETS

10. If four hot dogs and three sodas cost $7.00 and twelve hot dogs and twelve sodas cost $15.00, what is the cost of one hot dog and one soda?

      a. $0.50
      b. $0.75
      c. $1.33
      d. $1.88
      e. $2.08

11. The average of two numbers is 90. If the difference between the numbers is 12, what is the product of the two numbers?

      a. 8064
      b. 8100
      c. 8400
      d. 8640
      e. 9600

12. Ava and Ella have a combined age of 50.   In ten years, one-half of Ava's age will be equal to three-quarters of Ella's current age. How old is Ava now?

      a. 18
      b. 24
      c. 26
      d. 30
      e. 32

Answer Key: Word Problems with Two Variables

1. In this case, we can write two equations – one for the number of coins and the other for their value. As always, we must first define our variables. We will let = x the number of dimes and y = the number of quarters.

The first equation, which defines the *number* of coins, is simply x + y = 275
The second equation, which defines their *monetary worth*, is 0.10x + 0.25y = 50.00

To solve the problem for x, we must combine the equations in a way that eliminates y. First, we will multiply equation 2 by 100 to eliminate the decimals. When we do, we get:

x + y = 275
10x + 25y = 5000

Then, we can re-write equation 1 as y = 275 – x and substitute this value for y into equation 2. When we do, we get

10x + 25(275 – x) = 5000
10x + 6,875 – 25x = 5000
-15x = -1875
x= **125** dimes. Choice C is correct.
y = 275 – 125 = 150 quarters.

2. In this case, we can write two equations – one for the amounts of the Johnson's two investments and the other for the interest that they earn. As always, we must first define our variables. We will let = x the amount of money in savings bonds and y = the amount in the passbook savings account.

The first equation, which defines the *amount* of the investments, is simply x + y = 125,000

167

The second equation, which defines the *interest they earn*, is 0.075x + 0.03y = 7,500

To solve the problem for x, we must combine the equations in a way that eliminates y. First, we will multiply equation 2 by 1000 to eliminate the decimals. When we do, we get:

x + y = 125,000
75x + 30y = 7,500,000

Then, we can re-write equation 1 as y = 125,000 – x and substitute this value for y into equation 2. When we do, we get

75x + 30(125,000 – x) = 7,500,000
75x + 3,750,000 – 30x = 7,500,000
45x = 3750000
x = **$83,333.33** in savings bonds. Choice D is correct.
y = passbook savings account = 125,000 – 83,333.33 = $41,666.67

3. In this case, we can write two equations – one for the number of tickets and the other for their cost. As always, we must first define our variables. We will let = x the number of adult tickets and y = the number of children's tickets.

The first equation, which defines the *number* of tickets sold, is x + y = 800
The second equation, which defines the *cost* of the tickets, is 50x + 20y = 25,000

To solve the problem for x, we must combine the equations in a way that eliminates y. The fastest way is to re-write equation 1 as y = 800 – x and substitute this value for y into equation 2. When we do, we get

50x + 20(800 – x) = 25,000
50x + 16,000 – 20x = 25,000
30x = 9,000
x = **300** adult tickets sold. Choice A is correct.
y = 800 – 300 = 500 children's sold

4. In this case, we can write two equations – one for the speed of the planes and the other for the distance they travel. As always, we must first define our variables. We will let x = Plane B's speed and y = Plane A's speed.

The first equation, which defines the *speed* of the planes, is simply y = 4x
The second equation, which defines the *distance* they travel, is 3x + 3y = 5,000

To solve the problem for x, we must combine the equations in a way that eliminates y. The fastest way is to substitute equation 1 into equation 2. When we do, we get

3x + 3(4x) = 5,000
15x = 5,000
x = **333.33** = Plane B's speed. Choice B is correct.
4x = 1333.33 = Plane A's speed

5. In this case, we can write one equation for the first condition and a second equation for the second condition. As always, we must first define our variables. We will let = x the larger number and y = the smaller number.

The first equation, which defines the first condition, is x + y = 24
The second equation, which defines the second condition, is 3x – 2y = 17

To solve the problem for x, we must combine the equations in a way that eliminates y. The fastest way is to re-write equation 1 as y = 24 – x and substitute this value for y into equation 2. When we do, we get

3x – (2)(24 – x) = 17
3x – 48 + 2x = 17
5x = 65
x = **13** = larger number. Choice C is correct.
y = 24 – 14 = 11 = smaller number

6. In this case, we can write two equations – one for the amount of each solution and the other for the % of acid in each. As always, we must first define our variables. We will let = x the amount of 10% acid and y = the amount of 30% acid.

The first equation, which defines the *amount* of each solution, is simply x + y = 300
The second equation, which defines the *% of acid* in each solution, is 10x + 30y = 25(300)

To solve the problem for x, we must combine the equations in a way that eliminates y. We can re-write equation 1 as y = 300 – x and substitute this value for y into equation 2. When we do, we get:

10x + 30(300 – x) = 25(300)
10x + 9,000 – 30x = 7500
-20x = -1,500
x = **75** gallons of 10% acid. Choice A is correct.
y = 300 – 75 = 225 gallons of 30% acid.

7. In this case, we can write one equation for the first condition and a second equation for the second condition. As always, we must first define our variables. We will let = x the cost of one pair of shoes and y = the cost of one pair of socks.

The first equation, which defines the first condition, is 6x + 8y = 995
The second equation, which defines the second condition, is 4x + 12y = 750

To solve the problem for x, we must combine the equations in a way that eliminates y. We can do this by multiplying the first equation by 3 and the second equation by 2. When we do, we get

18x + 24y = 2,985
8ex+ 24y = 1,500

If we subtract the second equation from the first, we get 10x = 1,485. Therefore, x = **$148.50** = the cost of one pair of shoes. Choice E is correct.

8. In this case, we can write two equations – one for the total amount of funds and the other for the respective shares that were given to each sibling. As always, we must first define our variables. We will let = x the brother's share and y = the sister's share.

The first equation, which defines the amount of money invested, is simply x + y = 500,000
The second equation, which defines how the shares are divided, is y = 3x – 10,000

To solve the problem for x, we must combine the equations in a way that eliminates y. When we do, we get:

x + (3x – 10,000) = 500,000
4x – 10,000 = 500,000
4x = 510,000
x = **$127,500** = the brother's share. Choice B is correct.
y = 3($127,500) - $10,000 = $372,500 = the sister's share

9. In this case, we can write two equations – one for the number of coins and the other for their value. As always, we must first define our variables. We will let = x the number of nickels and y = the number of quarters.

The first equation, which defines the *number* of coins, is simply x + y = 3,500
The second equation, which defines their *monetary worth*, is 0.05x + 0.25y = 750.00

To solve the problem for x, we must combine the equations in a way that eliminates y. First, we will multiply equation 2 by 100 to eliminate the decimals. When we do, we get:

x + y = 3,500
5x + 25y = 75000

Then, we can re-write equation 1 as y = 3,500 – x and substitute this value for y into equation 2. When we do, we get

5x + 25(3500 – x) = 75000
5x + 87,500 – 25x = 75000
-20x = -12,500
x= **625** nickels. Choice A is correct.
y = 3,500 – 625 = 2,875 quarters.

10.   In this case, we can write one equation for the first condition and a second equation for the second condition. As always, we must first define our variables. We will let = x the cost of one hot dog and y = the cost of one soda.

The first equation, which defines the first condition, is 4x + 3y = 7
The second equation, which defines the second condition, is 12x + 12y = 15

To solve the problem for x, we must combine the equations in a way that eliminates y. First, we will multiply equation 1 by 4. When we do, our equations become

16x + 12y = 28
12x + 12y = 25

Next, we will subtract equation 2 from equation 1. When we do, we get 4x = 3. Therefore,

x = ¾ = 75 cents = the cost of one hot dog.

To solve for y, the cost of one soda, we must plug the value for x back into one of our equations. When we do, we discover that

(4)(0.75) + 3y = 7
3 + 3y = 7
3y = 4
y = 4/3 = $1.33 = the cost of one soda

The cost of one hot dog *and* one soda is therefore $0.75 + $1.33 = **$2.08**. Choice E is correct.

11. The trickiest part of this question is figuring out what you are being asked to calculate, which is the *product* of the two numbers in the original average. There's nothing particularly obvious or intuitive about this question – and there aren't any shortcuts. To solve it, we simply need to complete several routine calculations.

In this case, we can write one equation for the first condition and a second equation for the second condition.   As always, we must first define our variables. We will let = x the smaller number and y equal the larger number.

The first equation, which defines the first condition, is (x + y)/2 = 90
The second equation, which defines the second condition, is x – y = 12

First, let's re-write both equations in a clearer manner.
If we multiply equation 1 by 2, we get x + y = 180
If we re-write equation 2, we get y = x -12

To solve the problem for x, we must combine the equations in a way that eliminates y. When we do, we get:

x + (x – 12) = 180
2x -12 = 180
2x = 192
x = 96
y = 96 - 12 = 84.

The question asks us the *product* of these numbers, which is (96)(84) = **8,064**. Choice A is correct.

12. In this case, we can write one equation for the first condition and a second equation for the second condition.   As always, we must first define our variables. We will let = Ava's age and y = Ella's age.

The first equation, which defines the first condition, is x + y = 50

The second equation, which defines the second condition, is $(x + 10)/2 = \frac{3}{4}y$

To solve the problem for x, we must combine the equations in a way that eliminates y. The fastest way to accomplish this is to re-write equation 1 as $y = 50 - x$ and substitute this value for y in equation 2. But first, let's multiply equation 2 by 4 to eliminate the fractions. When we do, we get:

$2(x + 10) = 3y$

Now, let's substitute $50 - x$ for y:

$2x + 20 = 3(50 - x)$
$2x + 20 = 150 - 3x$
$5x = 130$
$x = \mathbf{26}$ = Ava's age
$y = 50 - 26 = 24$ = Ella's age. Choice C is correct.

To check our results, let's confirm that the conditions hold: In 10 years, Ava will be 36 and Ella will be 34. Half of Ava's age (18) is indeed ¾ of Ella's current age.

Chapter 20: Word Problems w/ Quadratic Equations

The most recent versions of the SAT, GRE and GMAT include problems that include an exponent of two. To solve this type of word problem, students must translate the information into a quadratic equation and solve for the non-negative root.

The following examples show typical problems on the SAT, GRE, and GMAT – and the best way to approach them.

Example 1: Quadrilaterals w/ Unknown Side Lengths

If a rectangular mailbox has an area of 12 square feet, and its length is 4 feet longer than its width, what is the width of the mailbox?

    a.   1
    b.   2
    c.   3
    d.   4
    e.   6

Solution: First, let's define our variables.   We will let x = the length of the mailbox. Therefore, its width = x - 4 and its area (Length x Width) = x(x - 4). Our equation becomes:

$x(x - 4) = 12$
$x^2 - 4x - 12 = 0$
$(x - 6)(x + 2) = 0$

Therefore, x = - 2 and 6. Since the length of the side cannot be negative, we can discard the -2 root. The length of the mailbox is 6 and the width is 6 – 4 = 2. Choice B is correct.

Example 2: Multiplying Unknown Integers

Ben has three times as many baseball cards as Amy. If the product of the squares of each number is 160, how many baseball cards does Amy have?

    a.   1
    b.   2
    c.   3
    d.   4
    e.   5

Solution: First, let's define our variables.   We will let x = the number of Amy's cards and 3x = the number of Ben's cards. Therefore, the squares of the two numbers are x^2 and $9x^2$. Our equation therefore becomes:

$x^2 + 9x^2 = 160$
$10x^2 = 160$
$x^2 = 160/10 = 16$
$\sqrt{x} = 16$
$x = +4$ and $- 4$
Amy has 4 baseball cards. Ben has 3(4) = 12. Choice D is correct.

Example 3: Ages

Rachel is 2 years older than Lisa. If the product of their ages is 120, how old is Rachel?

   a.   4
   b.   6
   c.   8
   d.   10
   e.   12

Solution: First, let's define our variables.   We will let x = Lisa's age. Therefore, Rachel's age = x + 2. Since the product of their ages is 120, our equation becomes:

$x(x + 2) = 120$
$x^2 + 2x - 120 = 0$
$(x - 10)(x + 12) = 0$

Therefore, x = - 12 and +10. Since a person's age cannot be negative, we can discard the -12 root. Therefore, Lisa's age = 10 and Rachel's age = 10 + 2 = 12. Choice E is correct.

Example 4: Comparing Geometric Figures

The length of a rectangular jewelry box is three inches greater than twice the length of a square wall safe. The width of the jewelry box is 2 inches less than the width of the safe. If the jewelry box and the wall safe are equal in area, what is the length of the wall safe?

   a.   1
   b.   2
   c.   3
   d.   4
   e.   5

Solution: First, let's define our variables. We will let x = the length of the wall safe. Therefore, the length of the jewelry box = 2x + 3 and the width = x – 2.   Since the areas of the jewelry box and the wall safe are equal, our equation becomes:

$(2x + 3)(x - 2) = x^2$
$2x^2 - 4x + 3x - 6 = x^2$
$2x^2 - 1x - 6 - x^2 = 0$
$x^2 - 1x - 6 = 0$
$(x - 3)(x + 2) = 0$

Therefore, x = - 2 and + 3. Since the length of a side cannot be negative, we can discard the -2 root. Therefore, the side length of the wall safe is 3 inches.   Choice C is correct.

Word Problems w/ Quadratic Equations: MODERATE - HARD

1. The length of a rectangular gift box is 4 inches shorter than its width. If the area of the box is 572 square inches, what is its length?

   a.   18
   b.   20
   c.   22
   d.   26
   e.   28

2. Jenny has twice as many swimming medals as Cindy. If the product of the squares of each number is 180, how many medals does Jenny have?

    a.   6
    b. · 8
    c.   12
    d.   16
    e.   24

3. Ben is 11 years older than Patrick. If the product of their ages is 180, how old is Patrick?

    a.   3
    b.   9
    c.   12
    d.   20
    e.   33

4. To adhere to local zoning laws, an architect must reduce the size of a square building by 800 square yards. When she does, the area of the building is equal to five times its perimeter. What was the original area of the building (in square yards)?

    a.   20
    b.   40
    c.   400
    d.   1,600
    e.   3,200

5. The length of a rectangular First Aid kit is two inches less than twice the length of a square defibrillator. The width of the First Aid kit is 4 inches longer than the side length of the defibrillator. If the First Aid kit and the defibrillator are equal in area, what is the side length of the defibrillator?

    a.   2
    b.   3
    c.   4
    d.   6
    e.   8

6. Integer X is equal to Integer Y + 8. If the product of Integer X and Integer Y is 20, what is Integer X?

    a.   -10
    b.   -5
    c.   -2
    d.   2
    e.   5

7. $A + B = 50$. $A^2 - B^2 = 500$. What is the larger number?

    a.   15
    b.   20
    c.   25
    d.   30
    e.   40

8. If a rectangular Rubbermaid storage unit has an area of 63 square feet, and its length is 2 feet longer than its width, what is the width of the storage unit?

      a.   1
      b.   2
      c.   3
      d.   4
      e.   6

9. The difference between two positive numbers is 40. If we square the larger number and subtract twenty times the smaller number from its square, the result is 3,200. What is the larger number?

      a.   20
      b.   45
      c.   50
      d.   60
      e.   80

10. A rectangular shipping container has a perimeter of 64 and an area of 240. What is the length of its shortest side?

      a.   8
      b.   12
      c.   20
      d.   24
      e.   32

Answer Key Word Problems: w/ Quadratic Equations

1. First, let's define our variables.   We will let x = the length of the gift box. Therefore, its width = x + 4 and its area (Length x Width) = x(x + 4). Our equation becomes:

$x(x + 4) = 572$
$x^2 + 4x - 572 = 0$
$(x - 22)(x + 26) = 0$

Therefore, x = 22 and -26. Since a length cannot be negative, we can discard the -26 root. The length of the rectangle is 22 and the width is 22 + 4 = **26**. Choice C is correct. .

2. First, let's define our variables.   We will let x = the number of Cindy's medals and 2x = the number of Jenny's medals. Therefore, the squares of the two numbers are x^2 and $4x^2$. Our equation therefore becomes:

$x^2 + 4x^2 = 180$
$5x^2 = 180$
$x^2 = 180/5 = 36$
$\sqrt{x} = 36$
x = +6 and – 6
Cindy has 6 medals. Jenny has 2(6) = **12** medals. Choice C is correct.

3. First, let's define our variables.   We will let x = Patrick's age. Therefore, Ben's age = x +11. Since the product of their ages is 180, our equation becomes:

$x(x + 11) = 180$
$x^2 + 11x - 180 = 0$
$(x - 9)(x + 20) = 0$

Therefore, x = - 20 and +9. Since a person's age cannot be negative, we can discard the -20 root. Therefore, Patrick's age = 9 and Ben's age = 9 + 11 = **20**. Choice B is correct.

4. First, let's define our variables.   We will let x = the side length of the building. Therefore, the perimeter = 4x. Therefore, our equation becomes:

$x^2 - 800 = 5(4x)$
$x^2 - 20x - 800 = 0$
$(x + 20)(x - 40) = 0$

Therefore, x = - 20 and +40. Since the length of a building cannot be negative, we can discard the -20 root. Therefore, the side length of the building is 40 yards and its area is (40)(40) = **1,600** square yards. Choice D is correct.

5. First, let's define our variables. We will let x = the side length of the defibrillator. Therefore, the length of the First Aid kit = 2x + 6 and the width = x - 4.   Since the areas of the First Aid kit and the defibrillator are equal, our equation becomes:

$(2x + 6)(x - 4) = x^2$
$2x^2 - 8x + 6x - 24 = x^2$
$x^2 - 2x - 24 = 0$
$(x - 6)(x + 4) = 0$

Therefore, x = - 4 and +6. Since the length of a side cannot be negative, we can discard the -4 root. Therefore, the side length of Square B is **6** inches.   Choice D is correct.

6. First, let's define our variables.   We will let x = Integer X and x – 8 = Integer Y. Since their product is 152, our equation becomes:

$x(x - 8) = 20$
$x^2 - 8x - 20 = 0$
$(x - 10)(x + 2) = 0$

Therefore, x = 10 and -2. Since the problem does not specify that the integers must be positive, we must test both roots in our original equation to confirm that they both hold.

If Integer X = 10, then Integer Y = 10 – 8 = 2. (10)(2) = 20
If Integer X = -2, then Integer Y = -2 – 8 = -10. (-10)(-2) = 20

Hence, both roots are correct. The only answer choice that includes one of them is Choice C, **-2**.

7. First, let's define our variables.   We will let x = A. Therefore, B = 50 – x. If the difference between their squares is 25, our equation becomes:

$(50 - x)^2 - x^2 = 500$
$(50 - x)(50 - x) - x^2 = 500$
$2,500 - 50x - 50x + x^2 - x^2 = 500$
$2,500 - 100x = 500$
$2,000 = 100x$
$X = 20$
$50 - X = 30.$ Choice D is correct.

8. First, let's define our variables.   We will let x = the length of the storage unit. Therefore, the width = x - 2 and the area of the storage unit (Length x Width) is x(x - 2). Our equation becomes:

$x(x - 2) = 63$

$x^2 - 2x - 63 = 0$
$(x - 9)(x + 7) = 0$

Therefore, x = 9 and -7. Since the length of the side cannot be negative, we can discard the -7 root. The length of the storage unit is 9 and the width is 9 – 2 = 7. Choice B is correct.

9. From the problem, we know that x – y = 40 and $x^2 - 20y = 3,200$. Thus, x = y + 40. We can combine the two equations to solve for y.

$(y + 40)^2 - 20y = 3,200$
$y^2 + 80y + 1600 - 20y = 3,200$
$Y^2 + 60y - 1600 = 0$
$(y + 80)(y - 20) = 0$

We must discard -80 because it is not a positive number. Hence, y = 20 and x = 60. Choice D is correct.

10. First, let's define our variables. For a rectangle, the Perimeter = 2(Length) + 2(Width). Hence,

64 = 2(Length) + 2(Width)
32 = Length + Width.
Therefore, we can let Length = x and Width = 32 – x.

The area of the shipping container = (Length)(Width) = (x)(32 – x) = 240. Therefore,

$32x - x^2 = 240$.
$32x - x^2 - 240 = 0$. To work with positive numbers, we will multiple both sides of the equation by -1.
$x^2 - 32x + 240 = 0$
$(x - 12)(x - 20) = 0$

Therefore, x = 12 and 20. The smallest solution is 12, which is Choice B.

To test our answers, we can plug them into our original formulas:

Area: L x W = (20)(12) = 240
Perimeter: 2L + 2W = 40 + 24 = 64

Chapter 21: Geometry

In recent years, nearly 20% of the questions in the quantitative section of the SAT, GRE and GMAT are geometry topics, including:

Coordinate geometry
Lines and angles
Triangles
Circles
Squares, rectangles, and other polygons
Cubes and others solids

Not surprisingly, the test writers have predictable – and sneaky - ways of testing your understanding of these areas. Before we present the most common types of word problems, we'd like to offer several caveats regarding geometry concepts on the exam:

1. At the beginning of each quantitative section of the exam, the test writers present a wealth of figures and formulas for the most common geometric shapes. Consequently, there's no need to memorize complex formulas, because they will be provided for you.

Reference Information:

1. *Circles. Area $= \pi r^2$, Circumference $= 2 \pi r$*
2. *Rectangles: Area = Length X Width*
3. *Right Triangles: Area = ½ (Base) (Height)*
4. *Cubes: Volume = Length x Width x Height*
5. *Cylinders: Volume $= \pi r^2 h$*
6. *Pythagorean Theorem: for right triangles $c^2 = a^2 + b^2$*

As you might expect, however, only a few questions will be so simple that you can simply plug numbers into formulas. Instead, the writers will include more difficult questions at the end of the quantitative section to test how well you can APPLY that information to real-world problems. For students who hope to achieve a top score on the quantitative portion of the exam, it is essential to solve these problems quickly and efficiently.

2. A typical question might ask you to determine the change in the area of a triangle or rectangle, if one side is lengthened and another is shortened. Alternatively, the writers may ask what happens to the circumference of a circle if its diameter doubles. As you might expect, these questions are filled with traps, pitfalls, and misleading answer choices. Read carefully. Be sure that you know what you are being asked to find or do. Some problems are far easier than they seem, because they are written in a convoluted manner.

3. In many cases, you will need to draw a diagram to solve a word problem. Sometimes, the test writers will offer a sketch of the scenario for you to use. Other times, they will present the problem verbally, which places the burden on *you* to map out the scenario. In many cases, a diagram is the fastest way to assess a problem, organize information, and find the solution.

4. Most figures on the test are drawn to scale. If they are not, the test writers will advise you accordingly. On a practical basis, what does this mean? *Figures that are not drawn to scale are usually presented in a misleading manner.* The moment that you read "not drawn to scale," stop relying on the figure for any sort of guidance or insight. The test writers have been known to draw triangles in which an angle APPEARS to be 90 degrees, but is not. Alternatively, it may appear that a line bisects a side of the triangle, when it actually doesn't. The only way to approach these problems is to *disregard the figures* and work solely with the numerical information that you are given. The numbers won't mislead you, but the figure probably will.

5. Be prepared to break complex figures into smaller, simpler ones. Many times, a diagram will show an odd-shaped polygon and ask you to determine an area, side length, or perimeter. Upon closer inspection, the polygon is actually two triangles that share a common side. Or, it is a rectangle and a triangle that share a common side. These problems are usually easily solved using the Pythagorean theorem or another basic geometric formula. This "trick" will enable you to solve a number of geometry questions on the exam that you could not tackle any other way.

Chapter 22: Triangles

Without a doubt, the most popular geometry topic on the SAT, GRE, and GMAT is triangles. Before we present the most typical types of word problems you are likely to see, let's review the basics.

Triangles are closed, three-sided figures in a single plane whose sides are straight lines.

Interior Angles: the 3 interior angles of any triangle must add up to 180 degrees

Exterior angles: the exterior angle in a triangle is one that extends outside the figure. Mathematically, the exterior angle is equal to the sum of the two remote interior angles.

Area of a Triangle: 1/2 (Base) (Height)

The height is the perpendicular distance between the side that is chosen as the base and the opposite vertex.

Triangle Inequality Theorem: the length of one side of a triangle must be *greater than the difference and less than the sum of* the lengths of the other two sides.

Example: If a problem states that the length of one side of a triangle is 3 and the length of another side is 7, then the length of the third side must be greater than 7 -3 = 4 and less than 7 + 3 = 10.

Types of Triangles

Similar Triangles: have the same shape; corresponding angles are equal and corresponding sides are proportional.

Isosceles Triangles: have *two equal sides*. Additionally, the angles opposite the equal sides, called base angles, are also equal.

Equilateral Triangles: *all three sides (and all three angles) are equal.* All three angles in an equilateral triangle measure 60 degrees, regardless of the lengths of sides.

Congruent Triangles: identical in size and shape.

Scalene Triangles: no two sides (or angles) are equal.

RIGHT TRIANGLES: by definition, a right triangle contains a 90 degree angle. The side opposite the 90 degree is called the hypotenuse.

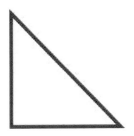

According to the **Pythagorean Theorem,** which holds for *all right triangles*, the square of the length of the hypotenuse equals the sum of the squares of the other two sides. Mathematically,

Length of Hypotenuse^2 = Length of First Side^2 + Length of Second Side^2

Example: If ABC is a right triangle with a right angle at B, and if AB = 6 and BC = 8, what is the length of AC?

Use the Pythagorean theorem, $AB^2 + BC^2 = AC^2$ (6)(6) + (8)(8) = 100. AC = 10

Popular Types of Right Triangles

3-4-5 Triangle: If a right triangle has a leg-to-leg ratio of 3:4, or if the leg-to-hypotenuse ratio is 3:5 or 4:5, it is a 3-4-5 triangle. In this case, we don't need to use the Pythagorean theorem to find the length of the third side. We can just figure out what multiple of 3-4-5 it is.

5-12-13 Triangle: If a right triangle has a leg-to-leg ratio of 5:12, or if the leg-to-hypotenuse ratio is 5:13 or 12:13, then it is a 5-12-13 triangle. In this case, we don't need to use the Pythagorean theorem to find the third side. We can just figure out what multiple of 5-12-13 it is.

30-60-90 Triangle: the sides of a 30-60-90 triangle are in a ratio of $x : x\sqrt{3} : 2x$. We don't need to use the Pythagorean theorem.

45-45-90 Triangle: the sides of a 45-45-90 triangle are in a ratio of $x : x : x\sqrt{2}$

As you probably suspect, the underlying theory of triangles will only take you so far on the SAT, GRE, and GMAT. Although there will certainly be one or two basic questions that will require you to plug numbers into formulas, most of them will require a higher – and more practical - level of thinking. Here is a review of the most common types of triangle word problems on the exams.

Example 1: Interior Angles

In triangle XYZ, angle Y is twice angle X and angle Z is 40 degrees more than angle Y. How many degrees are in angle Y?

      a.   28
      b.   36
      c.   56
      d.   60
      e.   96

Solution: Knowing that the three angles must total 180 degrees, we can solve this problem by using a simple algebraic equation. First, we must define our variables. We will let x = angle X, 2x = angle Y, and 2x + 40 = angle Z. Therefore, our equation becomes: x + 2x + (2x + 40) = 180. Solving for X, we find that: Angle X = 28 degrees, Angle Y = 56 degrees, and Angle Z = 96 degrees. Choice C is correct.

Example 2. Exterior Angles

In Triangle XYZ, angle X is twice as large as angle Y. The exterior angle at Z is 120 degrees. How many degrees are in angle X?

  a. 30
  b. 40
  c. 80
  d. 90
  e. 100

Solution: By definition, the exterior angle is equal to the sum of the two remote interior angles. If angle X is twice as large as angle Y, then their sum is 2x + 1x = 3x = 120. Hence,

3x =120
x = 40 = angle Y
2x = 80 = angle X. Choice C is correct.

Example 3: Triangle Inequality Theorem

In Triangle Q, the length of one side is 15 and the other side is 35. Which of the following could NOT be the length of the third side?

  a. 18
  b. 25
  c. 30
  d. 40
  e. 45

Solution: According to the triangle inequality theorem, the length of one side of a triangle must be greater than the difference and less than the sum of the lengths of the other two sides.

Therefore, in Triangle Q, the length of the third side must be greater than 35 – 15 = 20 and less than 15 + 35 = 50. All of the answer choices are between 20 and 50 except Choice A.

Example 4: Comparing Triangles to Circles

If a triangle of base 6 has the same area as a circle of radius 6, what is the altitude of the triangle?

  a. 3π
  b. 6π
  c. 12π
  d. 24π
  e. 36π

Solution: The area of the circle is $\pi r^2 = \pi(6)(6) = 36\pi$. In the triangle, the area = 1/2 (Base) (Height). We will let x = the height. Thus, for this triangle, 1/2 (6)x =36 π. x = 12 π. Choice C is correct.

Example 5: Isosceles Triangles

The vertex angle of an isosceles triangle is G degrees. How many degrees are there in one of the base angles?

  a. 90 – 2G
  b. 180 – G
  c. 1/2(90 – G)
  d. 1/2(180 – G)
  e. 180 – G

Solution: By definition, an isosceles triangle has two equal sides. Additionally, the angles opposite the equal sides, called base angles, are also equal. Since the vertex angle = G, the sum of the other two angles = 180 – G. Each base angle therefore contains 1/2(180 – G) degrees. Choice D is correct.

Example 6: Coordinate Geometry

The vertices of a triangle are (6,2), (6,9) and (14,2). What is the area of the triangle?

    a. 24
    b. 28
    c. 48
    d. 56
    e. 64

Solution: If we plot the points on a graph, we can easily see that they form a right triangle with a 90 degree angle at point (6,2). Therefore, we can use the formula Area = ½(Base)(Height) to solve the problem.

In this case, the Base is 14 – 6 = 8 and the Height is 9 – 2 = 7.
The area of the triangle is therefore ½(8)(7) = 28. Choice B is correct.

Word Problems with Triangles: EASY - MODERATE

1. If the perimeter of an isosceles triangle is 64 and its base is 16, find the length of one of the equal sides.

    a. 18
    b. 20
    c. 24
    d. 26
    e. 28

2. Each of the equal sides of an isosceles triangle is four less than three times its base. If the perimeter is 90, what is the base of the triangle?

    a. 12
    b. 14
    c. 15
    d. 18
    e. 28

3. The base of a triangle is 16 more than the height. If the area of the triangle is 256 square inches, what is its height?

    a. 4
    b. 8
    c. 16
    d. 32
    e. 36

4. The angles of a triangle are in the ratio of 3:4:5. What is the measurement (in degrees) of the largest angle?

    a. 45
    b. 60
    c. 70
    d. 75
    e. 80

5. If a triangle of base 16 has the same area as a circle of diameter 16, what is the altitude of the triangle?

    a. 4π
    b. 8π
    c. 12π
    d. 16π
    e. 32π

6. A base angle of an isosceles triangle is 30 degrees. How many degrees are in the vertex angle?

    a.   100
    b.   110
    c.   120
    d.   140
    e.   150

7. The vertices of a triangle are (8,3), (8,10) and (20,3). What is the area of the triangle?

    a.   25
    b.   36
    c.   42
    d.   48
    e.   50

8. The perimeter of triangle ABC is 125. If AB = 45 and BC = 55, what is the length of AC?

    a.   25
    b.   45
    c.   75
    d.   80
    e.   90

9. If Jake walks south for 50 yards, then west for 120 yards, then walked directly back to his starting point on a diagonal, how many yards did he walk altogether?

    a.   170
    b.   255
    c.   270
    d.   290
    e.   300

10. A delivery truck traveled west for 30 miles, then south for 50 miles, then returned directly to his starting point on a diagonal. If the truck gets 8 per gallon of gas, how many gallons of gas will the truck use on the trip?

    a.   10
    b.   12
    c.   16
    d.   18
    e.   20

11. In triangle MNO, angle M is one-half angle N and angle O is 20 degrees more than angle M. How many degrees are in angle O?

     a. 40
     b. 45
     c. 50
     d. 55
     e. 60

12. In Triangle D, the length of one side is 21 and the other side is 36. Which of the following could possibly be the length of the third side?

     a. 13
     b. 14
     c. 16
     d. 60
     e. 63

13. Which of the following sets of numbers *cannot* represent the lengths of the sides of a right triangle?

     a. 10, 24, 26
     b. 3.7, 11.9, 12.5
     c. 9, 26, 31
     d. 4, 15, 15.5
     e. 15, 36, 39

14. In Triangle CAT, CA = AT. If angle A = 3x – 20 and angle C = 1.5x + 115, how many degrees are in angle T?

     a. 30
     b. 45
     c. 60
     d. 75
     e. 90

15. In Triangle DOG, angle D is six times as large as angle O. The exterior angle at G is 140 degrees. How many degrees are in angle O?

     a. 20
     b. 40
     c. 100
     d. 120
     e. 140

16. In Triangle BIG, the angles are in a ratio of 2:3:5. What is the largest angle?

     a. 18
     b. 36
     c. 54
     d. 72
     e. 90

Word Problems with Triangles: AS HARD AS IT GETS

17. The perimeter of right triangle DEF is 144 inches. If we connect the midpoints of the three sides of DEF, we can form a smaller triangle. What will its perimeter be?

     a.   12
     b.   36
     c.   48
     d.   64
     e.   72

18. A rectangle with sides of 60 and 84 inches is completely inscribed in a circle. If all four corners of the rectangle touch the circumference of the circle, what is the area of the circle?

     a.   144 π
     b.   1,260π
     c.   2,520 π
     d.   2,664 π
     e.   5,040 π

19. A United Airlines jet leaves O'Hare Airport at 6 am and travels directly west at a speed of 700 mph. A US Air jet leaves the same airport at 9 am and travels due north. At 10 am, the two jets are exactly 3,000 miles apart. What is the speed of the USAir jet (in mph)?

     a.   700
     b.   774
     c.   1,077
     d.   1,474
     e.   It cannot be determined from the information given.

Answer Key: Word Problems with Triangles

1. Perimeter = sum of all three sides = 16 + 2x = 64. Therefore, 2x = 48. x = **24.** Choice C is correct.

2. Let x be the length of the base. Perimeter = sum of all three sides = 90 = x + 2(3x - 4) = 7x – 8. Thus, 7x = 98. x = **14.** Choice B is correct.

3. Area = ½(Base)(Height). Here, we will let x = the height and x+16 = the base. Therefore,

$256 = ½ x(x + 16)$
$512 = x^2 + 16x$
$0 = x^2 + 16x – 512$
$0 = (x - 16)(x + 32)$. The height = 16 inches. The base = X + 16 = **32** inches. Choice C is correct.

4. 3x + 4x + 5x = 180, so 12x = 180, x = 15, 3x = 45, 4x = 60, 5x = 75. Choice D is correct.

5. The area of the circle is $\pi r^2 = \pi(8)(8) = 64\pi$.

In the triangle, the area = 1/2 (Base) (Height). We will let x = the height. Thus, for this triangle, the area = 1/2 (16)x =64 π. x = **8 π.** Choice B is correct.

6. By definition, an isosceles triangle has two equal sides. Additionally, the two opposite angles, which are called base angles, are also equal. If one of the base angles = 30 degrees, then the second base angle also equals 30 degrees. The vertex angle is therefore 180 – 60 = **120** degrees. Choice C is correct.

7. If we plot the points on a graph, we can easily see that they form a right triangle with a 90 degree angle at point (8,3). Therefore, we can use the formula Area = ½(Base)(Height) to solve the problem.

In this case, the Base is 20 – 8 = 12 and Height is 10 – 3 = 7.
The area of the triangle is therefore ½(7)(12) = **42**. Choice C is correct.

8. 45 + 55 + AC = 125. AC = **25**. Choice A is correct.

9. The area that Jake walked is a "special" right triangle with sides equal to 50, 120 and 130. Therefore, the total distance Jake walked is the perimeter of that triangle, which is 50 + 120 + 130 = **300** yards. Choice E is correct.

10. The area the truck traveled is a right triangle with side lengths of 30 and 50. Using the Pythagorean theorem, we can use this information to determine the length of the hypotenuse:

$(30)^2 + (50)^2 = x^2$
$900 + 2,500 = 3,400 = x^2$
$x = 58.31$ miles.

The total distance traveled is the perimeter of that triangle, or 30 + 40 + 58.31 = 128.31 miles/ 8 mpg = **16** gallons. Choice C is correct.

11. Knowing that the three angles must total 180 degrees, we can solve this problem by using a simple algebraic equation. First, we must define our variables. We will let x = angle M, 2x = angle N, and x + 20 = angle O. Therefore, our equation becomes: x + 2x + (x + 20) = 180.

Solving for x, we find that: 4x = 160. Therefore, Angle M = 40 degrees; Angle N = 80 degrees; Angle O = 40 + 20 = **60** degrees. Choice E is correct.

12. According to the triangle inequality theorem, the length of one side of a triangle must be greater than the difference and less than the sum of the lengths of the other two sides. Therefore, in Triangle D, the length of the third side must be greater than 36 – 21 = 15 and less than 36 + 21 = 57. The only answer choice between 15 and 57 is Choice C.

13. Although this is a geometry question, it adds an additional level of trickery by asking which answer could NOT be correct. To solve, we must use the relationship that is defined by the Pythagorean theorem: *the squares of the two shorter sides MUST equal the square of the third side.*

Therefore, for these five answer choices, you must run through the calculations as quickly as you can. When you do, you will discover that they are ALL correct answer choices, except for Choice c. If we square 9 and 26, and add those numbers together, they do NOT equal the square of 31. Since the question asks us to identify the *one incorrect answer*, we must select Choice C.

14. If sides CA and AT are equal, then their angles are also equal. Hence,

3x – 20 = 1.5x + 115
1.5x = 135
x = 90 degrees. Choice E is correct.

15. By definition, the exterior angle is equal to the sum of the two remote interior angles. If angle D is six times as large as angle O, then their sum is 6x + 1x = 7x. Hence,

7x =140
x = 20 = angle O
6x = 120 = angle D. Choice A is correct.

16. The sum of all interior angles is 180 degrees. In this case, we can represent the three angles by 2x, 3x, and 5x, respectively. Therefore, our equation becomes:

2x + 3x + 5x = 180
10x = 180
x = 18

The smallest angle is 2x = 36, the middle angle = 3x = 54, and the largest angle is 5x = 90. Choice E is correct.

17. The new triangle will have sides that are one-half the length of those in triangle DEF. Hence, its perimeter will be one-half of DEF, which is **72.** Choice E is correct.

18. I know what you're thinking. This chapter is supposed to be about triangles; why are we including a question about circles and rectangles? Because this is **exactly** the type of problem you are going to see on the SAT, GRE and GMAT..... and you need the Pythagorean theorem to solve it.

In this situation, the diagonal of the rectangle is equal to the diameter of the circle. Because the rectangle can also be viewed as two triangles that share the diagonal as a common side, we can use the Pythagorean theorem to calculate its length.

Accordingly, the square of the diagonal is equal to (60)(60) + (84)(84) = 3,600 + 7,056 = 10,656. This means that the diameter of the circle is the square root of 10,656, or 103.22; the radius is therefore 51.6. Now, we can calculate the area of the circle, which is $(51.6)^2(\pi)$, = **2,664 π.** Choice D is correct.

19. The scenario can be depicted as a right triangle in which the hypotenuse = 3,000 miles. The United Airlines jet flew west for 4 hours. Since Distance = Rate x Time, Distance = 700 x 4 = 2,800 miles.

In contrast, the jet that flew north for traveled for one hour, so its Distance = Rate x Time = Rate X 1, or Distance = Rate.   To find this distance, which is the same as the rate, we must solve the following equation:

Distance (United Flight) + Distance (USAir Flight) = Total Distance

$2,800^2 + d^2 = 3,000^2$
$d^2 = 3,000^2 - 2,800^2 = 9,000,000 - 7,8400,000 = 1,160,000$
D = **1077** mph. Choice C is correct.

Chapter 23: Circles

Before we present any problems with circles, let's review some essential definitions. Circles are closed, curved figures in a single plane in which all points on the curve are of equal distance from the center.

A **radius (r)** of a circle is a line segment from the center to any point on the circle.

A **chord** is a line segment whose endpoints are on the circle.

A **diameter (d)** of a circle is a chord that passes through the center of the circle. The diameter of a circle is twice its radius and the longest distance between two points on the circle.

The **circumference** is the length around the circle. Mathematically, the circumference is: π **d** or **2 π r**

> *Example*: if the radius of a circle is 3, the circumference is $2 \times \pi \times 3 = 6 \pi$.

An **arc** is a portion of a circle, usually measured in degrees.

> The entire circle is 360 degrees
> A semicircle (half a circle) is 180 degrees
> A quarter of a circle is an arc of 90 degrees

The **length of an arc:** If *n* is the measure of the arc's central angle (in degrees), then the formula is:

Length of an Arc = (n/360)(2πr)

Example: A circle has a radius of 5. The measure of the central angle is 72°. The arc length is (72/360) (2π) (5) = 2π

Example: If a circle of radius 3 feet has a central angle of 60 degrees, the length of an arc intercepted by this central angle is (60/360) (2)(3) π = π feet

The **Area of a Circle** equals π r^2

A **sector** is a piece of the area of a circle. If *n* is the degree measure of the sector's central angle, then the formula is:
Area of a Sector = (n/360)π r^2

As you probably expect, the SAT, GRE and GMAT have predictable ways of testing these concepts in different types of word problems. Here are the most common examples (with solutions), followed by numerous problems for you to tackle on your own time.

Example 1. Plugging Numbers into Formulas

What is the diameter of a circle with an area of 196π?

> a. 7
> b. 14
> c. 16
> d. 28
> e. 32

Solution: For geometry topics, this problem is as straightforward as it gets – you are given the area of a circle and asked to determine its diameter. To solve, just use the formula for the area of a circle: Area $= \pi r^2$. In this case 196 $= \pi r^2 = \pi(14)(14)$. If the radius of the circle is 14, its diameter is 14 + 14 = 28. Choice D is correct.

Example 2: % Increase and Decrease

If the diameter of a circle increases by 50%, by what percent will the area of the circle increase?

    a.   25%
    b.   50%
    c.   100%
    d.   125%
    e.   175%

Solution: The test will undoubtedly include a question or two about the increase or decrease of a circle's area, radius, or diameter. In this case, the answers are in %, rather than actual numbers, which means that the best way to solve the problem is to select values for the diameter of the circle and determine the effect on its area.

The area of the circle $= \pi r^2$. If the diameter is 4, the radius is 2 and the area is 4π. If we increase the diameter by 50% to 6, the new radius is 3 and the new area is 9π. The percent increase is (9 - 4)/4 = 5/4, or 125%.

To verify that this answer is correct, let's try another set of numbers. If the diameter is 10, the radius is 5 and the area is 25π. If we increase the diameter by 50% to 15, the new radius is 7.5 and the new area is 56.25π. The percent increase is (56.25 - 25)/25 = 5/4, or 125%. Choice D is correct.

Example 3: Concentric Circles: Geometric Probability

Two concentric circles exist in a plane. If the larger circle has a diameter of 36 and the small circle has a diameter of 12, what is the probability that any point chosen at random from the large circle will also be in the small circle?

    a.   6.25%
    b.   11.11%
    c.   12.50%
    d.   25.00%
    e.   33.33%

Solution: The area of the large circle is (18)(18) π, or 324π, while the area of the small circle is (6)(6)π, or 36π. To determine the probability of any given point being in both circles, we simply divide the two quantities and convert to a percentage: Area of the small circle / Area of the large circle = $36\pi/324\,\pi$, or 0.111, or 11.11%. The correct answer is Choice B.

Example 4: Coordinate Geometry

What is the radius of the circle that passes through the point (10, 8) and has its center at (2, 2)?

    a.   1
    b.   2
    c.   5
    d.   8
    e.   10

Solution: This problem gives us two pieces of information about the circle – its center coordinates (2, 2) and a point on its circumference (10, 8). We can use the distance formula to find the radius of the circle:

Radius $= \sqrt{\{(10 - 2)(10 - 2) + (8 - 2)(8 - 2)\}}$
Radius $= \sqrt{\{(8)(8) + (6)(6)\}} = \sqrt{(64 + 36)} = \sqrt{100} = 10$

Thus, the radius of the circle is 10. Choice E is correct.

Word Problems w/ Circles: EASY - MODERATE

1. If the ratio of the areas of Circle A and Circle B is 16π to 36π, what is the ratio of the circumference of Circle A to Circle B?

    a.   1/3
    b.   1/4
    c.   2/5
    d.   2/3
    e.   3/4

2. If the diameter of a circle increases by 100%, by what percent will the area of the circle increase?

    a.   50%
    b.   100%
    c.   150%
    d.   200%
    e.   300%

3. Jenny is making holiday decorations from a large piece of velvet fabric. How many circles, each with a 6-inch radius, can Jenny cut from a rectangular piece of the fabric, which measures 84 inches x 204 inches?

    a.   64
    b.   124
    c.   119
    d.   238
    e.   476

4. A pizza is divided into slices of equal size, each with a side length of 7. Assuming that each slice meets at the center of the pizza, what is the pizza's circumference?

    a.   7
    b.   49
    c. 7π
    d. 14π
    e. 49π

5. A rectangle that measures 9 inches by 16 inches is completely inscribed in a circle. If all four corners of the rectangle touch the circumference of the circle, what is the area of the circle?

    a. 12π
    b. 36π
    c. 84π
    d. 144π
    e. 720π

6. If the radius of a circle is decreased by 30%, by what percent is its area decreased?

    a.   30
    b.   36
    c.   49
    d.   51
    e.   60

7. A circle is inscribed in a square whose side is 48. What is the area of the circle?

    a. 24π
    b. 48π
    c. 576π
    d. 2,304π
    e. It cannot be determined from the information given.

8. If the radius of a circle increases by 8, how much will its circumference increase?

    a. 4 π
    b. 8 π
    c. 16 π
    d. 32 π
    e. 64 π

9. For a circle whose center is X, arc YZ contains 80 degrees. How many degrees are in angle YXZ?

    a. 20
    b. 40
    c. 45
    d. 50
    e. 100

10. The clock at the Capitol Building has an hour hand that is 12 feet long. How many feet will the top of the hand move between the hours of midnight and eight am?

    a. 16π
    b. 18π
    c. 24π
    d. 36π
    e. 48π

11. What is the area of the circle that passes through the point (5, 4) and has its center at (1, 1)?

    a. 5π
    b. 10π
    c. 20π
    d. 25π
    e. 125π

12. The typical tire for a passenger car has a radius of 48 inches. How many feet will the tire cover in 300 revolutions?

    a. 2,400π
    b. 4,800π
    c. 9,600π
    d. 14,440π
    e. 28,880π

13. If the area and circumference of Circle X are equal, what is the diameter of Circle X?

    a.   1
    b.   2
    c.   4
    d.   8
    e.   It cannot be determined from the information given.

14. How many degrees are included between the hands of a clock when the time is 2 pm?

    a.   15
    b.   20
    c.   30
    d.   45
    e.   60

Word Problems w/ Circles: AS HARD AS IT GETS

15.   A designer is building a circular clock for the front of an old historic building. After he presents his design to the planning committee, they ask him to make it larger. The designer increases the diameter of the clock until its area is 30% larger than it was originally. Then, in the final stages of revision, the designer again enlarges the diameter of the clock by an additional 20%. How much larger is the diameter of the final clock than the original clock?

    a.   10%
    b.   25%
    c.   50%
    d.   56%
    e.   63%

16. Kelly obtained a recipe for a black velvet wedding cake from the Rachael Ray show. The original recipe made a single round layer cake with a diameter of 8 inches. For her upcoming wedding, Kelly wants to expand the recipe to make a single round layer cake with a diameter of 28 inches. If the original cake required 4 cups of sugar, how many cups of sugar will the larger cake require (assuming the two cakes are equal in thickness)?

    a.   12.25
    b.   18
    c.   24
    d.   48
    e.   49

Answer Key: Word Problems w/ Circles

1. The ratio of the areas of Circle A to Circle B is $16\pi/36\pi$. Since the area of each circle is πr^2, then the radius of Circle A = 4 and the radius of Circle B is 6. We can use this information to calculate the circumference of each.

The circumference of Circle A $=2\pi r = 2\pi(4) = 8\pi$
The circumference of Circle B $=2\pi r = 2\pi(6)= 12\pi$

The ratio of the circumferences of Circle A to Circle B = 8/12 or 2/3. Choice D is correct.

2. The fastest way to solve is to select values for the diameter of the circle and determine the effect on the area. If the diameter is 4, the radius is 2 and the area is 4π. Increasing the diameter by 100% to 8 makes the new radius 4 and the new area 16π. The percent increase is (16 - 4)/4 = 12/4, or 300%.

Let's confirm our answer with another set of numbers. If the diameter is 10, the radius is 5 and the area is 25π. Increasing the diameter by 100% to 20 makes the new radius 10 and the new area 100π. The percent increase is (100 - 25)/25 = 75/25, or 300%. Choice E is correct.

3. In this case, we are cutting a rectangular piece of fabric into smaller, circular pieces. If the circles have a 6-inch radius, then their diameter is 12 inches. For a piece of fabric measuring 84 inches by 204 inches, we can lay 204/12 - or 17 - circles across the *length* of the fabric.

Since the width of the fabric is 84 inches, we can make 84/12, or 7 total rows of circles. Therefore, Jenny can make 17 x 7 = 119 total circles. Choice C is correct.

4. Circumference = π x Diameter   If the radius is 7, the circumference= 14π. Choice D is correct.

5. In this situation, the diagonal of the rectangle is equal to the diameter of the circle. Because the rectangle can also be viewed as two triangles that share the diagonal as a common side, we can use the Pythagorean theorem to calculate its length.

Accordingly, the square of the diagonal is equal to (9)(9) + (16)(16) = 81 + 256 = 337. This means that the diameter of the circle is the square root of 337, or 18.36; the radius is therefore 9.18.

Now, we can calculate the area of the circle, which is $(9.18)(9.18)(\pi)$, = 84π. Choice C is correct.

6. If the radii of the two circles have a ratio of 10:7, their areas have a ratio of 100:49. Therefore, the decrease is 51 out of 100, or 51%.

Alternatively, you can try a few numbers to reach the same answer. Let's assume that a circle has a radius of 10. Its area is 100π. If we reduce the radius by 30% - to 7 – the area becomes 49π. Once again, the % reduction is 51%. Choice D is correct.

7. If the square has a side of 48, then the diameter of the circle is also 48. The radius is therefore 24, which makes the area of the circle $\pi(24)(24) = 576\pi$. Choice C is correct.

8. The circumference of the circle $=2\pi r$. Hence, the question is asking us to determine the difference between the first circumference and the second.

First circumference = $2\pi r$
Second circumference = $2\pi(r + 8) = 2\pi r + 2\pi(8) = 2\pi r + 16\pi$

The difference between the two circumferences – which is the amount that it increases – is equal to 16π. Choice C is correct.

9. According to the problem, angle X = 80 degrees. Since it is a central angle, it creates an isosceles triangle within the circle, with YX and XZ as equal sides. Angles Y and Z are therefore equal, with a sum of 180 - 80 = 100 degrees. Angle YXZ is therefore 50. Choice D is correct.

10. The clock at the railroad station is a circle with a radius of 12 feet. The total circumference is $2\pi r = 2\pi(12) = 24\pi$. In eight hours, the hour hand will move across two-thirds of the circumference of the circle, which is $(2/3)24\pi = 16\pi$. Choice A is correct.

11. This problem gives us two pieces of information about the circle – its center coordinates (1, 1) and a point on its circumference (5, 4). We can use the distance formula to find the radius of the circle:

Radius = $\sqrt{(5 - 1)(5 - 1) + (4 - 1)(4 - 1)}$

Radius = $\sqrt{(4)(4)+(3)(3)} = \sqrt{(16 + 9)} = \sqrt{25} = 5$

Thus, the radius of the circle is 5. The Area of the circle = $(5)(5)\pi = 25\pi$. Choice D is correct.

12. The tire is a circle with a radius of 48. The distance it covers in one revolution is simply the circumference of the tire. Since the circumference = $2\pi r$, we know that the tire covers $2\pi(48/12) = 8\pi$ feet in one revolution. Therefore, for 300 revolutions, the tire covers 2400π feet. Choice A is correct.

13. The area of Circle X = πr^2 while the circumference of Circle X = $2\pi r$. If these qualities are equal, then $\pi r^2 = 2\pi r$, which simplifies to r = 2. The diameter of Circle X is therefore 4.

14. The clock is a circle with a circumference of 360 degrees. Each number on the clock included 1/12 of 360 degrees, or 30 degrees. At 2 pm, the hands would be 2(30) = 60 degrees apart. Choice E is correct.

15. Since we do not have any numbers, we can simply use any number for the original diameter of the clock. For simplicity, let's assume the original diameter was 2. Its radius therefore, was 1, which makes the original area = πr^2 =1π.

If the area of the clock increases by 30%, then the new area is = $1\pi + (0.30)(1)\pi = 1.30\pi$
If the area increases by an additional 20%, then the new area is $1.30\pi + (0.2)(1.30\pi) = 1.30\pi + 0.26\pi = 1.56\pi$.

Initially, for the first clock, the area = $\pi r^2 = \pi$
For the final clock, the area = $\pi r^2 = 1.56\pi$

The new radius is therefore the square root of 1.56, or 1.25. The new diameter is 2.50.

Hence, the new radius and diameter of the final clock are **25%** larger than those of the original clock. Choice B is correct.

16. The original cake had a diameter of 8 inches. Hence, its area was $(4)(4)\pi = 16\pi$.
The second cake has a diameter is 28 inches. Hence, its area was $(14)(14)\pi = 196\pi$.

196/16 = 12.25. Kelly will need to multiply the recipe by 12.25 to make the larger cake. (12.25)(4) = 49 cups. Choice E is correct.

Chapter 24: Squares, Rectangles & Polygons

A **rectangle** is a closed, four-sided figure with four right angles that exists in a single plane. The opposite sides – and the diagonals - are equal.

The **perimeter** of a rectangle is the sum of the lengths of the four sides, which is: 2(Length + Width).

The area of a rectangle = Length X Width

A **parallelogram** is a rectangle with two pairs of parallel sides. Additionally, both the opposite sides and opposite angles are equal. Further, the sum of all consecutive angles is 180 degrees.

The **area of a parallelogram** = Base X Height

A **square** is a *rectangle with four equal sides*. Thus, the perimeter of a square is equal to four times the length of one side.

The area of a square = Side Length ^{2}

Example 1: In a square with sides of length 2, the area is 2 x 2 = 4.
Example 2: In a square with sides of length 3, the area is 3 x 3 = 9.

Polygons are closed figures in a single plane whose sides are straight lines.

For any polygon, the **sum of the interior angles** is equal to **180(n – 2) degrees,** where n = the number of sides.

Figure	# Sides	Sum of Interior Angles
Triangle	3	180
Rectangle	4	360
Pentagon	5	540
Hexagon	6	720
Octagon	8	1,080
Nonagon	9	1,260
Decagon	10	1,440

A **regular polygon** is one in which all sides and angles are equal. The measure of **each internal angle** (in degrees) in a regular polygon = **180(n – 2)/n,** where n = the number of sides. Regular polygons can be inscribed inside and outside of circles. (In fact, the test writers *love* this type of scenario.)

Here is a review of the most common types of word problems about squares, rectangles, and polygons you are likely to encounter on the SAT, GRE and GMAT.

Example 1. Comparing Squares of Different Sizes

Square 1 has a side length of 3. Square 2 has a side length of 9. What is the ratio of their areas?

    a.   1:3
    b.   1:6
    c.   1:9
    d.   1:10
    e.   1:18

Solution: The area of Square 1 is (3)(3) = 9. The area of Square 2 = (9)(9) = 81. The ratio of 9 to 81 is 1:9. Choice C is correct.

Example 2: Using the Pythagorean Theorem

Find the area (in square feet) of a square whose diagonal is 12 feet.

    a.   36
    b.   72
    c.   144
    d.   288
    e.   576

Solution: Knowing the square is actually 2 triangles that share the same hypotenuse (the diagonal), we can use the Pythagorean theorem to solve for the length of a side.

$s^2 + s^2 = 12^2$
$2s^2 = 144$
$s^2 = 72$
Side length = 8.485 feet. Therefore, the area of the square = 72. Choice B is correct.

Example 3: Increasing & Decreasing Areas & Side Lengths

If the base of a parallelogram decreases by 25% and the height increases by 35%, by what percent does the area increase?

    a.   1%
    b.   5%
    c.   10%
    d.   15%
    e.   20%

Solution: The area of the original parallelogram = Base X Height. Let B = the length of the base and H = the height of the original parallelogram. If the base decreases by 25%, it becomes 0.75B. If the height increases by 35%, it becomes 1.35H. The new area is therefore: (0.75)B times (1.35)H = 1.0125 BH, which is 1.25% bigger than the original area. Choice A is correct.

Example 4: Practical Applications

A plumber wishes to cover a bathroom wall with colorful ceramic tiles, which each measure 1/2 inch by 3 inches. If the wall is a rectangle that measures 10 feet by 12 feet, how many ceramic tiles will the plumber need to complete the job?

    a.   1,152
    b.   1,728
    c.   11,520
    d.   17,280
    e.   25,290

Solution: The area of the wall is 10 feet x 12 feet, or 120 square feet. The area of one tile is 1/2 inch x 3 inches = 3/2 square inches, or 1.5 square inches.

First, for simplicity, we must convert the units of the tiles from square inches to square feet:
1.5 square inches (1 square foot/ 144 square inches) = 0.0104166 square feet.

Next, we must multiply the total area of the wall by the area of one tile to determine how many tiles we need: 120 square feet (1 tile/0.0104166 square feet) = 11,520 tiles, which is Choice C.

To hone your skills on these concepts, try the following word problems. Complete solutions are presented at the end of the chapter.

Word Problems: Squares, Rectangles & Polygons: EASY - MODERATE

1. The length of Rectangle B is six times its width. If the perimeter of Rectangle B is 280 feet, what is its length?

    a.   20
    b.   40
    c.   60
    d.   80
    e.   120

2. The side length of Square A is four times as long as the side length of Square B. If the sum of their perimeters is 1,200 cm, what is the area of Square B (in cm^2)?

    a.   60
    b.   240
    c.   600
    d.   3,600
    e.   57,600

3. What is the sum of the measure of the interior angles of a polygon having 11 sides?

    a.   1,320
    b.   1,600
    c.   1,620
    d.   1,800
    e.   1,980

4. A parallelogram with an area of 36 has a base of (x + 8) and a height of (x − 8). What is the exact measure of its height?

    a. 2
    b. 4
    c. 8
    d. 10
    e. 18

5. The Wilson family measured their rectangular backyard for a privacy fence. If the ratio of the length to width was 15:36, what was the diagonal of the enclosed area (in feet)?

     a.   24
     b.   36
     c.   39
     d.   48
     e.   It cannot be determined from the information given.

6. A parallelogram has an interior angle of 75 degrees. What is the measure of the adjacent angle (in degrees)?

     a.   75
     b.   90
     c.   105
     d.   115
     e.   285

7. Square X has a side of 17 inches, while square Y has a side of 27 inches. How much greater is the area of square Y than square X (in square inches)?

     a.   100
     b.   270
     c.   289
     d.   440
     e.   729

8. Karen inherited a valuable oil painting that she wants to have framed. If the painting is a rectangle, with a width of 48 inches and a length of 64 inches, how much framing, in linear feet, does Karen need to buy?

     a.   19
     b.   32
     c.   112
     d.   224
     e.   448

9. An octagon has seven interior angles that measure 80, 90, 105, 120, 125, 130 and 135. What is the measure of the eighth internal angle?

     a.   95
     b.   115
     c.   235
     d.   295
     e.   475

10. A city park is frequently used as an exercise path. If the park is a square, with each side 2,400 feet long, how many minutes would it take someone walking 600 feet per minute to walk the entire perimeter of the park?

     a.   8
     b.   12
     c.   16
     d.   20
     e.   40

11. Kelly has decided to decorate her room with a designer wallpaper that costs $18.45 per square foot. If her room measures 20 feet by 16 feet, how much will it cost Karen to buy the wallpaper?

   a. $59.04
   b. $354.24
   c. $590.40
   d. $1,180.80
   e. $5,904.00

12. Doug has looked everywhere for the right carpet for his living room, which measures 18 feet x 36 feet. Finally, at Designer Carpet Surplus, he finds the perfect carpet, which costs $25 per square yard. How much will it cost Doug to purchase enough of this carpet to cover his entire living room?

   a. $480
   b. $1,440
   c. $1,800
   d. $4,800
   e. $14,400

13. If the length of a rectangle increases by 33% and its width decreases by 64%, what is the overall effect on the area of the rectangle?

   a. It increases by 31%
   b. It remains the same
   c. It decreases by 16%
   d. It decreases by 31%
   e. It cannot be determined from the information given.

14. The church must replace 6 stained glass windows that were destroyed by a hurricane. The windows are squares that measure 13 feet on each side. If the stained glass costs $5.86 per square foot, how many of the windows can the church afford to replace if they have budgeted $4000 for the project?

   a. 2
   b. 3
   c. 4
   d. 5
   e. 6

15. How many degrees are there between two adjacent sides of a regular 14-sided figure?

   a. 140
   b. 154
   c. 180
   d. 216
   e. 280

16. Joe will cover his bathroom floor with ceramic tiles that measure 3 inches by 6 inches. If the room is a rectangle that measures 8 feet by 6 feet, how many tiles will Joe need to cover the floor?

   a. 48
   b. 92
   c. 196
   d. 384
   e. 760

17. If the base of a parallelogram increases by 12% and the height decreases by 18%, by what percent does the area change?

    a. 9% decrease
    b. 6% decrease
    c. 6% increase
    d. 10% increase
    e. 32% increase

18. The sides of a hexagonal shaped lot are 24.5 ft, 12.0 ft, 9.75 ft, 11.9 ft, 34.0 ft and 21.6 ft. If the cost of chain link fencing is $36.00 per linear yard, how much will it cost the owner of the lot to buy a fence to secure the entire lot?

    a. $1,222
    b. $1,365
    c. $1,643
    d. $4,086
    e. $4,104

19. Squares X, Y and Z have side lengths of 6, 7, and 8, respectively. What is the sum of the areas of squares X, Y and Z?

    a. 42
    b. 84
    c. 144
    d. 149
    e. 168

20. Square R is divided into 4 smaller squares of equal size. If the perimeter of square R is 12, what is the perimeter of each individual smaller square?

    a. 3/2
    b. 2
    c. 3
    d. 4
    e. 6

21. The perimeter of a 9-sided figure is 54 feet. If each side is extended by 2 feet, what is the perimeter of the new figure?

    a. 66
    b. 72
    c. 81
    d. 84
    e. It cannot be determined from the information given.

22. The area of Square G is 144. H is one-third the perimeter of Square G. What is the value of H?

    a. 16
    b. 18
    c. 24
    d. 36
    e. 48

Word Problems: Squares, Rectangles & Polygons: AS HARD AS IT GETS

23. The perimeter of Square X is twelve times the perimeter of Square Y. What is the relationship between the areas of Square X and Square Y?

     a.   The area of Square X is 4 times as large as the area of Square Y.
     b.   The area of Square X is 6 times as large as the area of Square Y.
     c.   The area of Square X is 12 times as large as the area of Square Y.
     d.   The area of Square X is 144 times as large as the area of Square Y.
     e.   It cannot be determined from the information given.

24. When Parallelogram P is plotted on a graph, it has four endpoints. If three of those points are (3, 1), (-1, -3) and (-3, 0), what is the fourth endpoint?

     a.   (-4, 1)
     b.   (-1, 4)
     c.   (4, 1)
     d.   (0, -3)
     e.   (1, 4)

25. After her honeymoon, Lisa decided to transform her wedding invitation into a piece of framed artwork for her living room. To do so, she enlarged the length and width of her rectangular wedding invitation by 80%. Unfortunately, the resulting invitation was too large for the custom frame Lisa ordered, so she reduced the length and width of the invitation by 50%. The area of the final invitation is what percent larger (or smaller) than the area of the original?

     a.   19% smaller
     b.   40% smaller
     c.   10% larger
     d.   19% larger
     e.   40% larger

26. A kennel owner has 1,400 feet of fencing to create a rectangular dog run. According to the architect's plan, the length of the run is 100 feet more than twice times its width. What will the length of the dog run be (in feet)?

     a.   100
     b.   200
     c.   300
     d.   400
     e.   500

Answer Key: Squares, Rectangles & Polygons

1. The perimeter of Rectangle A is 2(Length) + 2(Width). In this case, we will let the width = X and the length = 6x. Our formula for the perimeter is therefore:

2x + 2(6x) = 280
2x + 12x = 280
14x = 280
x = 20 = width
6x = **120** = length. Choice E is correct.

2. We will let x= the side length of Square B. Therefore, 4x = the perimeter of Square B.

We will let 4x = side length of Square A. Therefore, 16x = the perimeter of Square B.
4x + 16x = 1,200
20x = 1,200
x = 60 = length of Square B

Area of Square B = (60)(60) = **3,600** cm^2. Choice D is correct.

3. The sum of the interior angles is equal to 180(11 – 2) degrees = 180(9) = **1,620** degrees. Choice C is correct.

4. The area of a parallelogram is equal to its base times its height. Therefore,

(x + 8)(x – 8) = 36
x^2 – 64 = 36
x^2 = 100
x = 10
The base of the parallelogram = 10 + 8 = 18 and its height is 10 – 8 = **2**. Choice A is correct.

5. This is one of those annoying "trick" questions for which the SAT is notorious. Most students scramble furiously to calculate an area by using the numbers in the ratio, but it is not necessary.   If the ratio of the length to width is 15:36, then the diagonal will be **39**, because it is a multiple of a 5-12-13 special triangle. Choice C is correct.

6.The adjacent angle = 180 –75 = **105** degrees. Choice C is correct.

7. Area of Y = 27 x 27 = 729 square inches. Area of X = 17 x 17 = 289 square inches. 729 – 289 = **440** square inches. Choice D is correct.

8. The perimeter of a rectangle is 2L + 2W = 2(48) + 2 (64) = 224 inches. But this is not our answer – we must first convert the units from inches to feet by dividing by 12. 224/12 = 18.7 = **19** linear feet. Choice A is correct.

9. For an octagon, the sum of the interior angles is equal to 180(8 – 2) = 1080 total degrees, so 80 + 90 + 105 + 120 + 125 + 130 + 135 + X = 1080. X = **295** degrees. Choice D is correct.

10. If the park is a square with a side length of 2,400 feet, the perimeter is 2,400 (4), or 9,600 feet. Someone walking 600 feet per minute would take 9,600/600, or **16** minutes to walk the perimeter of the park. Choice C is correct.

11. Area = (20)(16) = 320 square feet x $18.45/square foot = **$5,904**. Choice E is correct.

12. First, we must convert our room measurements into yards: 18 feet = 6 yards, while 36 feet = 12 yards. Therefore, the area of Doug's room is (6)(12) = 72 square yards.   (72)(25) = **$1,800**. Choice C is correct.

13. The area of a rectangle is equal to its length times its width. Therefore, the new area will be equal to the new length (which is 1.33 times its old length) times its new width (which is 0.64 times its old width).   When we multiply them together, we find that the new area is (1.33)(0.64), or **0.84** times the original area. Thus, Choice C is correct.

14. Area of each window = (13)(13) = 169 square feet x $5.86 = $990.34 per window. The church can replace **4** windows for $3,961.36. Choice C is correct.

15. The measure of each internal angle (in degrees) in a regular polygon = 180(n – 2)/n, where n = the number of

sides. Hence, for a regular 14-sided figure, the measure of each angle is 180(14 − 2)/14 = 2,160/14 = **154.29** degrees. Choice B is correct.

16. The area of the room is 8 x 6 = 48 square feet. The area of one tile is (0.25 foot) x (0.5 foot) = 0.125 square feet. Therefore, to cover the entire floor, Joe will need: 48 square feet (1 tile/0.125 square feet) = **384** tiles. Choice D is correct.

17. The area of the original parallelogram = Base X Height. Let B = the length of the base and H = the height of the original parallelogram.

If the base increases by 12%, it becomes 1.12B. If the height decreases by 18%, it becomes 0.82H. The new area is therefore: (1.12)B (0.82)H = 0.9184BH, which is **9.18**% smaller than the original area. Choice A is correct.

18. The perimeter of the lot is the sum of its six sides, or 24.5 + 12 + 9.75 + 11.9 + 34 + 21.6 = 113.75 feet / 3 = 37.9 yards. 37.9 x $36 = **$1,365**. Choice B is correct.

19. The sum of the areas is $6^2 + 7^2 + 8^2 = = 36 + 49 + 64 = $ **149**. Choice D is correct.

20. If Square R has a perimeter of 12, then its side length is 3. If Square 4 is divided into 4 smaller squares of equal size, then each smaller square has side lengths that are one-half as long as those of Square R, or 3/2. The perimeter of the smaller squares is therefore 4(3/2), which is 6, which is one-half the perimeter of Square R. Choice E is correct.

21. If we add 2 feet to the length of each side, the perimeter will increase by (9)(2) = 18. Therefore, the new perimeter is 54 + 18 = **72**. Choice B is correct.

22. If the area of Square G is 144, then its side length is 12. The perimeter of Square G is (12)(4) = 48. One-third of its perimeter is 48/3 = **16**. Choice A is correct.

23. Square Y = side length 1 = perimeter = 4. Area = (1)(1) = 1
Square X = side length 12 = perimeter = 48. Area = (12)(12) = 144

To check, let's try a second set of numbers:

Square Y = side length 2 = perimeter = 8. Area = (2)(2) = 4
Square X = side length 24 = perimeter = 96. Area = (24)(24) = 576

Choice D is correct.

24. Choice E is correct. To solve, you should plot the first three points, which will give you an idea of what the parallelogram looks like. It will ALSO allow you to eliminate answer choices that are in the wrong quadrant, such as Choices A, B, and D. Once you narrow down to Choices C and E, you can confirm the correct choice by their slopes.

25. For simplicity, let's assume that the original invitation had a length and width of 10, which made its area 100.

If the length and width are both increased by 80%, the new invitation is (10)(1.8) x (10)(1.8) = 18 x 18.
If the length and width are both reduced by 15%, the final invitation is (18)(0.50) x (18)(0.50) = 9 x 9.

The original area was 10 x 10 or 100. The new area is 9 x 9, or 81, which is a 19% decrease.

26. Using the information we have been given about the perimeter and area of the dog run, we can write two separate formulas for its length and width. Then, we can combine the two equations to solve for each.

Perimeter = 2L + 2W
1,400 = 2(100 + 2W) + 2W

1,400 = 200 + 4W + 2W
6W = 1,200
W = 200

Now, we can plug this value into the original equation to solve for the length:

2(L) + 2(200) = 1,400
2L = 1000
Length = **500**. Choice E is correct.

Chapter 25: Three-Dimensional Figures

The most sophisticated – and complex – geometric figures exist in three dimensions. This chapter will discuss cubes, rectangular solids, and cylinders, which are the most popular solids in SAT, GRE, and GMAT word problems. Before we proceed, let's review a few basic concepts:

Rectangular solids (or prisms): the surface of a rectangular solid consists of three pairs of identical faces. To find the surface area, we must add the area of each face. If the length is l, the width is w, and the height is h, the formula is:

$$\text{Surface Area} = 2lw + 2wh + 2lh$$

The **volume** of a rectangular solid = Length x Width x Height

A **cube** is a rectangular solid in which the length, width, and height are all equal. If a is the length of an edge of a cube, the volume = a^3

A **cylinder** is an enclosed three dimensional figure which has circular bases.

The volume of a cylinder = $\pi r^2 h$, where r = the radius of the base and h = the height of the cylinder.

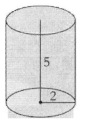

In the cylinder above, r = 2 and h = 5, so   Volume = $\pi (2)^2(5) = 20\pi$

A **sphere** is a three-dimensional figure that is perfectly round. It surface area is $4\pi r^2 h$ and its area is $4/3\pi r^3$

As you probably suspect, these underlying geometric theories will only take you so far on the SAT, GRE, and GMAT. Although there will certainly be one or two basic questions that will require you to plug numbers into formulas, most of them will require a higher – and more practical - level of thinking. Here is a review of the most common types of word problems about three-dimensional figures on the exam.

Example 1: Manipulating the Formulas

A cylindrical bucket has a diameter of 12 inches and a height of 14 inches. How many gallons will it hold of a liquid with a density of 84 cubic inches per gallon? (Use π = 3.1416)

- a.   18.85
- b.   37.70
- c.   75.40
- d.   504.00
- e.   1,583.37

Solution: The problem is asking us to determine the capacity, or volume, of a cylinder.   To do so, we can simply use the formula:

 Volume = $\pi r^2 h$ = (3.1416)(6)(6)(14) = 1,583.37 cubic inches. To convert our answer to gallons, we must divide by 84: 1,583.37 cubic inches/84 cubic inches per gallon = 18.85 gallons. Choice A is correct.

Example 2. Converting Surface Area to Volume…And Vice Versa

If the surface area of a cube is 486 square feet, how many cubic feet are there in the volume of the cube?

     a.   360
     b.   400
     c.   625
     d.   676
     e.   729

Solution: The surface area of the cube - 486 square feet - is composed of 6 equal sides. Thus,

$486 = 6x^2$, where x= a side of the cube.
$x^2 = 81$, or $x = 9$

The volume of the cube is $9^3 = 729$ cubic feet. Choice E is correct.

Example 3. Comparing One Type of Figure to Another

Find the edge (in centimeters) of a cube whose volume is equal to the volume of a rectangular solid that is 8 cm by 18 cm by 96 cm.

     a.   16
     b.   24
     c.   36
     d.   48
     e.   60

Solution: The volume of the rectangular solid is Length x Width x Height = 8 x 18 x 96 = 13,824

The volume of the cube = $13,824 = (Side\ length)^3$
Side length = 24. Choice B is correct.

Word Problems: Three-Dimensional Figures: EASY - MODERATE

1. According to veterinary guidelines, each dog in a boarding kennel must have 4,500 cubic feet of individual space. If the kennel room measures 32 feet by 72 feet by 96 feet, how many dogs can legally be housed there?

     a.   36
     b.   39
     c.   45
     d.   49
     e.   54

2. A researcher pumps 100% nitrogen gas into an experimental chamber at a rate of 30 cubic inches per second. If the chamber's dimensions are 15 inches by 24 inches by 48 inches, how many minutes will it take the researcher to fill the chamber with nitrogen?

     a.   9.6
     b.   57.6
     c.   96
     d.   576
     e.   5,760

3. A Brinks truck is making a special delivery of 24 gold bars to the U.S. Treasury. Each bar is 3 feet long, 6 inches wide and 12 inches deep. If the gold is certified to weigh 3 ounces per cubic inch, how many pounds does each bar weigh?

    a.   54
    b.   486
    c.   864
    d.   1,296
    e.   7,776

4..If the surface area of a cube is 726 square feet, how many cubic feet are there in the volume of the cube?

    a.   121
    b.   1,331
    c.   1,452
    d.   2,904
    e.   7,260

5. A gourmet food company has developed a special low calorie fat that it sells in cubic blocks. If the weight of the fat is 36 pounds per cubic foot, and the edge of the cubic container is 8 inches, what is the weight of a block of the fat (in pounds)?

    a.   10.67
    b.   12.33
    c.   24.33
    d.   40.67
    e.   67.33

6. Thanks to an unexpected breeze, a beach ball with a radius of 6 inches rolls down a 400 yard stretch of sand. How many revolutions does the ball make on its path?

    a.   240/π
    b.   400/π
    c.   600/π
    d.   800/π
    e.   1,200/π

7. A gardener will fill a plot that is 4 inches deep, 30 feet long and 10 feet wide with colorful cypress mulch. If the mulch costs $1.50 per cubic foot, how much will it cost the gardener to fill the entire plot?

    a. $75
    b. $150
    c. $300
    d. $1200
    e. $1800

8. A mail order company uses a rectangular shipping carton, which has a volume of 512 cubic centimeters. If the length of the box is twice the height, and the width of the box is twice the length, what is the height of the box (in centimeters)?

    a.   2
    b.   4
    c.   8
    d.   12
    e.   16

9. Jill is filling the wading pool in her backyard with a garden hose at a rate of 300 cubic inches per minute. The pool is a cylinder with a diameter of 36 inches and a depth of 8 inches. How many minutes will it take Jill to completely fill the wading pool? (Use π = 3.1416)

     a.   18
     b.   27
     c.   30
     d.   36
     e.   48

10. How much larger is the surface area (in cubic feet) of a cube with an edge of 5 feet than a cube with an edge of 3 feet?

     a.   25
     b.   27
     c.   98
     d.   125
     e.   152

11. A wholesale dairy sells blocks of butter in cubic containers that have an edge of 20 inches. If the butter weighs 32 pounds per cubic foot, what is the weight of a single cube of butter (to the nearest tenth of a pound)?

     a.   2.75
     b.   4.60
     c.   53.33
     d. 106.65
     e. 148.15

12. Find the edge (in inches) of a cube whose volume is equal to the volume of a rectangular solid that is 2 in by 36 in by 81 in.

     a.   9
     b.   18
     c.   27
     d.   36
     e.   54

13. A mechanic must store his leftover antifreeze in a tank in his garage.   His largest tank is a cylinder with a radius of 14 and a height of 16 inches. If the antifreeze has a density of 12 cubic inches per gallon, how many gallons of it will fit in the bucket? (Use π = 3.1416)

     a.   205
     b.   261
     c.   421
     d.   704
     e.   821

14. Argon gas is pumped into a tank at a rate of 42 cubic inches per second. If the chamber's dimensions are 12 inches by 24 inches by 42 inches, how many minutes will it take for the tank to be completely filled with gas (to the nearest tenth of a minute)?

     a.   4.8
     b.   9.6
     c.   28.8
     d.   57.6
     e.   288.0

15. An eBay member earns her living selling miniature versions of the Rubik's cube, which each have a side length of 3 inches. When she prepares an order for a wholesale customer, the only shipping carton the seller has available is 4 feet x 3 feet x 2 feet. How many cubes can she fit in the shipping carton?

    a.   96
    b.   512
    c.   1,536
    d.   4,608
    e.   13,824

16. The Post Office will not accept any packages for which the height plus the girth exceeds 120 inches. Wal-Mart sells a rectangular shipping carton whose base is 20 inches by 24 inches. What is the maximum height this carton can be to adhere to the Post Office requirements (in inches)?

    a.   12
    b.   16
    c.   24
    d.   32
    e.   76

17. At the Nabisco plant in Carson City, the workers must fill a cylindrical storage tank with Oreo flavored frozen yogurt. The tank is 20 feet tall and has a radius of 5 feet. If one cubic foot of frozen yogurt = 7.481 gallons, how many gallons of frozen yogurt will the storage tank hold?

    a.   210
    b.   500
    c.   1570
    d.   11,751
    e.   15,700

18. The volume of a sphere varies directly with the cube of its radius. If a sphere has a radius of 10 inches and a volume of 1500 cubic inches, then what is the volume of a sphere that has a radius of 2 inches (in cubic inches)?

    a.   8
    b.   12
    c.   200
    d.   300
    e.   800

Word Problems: Three-Dimensional Figures: AS HARD AS IT GETS

19. A rectangular solid has a volume of 37 cubic inches. All of it side lengths are integers. What is the surface area of the rectangular solid (in cubic inches)?

    a.   76
    b.   146
    c.   149
    d.   150
    e.   222

20. A backyard swimming pool that is rectangular in shape holds 180,000 cubic feet of water. If the pool is 80 feet long and 120 feet wide, how deep will the water be if the pool is 75% full (to the nearest foot)?

    a.   10
    b.   12
    c.   14
    d.   15
    e.   18

21. If one cubic foot of water equals 7.8 gallons, how long it take for a faucet that flows at a rate of 18 gallons/minute to file a cube that is 42 feet on each side (in hours)?

    a.   68.6
    b.   535.0
    c.   4,116.0
    d.   9,631.3
    e. 32,105.0

22. Which of the following rectangular solids has the same volume as a sphere with a radius of 5? (Use $\pi = 3.1416$)

    a.   A cube with a side length of 10.
    b.   A cube with a diagonal of 5.
    c.   A rectangular solid with a length of 5, a width of 10, and a height of 10.
    d.   A rectangular solid with a length of 2, a width of 2, and a height of 131.
    e.   A rectangular solid with a length of 3, a width of 3, and a height of 58.

23. At the end of a shift, a confectionary worker must drain the contents of a cylindrical tank of chocolate liqueur into a rectangular storage tank. The cylindrical tank, which has a diameter of 24 feet and a height of 5 feet, is three-quarters full at the end of the shift. If the rectangular storage tank is measures 15 feet by 18 feet by 21 feet, what percentage of it will the chocolate liqueur fill? (Use $\pi = 3.1416$)

    a.   19.9%
    b.   29.9%
    c.   34.9%
    d.   39.9%
    e.   119.7%

24. The length, width, and height of a standard size shipping carton are A, B, and C, respectively. If A, B, and C are all different prime integers between 1 and 15, which of the following could NOT be the volume of the shipping carton?

    a.   105
    b.   110
    c.   120
    d.   130
    e.   190

25. A chef must divide a large block of fudge into smaller cubes for individual retail sale. His original block of fudge is a solid cube, with a total surface area of 5,400 square centimeters. If the chef cuts perfectly, and loses no fudge in the cutting process, how many solid cubes of fudge can he cut, each with a total surface area of 150 square centimeters?

    a.   36
    b.   43
    c.   72
    d.   180
    e.   216

26. A rectangular prism has a length that is three times its width, a height that is four times its length, and a volume that is twelve times its height. What is the length of the prism?

     a. 2
     b. 6
     c. 24
     d. 288
     e. It cannot be determined from the information given.

Answer Key: Word Problems -Three-Dimensional Figures

1. Volume = 32 x 72 x 96 = 221,184cubic feet / 4500 cubic feet per dog = **49** dogs. Choice D is correct.

2. Volume = (15)(24)(48) = 17,280 cubic inches /30 cubic inches per second = 576 seconds = **9.6** minutes. Choice A is correct.

3. Volume = (36)(6)(12) = 2,592 cubic inches x 3 oz/ inch = 7,776 oz./16 oz. per pound = **486** lbs. Choice B is correct.

4. The surface area of the cube - 726 square feet - is composed of 6 equal sides. Thus, 726 = $6x^2$, where x= a side of the cube. x^2 = 121, or x = 11. The volume of the cube is $(11)^3$ = **1,331** cubic feet. Choice B is correct.

5. Volume = (2/3)(2/3)(2/3) = 8/27 = 0.2963 cubic feet x 36 lb/cubic feet = **10.67** lb. Choice A is correct.

6. The ball has a diameter of 12 inches or 1 foot. Therefore, each revolution = 1 circumference = πd = 1π. If the total length the ball rolls is 400 yards or 1,200 feet, then it makes **1,200/π** revolutions. Choice E is correct.

7. Area = L x W x H = (1/3)(30)(10)=100 cubic feet x $1.50 per cubic feet = **$150.00**. Choice B is correct.

8. Let x = height of the box; length = 2x; width = 4x. x(2x)(4x) = $8x^3$ = 512. Therefore, x = **4**. Choice B is correct.

9. Our first step is to determine the capacity, or volume, of the pool, which is a cylinder.   To do so, we can simply use the formula: Volume = $\pi r^2 h$ = (3.1416)(18)(18)(8) = 8,143 cubic inches.

Next, we must divide the volume by the rate of the water (300 cubic inches per minute) to get the time required to fill the pool: 8,143 cubic inches/300 cubic inches per minute = **27.1** minutes. Choice B is correct.

10. Area 1 = 5 x 5 x 5 = 125 cubic feet. Area 2 = 3 x 3 x 3 = 27 cubic feet. 125 – 27 = 98 cubic feet. Choice C is correct.

11.   The side length is 20 inches = 5/3 feet. Therefore, the volume of the cube = $(5/3)^3$ = 4.63 cubic feet x 32 pounds/cubic foot = **148.15** pounds. Choice E is correct.

12. The volume of the rectangular solid is Length x Width x Height = 2 x 36 x 81 = 5,832 cubic inches.

The volume of the cube = 5,832 = (Side length)^3
Side length = **18** inches. Choice B is correct.

13. The problem is asking us to determine the capacity, or volume, of a cylinder. To do so, we can simply use the formula: Volume = $\pi r^2 h$ = (3.1416)(14)(14)(16) = 9,852.06 cubic inches

To convert this to gallons, we must divide by 12: 19,852.06/ cubic inches/12 cubic inches per gallon = **821** gallons. Choice E is correct.

14. Volume = (12)(24)(42) = 12,096 cubic inches/42 cubic inches per second = 288 seconds = **4.8** minutes. Choice A is correct.

15. The volume of an individual Rubik's cube is 3 x 3 x 3 = 27 cubic inches. The volume of the shipping carton is 48 x 36 x 24 = 41,472 cubic inches. 41,472/27 = **1,536** cubes. Choice C is correct.

16. The toughest part about this problem is realizing that the girth of a package = its perimeter, which is 2L + 2W. Thus,

H + 2L + 2W = 120
H + 2(20) + 2(24) = 120
H + 40 + 48 = 120

H = **32** inches. Choice D is correct.

17. Volume = $\pi r^2 h$= π(5)(5)(20) = 500π = 1570.80 cubic feet. Since 1 cubic foot = 7.481 gallons of ice cream, (1570.80)(7.481) = **11,751** gallons. Choice D is correct.

18. By definition, V= kr^3, where V = the volume of the sphere and r = the radius. Thus, 1,500 = k(10)^3 or K = 1.5. Volume = 1.5r^3, so 1.5 (2)(2)(2) = **12** cubic inches. Choice B is correct.

19. If the volume of the solid is 37 and the side lengths are integers, the only possibility is that the solid is a 1 x 1 x 37. In this case, the two ends are one-inch squares, which each have an area of 1. The other four sides are 1 x 37 rectangles, which each have an area of 37. The total surface area is therefore (1) + (1) + (4)(37) = 2 + 148 = **150** cubic inches. Choice D is correct.

20. Volume = L x W x H, so 180,000 = (80)(120)(H), or H = 18.75 feet. 75% of 18.75 = **14.06** feet. Choice C is correct.

21. When you encounter one of these "applied" problems, resist the urge to panic. Instead, read it carefully and develop a logical plan of attack. First, figure out which geometric figure is being discussed. In this case, it is a cubic tank.

Next, determine what you need to calculate to solve the problem.   Here, it is helpful to visualize a faucet filling up a large cubic tank with a side of 42 feet. The volume or capacity of the tank = 42 x 42 x 42 = 74,088 cubic feet.

Since 1 cubic foot = 7.8 gallons, 74,088 cubic feet = 577,886.40 gallons = the amount of water needed to fill the entire tank.

If the faucet flows at a rate of 18 gallons per minute, it will take 577,886.40/18 = 32104.8 minutes to fill the cube, or **535** hours. Choice B is correct.

22. The volume of a sphere = $4/3\pi r^3$. Hence, the volume of a sphere with a radius of 5 = 4/3(3.1416)(5)(5)(5) = 524. The correct answer choice must ALSO have a volume of 524.

The best way to solve the problem is to quickly check each answer choice. By definition, the volume of a rectangular solid = Length x Width x Height. When we check each answer choice, we find that Choice D is the correct answer: Volume = (2)(2)(131) = **524.**

Also note: Choice E is close (volume = 522), but it is not the *best* answer. That's what makes this problem so tricky – you need to check *all* of the answer choices for the best match.

23. Volume of a cylinder = $\pi r^2 h$ = (3.1416)(12)(12)(5) = 2,262 cubic feet.

Volume of the rectangular storage tank = L x W x H = (15)(18)(21) = 5,670 cubic feet.

But, the cylindrical tank is only ¾ full; therefore, the volume of chocolate is ¾(2,262 cubic feet) = 1,696.5 cubic feet. This amount of chocolate will fill 1,696.5/5,670 = **29.9%** of the rectangular storage tank. Choice B is correct.

24. To solve this problem, we must factor each answer choice to see which ones meet the criterion (3 different prime integers between 1 and 15). When we do, we discover that only Choice C could not be the volume of the carton.

105 = 3 x 5 x 7
110 = 2 x 5 x 11
120 = 2 x 2 X 2 x 15. Choice C is correct.
130 = 2 x 5 x 13
190 = 2 x 5 x 19

25. The original cube has six sides of equal area. The total surface area of 5,400 square centimeters is therefore the sum of the 6 sides, which each have an area of 5,400/6 = 900 square centimeters.

We can use this information to calculate the volume of the original cube. The area of each side = Length X Width = 900. The side length of the original cube is therefore the square root of 900, or 30. Hence, the volume of the original cube of fudge is (30)(30)(30) = 27,000 cubic centimeters.

In contrast, the smaller cubes of fudge have a total surface area of 150, which is the sum of 6 sides, which each have an area of 150/6 = 25 square centimeters.

We can use this information to calculate the volume of the smaller cubes. The area of each side = Length X Width = 25. The side length of each smaller cube is therefore the square root of 25, or 5. Hence, the volume of the smaller cubes are (5)(5)(5) = 125 cubic centimeters.

Finally, we must compare the two volumes to determine how many small cubes of fudge we can create from the larger one. The original cube has a volume of 27,000 cubic centimeters, while the smaller cubes have a volume of 125 cubic centimeters. We can therefore create 27,000/125 = **216** smaller cubes from the original one. Choice E is correct.

26. The tricky part of this question is figuring out what we are being asked, which is the length of the prism. To calculate it, we will use the formula Volume = Length X Width X Height. From the problem, we know that:

L = 3W
H = 4L = 4(3W) = 12W
Volume = 12H = 12(12W) = 144W

144w = (3w)(w)(12w)
144w = = 36w³
0 = w³ – 4w
0 = w(w² – 2) = w (w – 2)(w + 2)

Width = 2
Length = 3 X 2 = **6.** Choice B is correct.
Height = 12(2) = 24
Volume = (2)(6)(24) = 288

Note that the incorrect answer choices are the actual values of L, H, and Volume.

Chapter 26: SAT Only: Student Response Questions (Grid-Ins)

Grid-in questions on the SAT cover the same material as those in multiple choice format. The only difference is that students must provide an original answer, rather than select from one of five possible answer choices.

On a practical basis, this eliminates the chance to use the plug-in technique to test the individual answer choices. You also cannot just "guess" an answer to a problem that you don't know how to solve. The good news is that the grid-in word problems are usually less difficult than those in multiple choice format. As a result, the same strategies we covered in previous chapters are also applicable here.

Grid-in questions also offer a unique advantage: there is absolutely *no penalty for guessing*. Even if you fill in a totally useless answer, you will not lose the ¼ of a point that is deducted for wrong answers in the multiple choice sections of the exam. So, for grid-ins, take your best shot at every question. The only types of answers that **can't** be entered onto the grid (and are obviously wrong) are:

Negative numbers
Numbers greater than 9999
Any answer that includes a comma, a variable (such as x) or a symbol (such as π)
Mixed numbers (convert them to fractions before you enter them on a grid)
A square root or exponent

Sample Word Problems: Grid-Ins: EASY - MODERATE

1. If Greg splits his thousand dollar lottery prize evenly with his three brothers, after 30% is deducted from the winnings in taxes, how much will each of them receive (in dollars)?

2. If the prime numbers between 10 and 30 are added together, what is their sum?

3. What is the least positive three-digit integer that is divisible by both 5 and 11 and leaves a remainder of 3 when divided by 6?

4. A restaurant sold 5/6 of its stock of chicken cutlets. If it sold 150 chicken dinners, which used 3 cutlets per dinner, how many chicken cutlets are left?

5. Rick earns $6,000 per month, but pays 1/3 of his gross income in taxes. If he saves 1/7 of his take-home pay each month, but he receives no interest on the money, how much will Rick save in a given year (to the nearest whole dollar)?

6. Joe and Candy have a $100 gift certificate for a local restaurant, which must cover the complete cost of their meal, plus tax and tip. Assuming that they will pay 6% sales tax for the meal and leave a 20% tip, what is the most their food can cost?

7. Acme Grocery sells organic sesame seeds for 52.5 cents per ounce. If a wholesale customer purchases 50 pounds of the organic sesame seeds at a 20% discount, what is the total price they will pay (in dollars)?

8. Carla bought several items for her new house, including a bed for $550, two chairs for $125 each, three sets of curtains for $45 per set, and an area rug for $225. If Carla paid 5% sales tax for her purchase, what is the total amount that she spent?

9. If three workers can clean eighteen hotel rooms in one day, how many rooms can eleven workers clean in one day?

10. If thirteen less than eleven times a whole number is 306, find the number.

11. A general admission ticket to the symphony costs $32, while a student ticket costs $10.00. If a total of 800 people attended a Saturday concert and the total ticket sales were $12,400, how many student tickets were sold that day?

12. Sam is five times as old as Greg. Lori is 15 years older than Sam. If their combined age is 81, how old is Greg?

13. Stenographer 1 can type four times as fast as Stenographer 2. If they both spend an equal amount of time typing 1000 pages of data, how many pages will Stenographer 2 type?

14. A bartender is mixing Liquor A, which is 4% alcohol, with Liquor B, which is 20% alcohol, to yield Liquor C, which is 16% alcohol. To make a 4,000 ounce batch of Liquor C, how many ounces of Liquor B must be used?

15. What is the probability of getting a blue M&M from a dispenser that contains 50 red M&Ms, 75 green M&Ms, 100 blue M&Ms and 75 white M&Ms?

16. If the following sequence continues indefinitely, what will be the sum of the 500th term through the 505th term?

4,5,6,7,8,9,4,5,6,7,8,9,4,5,6,7,8,9,4,5,6,7,8,9,4,5,6,7,8,9,.......

17. David scored the following number of baskets during his first six basketball games: 5, 6, 9, 12, 4, and 8. How many baskets must he score in game 7 to have an average of 8 baskets per game for the entire 7-game season?

18. A hospital is conducting an efficiency study to determine the number of thermometers that are broken on any given day. For the first three weeks in July, the following daily values have been recorded: 5, 3, 7, 3, 6, 4, 8, 3, 7, 10, 3, 5, 9, 5, 3, 7, 2, 6, 5, 3, 7. What is the mode of this data set?

19. Ava and Ella have a combined age of 50. In ten years, one-half of Ava's age will be equal to three-quarters of Ella's current age. How old is Ava now?

20. What is the area of a right triangle whose legs are both equal to eight?

21. In quadrilateral ABCD, the sum of angles A, B and C = 7D. What is the value of angle D (in degrees)?

22. Find the number of sides of a polygon if the sum of the interior angles is 1,980 degrees?

23. For a rectangular box with a width of ½ foot, a length of 18 inches and a height of 2 feet, what is the total volume (in cubic inches)?

24. The sum of five consecutive integers is 410. What is the largest integer?

25. Ninety students are enrolled in classes at Rhode Island School of Design. Fifty-five are registered for drawing, twenty-eight have registered for watercolors, and fifteen have registered for both drawing and watercolors. How many have signed up for NEITHER drawing nor watercolors?

Answer Key for Sample Word Problems: Grid-Ins

1. The first step is to determine the actual amount that Greg won after taxes are deducted, which is 1000 – 300 = 700. Next, we must divide this figure by the total number of recipients, which is 4, to get **175**.

2. The prime numbers between 20 and 30 are 23 and 29. Their sum is **52**.

3. This problem is only difficult because it is presented as a grid-in, which means that we can't simply "check" the answer choices. Instead, we must solve it on our own.

Thankfully, there are not many numbers that are evenly divisible by both 5 and 11. We can simply start by listing the three-digit multiples of 11. When we reach one that is *also* a multiple of 5, we can check to see if it meets the second criterion in the problem.

110 is the first three-digit multiple of both 5 and 11. But, it leaves a remainder of 2 when divided by 6. Next, we must check 165, which meets both criteria; it is a multiple of both 5 and 11. It leaves a remainder of 3 when divided by 6. (27 x 6 = 162. 162 + 3 = 165.) Hence, the correct answer is **165.**

4. First, we must calculate the number of chicken cutlets the restaurant used, which is (150)(3) = 450. This number is equal to 5/6 of the total number of chicken cutlets in stock. Hence, 450/1 = 5/6. To determine the total number of cutlets, we simply cross multiply and divide: (450)(6) / 5 = 540. If the restaurant started with 540 cutlets and sold 450 of them, there were 540 – 450 = **90** left.

5. First, we must determine Rick's take-home pay, which is $6,000 (2/3) = $4,000 per month. If he saves 1/7 of it each month for one year, he will save $4,000(1/7)(12) = **$6,857.14**.

6. The total bill, which can be no more than $100, include the cost of the meal, 6% sales tax and a 20% tip. If we let x = the cost of the food, then the tax = 0.06x. The tip is 20% of the total cost of the food and the 6% tip. Algebraically, we can represent the tip as 0.20 (x + 0.06x) = 0.212x.

Since the total bill can be no more than $100, our final equation for the meal is:

Meal + Tax + Tip = 100, or x + 0.06x + 0.212x = 100, or 1.272x = 100. Solving for x, the cost of the meal must be less than **$78.62**. (Tax = $4.72, Tip = 16.67)

7. Sesame seeds are 0.525 dollars per ounce. The cost for 50 pounds = (50)(16)(0.525) = $420 x 0.80 = **$336**.

8. Carla spent 550 + 125(2) + 45 (3) + $225 = 550 + 250 + 135 + 225 = 1160 + (1160)(0.05)= **$1218.**

9. We can solve this problem by using a proportion: 3/18 = 11/x, Solve for **x =66**.

10. From the problem, we can easily write the following equation to solve for the unknown: 11x – 13 = 306
11x = 319
x = **29**

11. Let x = the number of general tickets; therefore, the number of student tickets is 800 – x. The total ticket sales equal the sum of general and student tickets, so:

32.00x + 10.00(800 – x) = 12,400
32 x + 8000 – 10x = 12400
22x = 4400
x = 200 general tickets; 800 – 200 = **600 student tickets**.

12. In this problem, we know the relationship among the ages of Sam, Lori, and Greg – and their combined age. We can use this information to build an equation to solve for Lori's age.

We will let Greg's age = x. Thus, Sam's age is 5x, while Lori's age 5x + 15. Since the sum of their ages is 81, our equation becomes:

x + 5x + (5x +15) = 81
11x + 15 = 81
11x = 66
x = **6** = Greg's age.

13. Let x = # of pages that Stenographer 2 types. 4x = # pages that Stenographer 1 types. x + 4x = 1500, so x= **200 pages**.

14. First, we must draw a table with the information that we know.

Ingredient	% Alcohol	Amount (oz)	Total Amount of Alcohol
Liquor A	4	4,000 - x	4 (4,000 – x)
Liquor B	20	x	20x
Liquor C	16	40,000	16(4,000)

The problem asks us to calculate the amount of Liquor B that is needed to create a blend with 15% alcohol. We will let x = the oz of Liquor B needed. Therefore, the amount of Liquor A needed = 4000 – x.

Since the total alcohol in Liquor C is the sum of the amounts in Liquors A and B, we can write an equation to solve for x: Alcohol in Liquor A + Alcohol in Liquor B = Total Alcohol in Liquor C
4(4,000 – x) + 20x = 16(,000)
16,000 – 4x + 20x = 64,000
16x = 48,000
X = **3,000** oz of Liquor B needed.

15. First, we must find the total: 50 + 75 + 100 + 75 = 300. Then, we can determine the fraction: 100/300 = **1/3.**

16. The series includes 6 digits that repeat indefinitely in the order: 4,5,6,7,8,9. The *sum of any six consecutive digits* will therefore be the sum of 4+5+6+7+8+9 =**39**.

17. 8 = (5 + 6 + 9 + 12 + 4 + 8 + x)/7, So, 8 = (44 + x)/7, so 56 = 44 + x, or x = 12. David must score **12 baskets** in the final game.

18. First, arrange the values in ascending order: 2, 3, 3, 3, 3, 3, 3, 4, 5, 5, 5, 5, 6, 6, 7, 7, 7, 7, 8, 9, 10. Then, find the value that occurs most often; in this case, it is **3,** which is the mode.

19. In this case, we can write one equation for the first condition and a second equation for the second condition. As always, we must first define our variables. We will let = Ava's age and y = Ella's age.

The first equation, which defines the first condition, is x + y = 50
The second equation, which defines the second condition, is (x + 10)/2 = ¾y

To solve the problem for x, we must combine the equations in a way that eliminates y. The fastest way to accomplish this is to re-write equation 1 as y = 50 – x and substitute this value for y in equation 2. But first, let's multiply equation 2 by 4 to eliminate the fractions. When we do, we get:

2(x + 10) = 3y

Now, let's substitute 50 – x for y:

$$2x + 20 = 3(50 - x)$$
$$2x + 20 = 150 - 3x$$
$$5x = 130$$
$$x = \mathbf{26} = \text{Ava's age}$$
$$y = 50 - 26 = 24 = \text{Ella's age.}$$

To check our results, let's confirm that the conditions hold: In 10 years, Ava will be 36 and Ella will be 34. Half of Ava's age (18) is indeed ¾ of Ella's current age.

20. Area = ½ (8)(8) =**32**.

21. A + B + C + D = 360. Here, D + 7D = 360, or 8D = 360. D = **45 degrees**.

22. 180 (X – 2) = 1,980, so X - 2 = 11, or X = **13 sides**.

23. V = L x W x H = 6 x 18 x 24 = **2,592 cubic inches**.

24. In this problem, we know that 5 consecutive numbers, when added together, equal 410. We will let the smallest of the 5 numbers = x. Therefore, the second, third, fourth and fifth consecutive numbers are equal to x + 1, x + 2, x + 3, and x + 4, respectively. Mathematically, we can represent their relationship by the following equation:

$$x + (x + 1) + (x + 2) + (x + 3) + (x + 4) = 410$$
$$5x + 10 = 410$$
$$x = 400/5 = 80 = \text{the smallest number.}$$
The largest number is x+4 = **84.**

25. To avoid counting students twice, we must divide them into four categories according to the following equation:

Drawing + Watercolors + Neither – Both = 90
55 + 28 + Neither - 15 = 90
Both = **22.**

Chapter 27: GRE Only: Quantitative Comparisons

The GRE presents a unique type of problem called the *quantitative comparison*. At first glance, the objective is simple. There is information in two columns – your job is simply to identify which quantity is larger. Not surprisingly, the GRE writers employ the same types of tricks and traps with quantitative comparisons as they do with multiple choice questions. Most importantly, they also present various types of word problems in both formats.

Here are our best tips for handling quantitative comparisons on the GRE, including 25 practical problems (and solutions).

Strategy 1. Know the directions cold, so that you don't have to look at them on the day of the exam:

Each question has two quantities to be compared: one in Column A and one in Column B. Compare the quantities taking into consideration any other information given and choose

Choose A if the quantity in Column A is *always* larger than the quantity in Column B.
Choose B if the quantity in Column B is *always* larger than the quantity in Column A.
Choose C is the two quantities are *always* equal.
Choose D if the relationship cannot be determined.

Strategy 2. Know what you are – and *aren't* – being asked to do. Quantitative comparisons simply require you to identify which quantity is larger…. or whether you can make that determination. You may – or may NOT – have to perform any calculations to compare the quantities. You also may not have to obtain the exact answer to a math problem – you simply need to determine which quantity is larger. From our experience, many students waste a lot of time on the GRE because they fail to make these distinctions. Don't do any more work than you need to.

Strategy 3. If one of the quantities contains a variable, you will need to plug-in *several* numbers to ensure that the relationship holds for positive numbers, negative numbers, zero, and fractions. For simplicity, test -1, 0, 1, 2 and ½.

Strategy 4. For problems that contain *two* variables, you must ALSO check the situation in which X = Y to ensure that the same relationship holds.

Strategy 5. To make a comparison easier, make the two quantities look alike. Consider the problem as an equality: whatever you do to one side (addition, subtraction, multiplication, division), you must do to the other.

Strategy 6. Whenever possible, cancel out numbers and expressions that are common to both sides. By doing so, you can easily see the comparison you are being asked to make.

Example: | **Column A** | **Column B**
| 1/6 + 2/13 + 5/7 | 2/13 + 5/7 + 1/12

Our first step is to eliminate the two common fractions from each column, which are 2/13 and 5/7. When we do, we find that the quantity in Column A is 1/6, while the quantity in Column B is 1/12. Thus, we can easily solve the problem without doing a single calculation.

Strategy 7. If Columns A and B contain numbers (and not variables), then a definitive relationship can always be determined. In these cases, Choice D is never correct.

Strategy 8. If the relationship between the values in Column A and B vary when you plug-in different variables, then you MUST choose Choice D. The relationship cannot be determined without further information.

Sample Word Problems: Quantitative Comparisons

Each question has two quantities to be compared: one in Column A and one in Column B. Compare the quantities taking into consideration any other information given and choose

Answer A - if the quantity in Column A is greater
Answer B - if the quantity in Column B is greater
Answer C - if the two quantities are equal
Answer D - if the relationship cannot be determined without further information.

1. A restaurant received 112 cans of Coca-Cola for their busy rush hour. Waitress A served 18 cans of Coca-Cola, waitress B served 11 cans, and 5 cans were consumed by each of the three cooks.

Column A	Column B
The number of remaining cans	70

2. **Column A**

	Column B
The largest integer less than 100 that leaves a remainder of 1 when divided by 17	85

3. **Column A**

	Column B
The number of 0.5 oz. chicken nuggets in a 2 lb. bag of chicken nuggets	64

4. Robert bought a condo with an unusual financing plan. He paid a down payment of $5,000, which was 1/12 of the cost of the condo, and agreed to pay the balance in 60 equal installments

Column A	Column B
Robert's monthly installment payment	$900

5. A year ago, *The Sopranos* won 15 Emmy awards. This year, the show won 3 Emmy awards.

Column A	Column B
500	The % decrease this change represents

6. George earns a base salary of $300 each week, plus a 20% commission on all sales. During the week of July 1, George sold $15,000 in merchandise.

Column A	Column B
George's total earnings the week of July 1	$3,300

7. Clare earns $675 per week as an accountant, but she pays 15% of her earnings in taxes.

Column A	Column B
$29,895	Claire's yearly take home pay

8. Jed bought 8 cartons of plants from a local nursery that offers a 5% discount for paying cash. Each plant cost $5.00 and there were 12 plants per carton.

Column A	Column B
The total cost for 8 cartons, assuming that Jed pays cash	$466

9.
Column A	Column B
The ratio of fifteen minutes to eight hours	1/32

10.
Column A	Column B
Eleven less than eleven times eleven	111

11. Five consecutive odd integers have a sum of 475.

Column A	Column B
159	The largest of the five integers.

12. Debbie put $7,500 into a CD that pays 4.95% simple annual interest and left it there for 6 years.

Column A	Column B
The total amount the CD was worth after 6 years	$9750.00

13. A Laundromat emptied its vending machines at the end of the night and found 312 quarters, 234 dimes, 443 nickels and 444 pennies. The owner will retain $50.00 of this amount for petty cash and deposits the rest at the bank.

Column A	Column B
The amount of the bank deposit	$78.99

14. Two delivery trucks are 640 miles apart. At midnight, they start to travel toward each other at rates of 50 and 30 miles per hour.

Column A	Column B
The number of hours before they pass each other	10

15. A cook is mixing 75% chocolate liqueur with 1,200 gallons of 50% chocolate liqueur to produce a mixture containing 60% chocolate liqueur.

Column A

The gallons of 75% chocolate liqueur needed

Column B

800

16. Employees at McDonalds either cook, clean or both. Ten percent of the employees cook, while twenty percent of the employees clean.

Column A

The percentage of employees that cooks and cleans

Column B

75%

17. A coin with one side heads and the other side tails is tossed four times.

Column A

The probability of getting 4 consecutive tails

Column B

1/32

18. The following sequence continues indefinitely. 9,8,7,6,5,4,9,8,7,6,5,4,9,8,7,6,5,4,9,8,7,6,5,4,9,8,7,6,5,4, ...

Column A

8

Column B

The 300th term

19. American Airlines is recording the number of on-time flights into and out of the Miami airport. The daily totals for one particular week are 1135, 1059, 1432, 2310, 1587, 1986, and 2131.

Column A

1578

Column B

The median of this data set

20. A right triangle has side lengths of 4 and 8.

Column A

The length of the hypotenuse

Column B

8

21. For a circle whose center is F, arc GH contains 40 degrees.

Column A	Column B
140	The # degrees in angle GFH

22. A square has a side length of 13.

Column A	Column B
The area of the square	52

23. Rectangle ABCD has a length of 15 and a width of 9.

Column A	Column B
48	The perimeter of the rectangle

24. A cube has a volume is 27 cubic centimeters.

Column A	Column B
Its surface area (in square centimeters)	54

25. In Triangle XYZ, the angles are in a ratio of 2:3:5.

Column A	Column B
18	The degrees in the smallest angle

Answer Key: Sample Word Problems: Quantitative Comparisons

1. This problem includes a lot of unnecessary words to confuse you. The actual calculation is simple: $112 - 18 - 11 - 3(5) = \textbf{68}$. Choice B is correct.

2. **86** ($17 \times 5 = 85$; $85 + 1 = 86$). Choice A is correct.

3. If each nugget weighs 0.5 oz, then 1 lb contains 32 nuggets; therefore, 2 lb = **64 nuggets**. Choice C is correct.

4. If the $5000 down payment is 1/12 the cost of the house, then the total cost is ($5000)(12) = $60,000. The remaining balance of $55,000 will be paid in 60 equal installments of 55,000/60 = $916.67 = **$917.** Choice A is correct.

5. 15-3 = 12. 12/15 x 100 = **80% decrease**. Choice A is correct.

6. George's total earnings = base salary + commissions = $300 + $15,000(0.20) = **$3300.** Choice C is correct.

7. Clare's total earnings are $675 (52) = $35,100(0.85) = **$29,835.00** Choice A is correct.

8. Jed's total cost will be (8)(12)($5.00) = $480(0.95)= **$456.** Choice B is correct.

9. Fifteen minutes = ¼ hour = **1/32** of 8 hours. Choice C is correct.

10. From the problem, we can easily write the following equation to solve for the unknown: 11(11) – 11 = 121 – 11 = **120.** Choice A is correct.

11. Our equation is:

x + (x + 2) + (x + 4) + (x + 6) + (x + 8) = 785
5x + 20 = 785
5x = 765
x = 153, X + 2 = 155, X + 4 + 157, X + 6 = 159, x + 8 = 161. The largest number is **161.** Choice B is correct.

12. Interest = Principal x Rate x Time. In this case, we have simple annual interest and we are asked to calculate the total amount at the end of 6 years:

Total = $7,500 + ($7,500)(0.0495)(6) = $7,5000 + $2227.50 = **$9727.50.** Choice B is correct.

13. We must determine the total amount of money in the machines and subtract $50 to find the total bank deposit. 312 quarters = $78; 234 dimes = $23.40; 443 nickels = $22.15; 444 pennies = $4.44. 78 + 23.40 + 22.15 + 4.43 – 50.00 = **$77.99**. Choice B is correct.

14. The first step for this type of problem is to draw a quick chart of what we know:

Truck	Distance	Rate	Time
A	50x	50	x
B	30x	30	x

Here, we can use the rate equation to determine the time at which the two delivery trucks will pass each other. By definition, they are traveling the same distance, which is 640 miles. Also by definition, that distance equals the SUM of the quantities (Rate x Time) for each truck. Hence, our equation becomes:
50x + 30x = 640
80x = 640. Thus, x = 8. They will pass after **8 hours**. Choice B is correct.

15. First, we must draw a table with the information we know.

Amount of Syrup	% Chocolate	Amount of Chocolate
x	75	75x
1,200	50	50(1,200)
1,200 + x	60	60(1200 + x)

The problem asks us to calculate the amount of syrup containing 75% chocolate liqueur that should be blended with syrup that is 50% chocolate liqueur to create a blend that is 60% chocolate liqueur. We will let x = the gallons of 75% syrup needed. Therefore, the total amount of syrup is = 1200 + x.

Since the total amount of chocolate liqueur in the blend is the sum of the amounts in the two original syrups, we can write an equation to solve for x:

75x + 50(1,200) = 60(1,200 + x)
75x + 60,000 = 72,000 + 60x
15x = 12,000
x = **800** gallons of syrup containing 75% chocolate liqueur are needed. Choice C is correct.

16. In this case, we have three distinct groups, which must add up to 100%. Since the original two groups are 10% and 20%, the remaining group must be 100 – 10 – 20 = **70**% of the total. Choice B is correct.

17. Probability = ½ x ½ x ½ x ½ = **1/16.** Choice A is correct.

18. The series includes 6 digits that repeat indefinitely in the order: 9,8,7,6,5,4. 301/6 = 50 + a remainder of 1. The 301st digit will be **9**. Choice B is correct.

19. First, arrange the numbers in ascending order: 1059, 1135, 1432, 1587, 1986, 2131, 2310. The middle number, **1587**, is the median. Choice B is correct.

20. Use the Pythagorean theorem to find the length: $a^2 + b^2 = c^2$, or $16 + 64 = c^2$, which is the square root of 80, or **8.94**. Choice A is correct.

21. According to the problem, angle F = 40 degrees. Since it is a central angle, it creates an isosceles triangle within the circle, with GF and FH as equal sides. Angles G and H are therefore equal, with a sum of 180 - 40 = 140 degrees. Angle YXZ is therefore **70 degrees**. Choice A is correct.

22. Area = L x W = 13 x 13 = **169**. Choice A is correct.

23. Perimeter = 2(15) + 2(9) = **48**. Choice C is correct.

24. The volume = s^3, where s is the length of a side. Thus, a side length is the cubic root of 27, or 3 centimeters. If the side of the cube is 3 cm, the area of one of its faces is (3)(3) = 9 square centimeters. Since a cube has 6 faces, its surface area is 6 x 9 = **54** square centimeters. Choice C is correct.

25. The sum of all interior angles is 180 degrees. In this case, we can represent the three angles by 2x, 3x, and 5x, respectively. Therefore, our equation becomes:

2x + 3x + 5x = 180
10x = 180
X = 18
The smallest angle is 2x = **36.** Choice B is correct.

Chapter 28: GMAT Only: Data Sufficiency Problems

In addition to multiple choice questions, the GMAT also presents *data sufficiency* problems. At first glance, the objective is simple. You are presented with a question, followed by two statements; you must then determine if either statement (or both) provide(s) adequate information to answer the question. Not surprisingly, the GMAT writers employ the same types of tricks and traps with data sufficiency questions as they do with multiple choice questions. Most importantly, they also present various types of word problems in both formats.

Here are our best tips for handling data sufficiency questions on the GMAT, including 25 practical problems (and solutions).

Strategy 1. Understand the premise of data sufficiency questions – and the specific instructions for them – before you take the exam. If possible, memorize the five answer choices:

Each of the following problems has a question and two statements, which are labeled (1) and (2). Use the data in (1) and (2), together with other available information (such as the number of hours in a day and the definition of clockwise), to determine if the statements are sufficient to answer the question. Then, select the appropriate answer choice:

A. **Statement 1 alone is sufficient but Statement 2 alone is not sufficient to answer the question asked.**
B. **Statement 2 alone is sufficient but Statement 1 alone is not sufficient to answer the question asked.**
C. **Statements 1 and 2 together are sufficient to answer the question but neither statement is sufficient alone.**
D. **Each statement alone is sufficient to answer the question.**
E. **Statements 1 and 2 are not sufficient to answer the question - additional data is needed.**

Strategy 2. Understand what you are being asked - and NOT asked - to do. Unlike the word problems on the GMAT, which test your basic mathematical skills, data sufficiency questions test your *reasoning ability*. To answer these questions, you do NOT need to solve the problem or crunch a lot of numbers. You simply need to determine whether or not you have enough information to do so with the two statements that are provided. From our experience, many students waste a lot of time on the GMAT because they fail to make this distinction.

Strategy 3. Once you know what the question is asking, determine what information you need to find the answer. For example, to determine the area of a rectangle, you will need to know the length and the width. Your answer choice will depend on whether or not Statement 1 and/or Statement 2 provide that information.

Strategy 4. Examine each statement separately. Does it provide a number or quantity that you need to answer the question? Does it add new information or simply repeat what is in the question stem? Or is it completely extraneous information?

Then, use the process of elimination. If Statement 1 is insufficient, then Choices A and D can immediately be eliminated. Likewise, if Statement 2 is insufficient, then Choices B and D can immediately be eliminated. Use this information to determine your plan of attack – and, if necessary, to guide your guessing strategy.

Strategy 5. Do not make any assumptions about the question or the two individual statements. Instead, use only the factual information that is provided. Also, do not rely upon a figure or diagram for geometry questions that ask you to determine the size of an angle or figure. The test writers often include misleading figures to imply relationships that do not actually exist.

Strategy 6. If the problem includes a variable, do not assume that it is a positive number or an integer. Variables such as x and y can conceivably be positive numbers, negative numbers, zero, and fractions.

Strategy 7. Read carefully. A common ploy is for Statements 1 and 2 to convey the same information in different ways. If this is the case, then the correct answer choice will be D or E. Even worse, one of the statements is usually needlessly complicated, simply to confuse you. The following statements, which initially seem quite different, actually say the same thing:

(1) a is 75% of b
(2) the ratio of b/a is 4:3

When you encounter two statements like this, re-state them in the same terms. By doing so, you can quickly conclude the relevance (and usefulness) of each one in the actual problem.

Strategy 8. Work through the data sufficiency questions in this publication to become proficient in this unusual type of problem. The more familiar you are with the underling math topics and the typical tricks of the test writers, the better you will perform on the day of the exam.

Sample Word Problems: Data Sufficiency

Use the following answer choices for the questions below:

A. Statement 1 alone is sufficient but Statement 2 alone is not sufficient to answer the question asked.
B. Statement 2 alone is sufficient but Statement 1 alone is not sufficient to answer the question asked.
C. Statements 1 and 2 together are sufficient to answer the question but neither statement is sufficient alone.
D. Each statement alone is sufficient to answer the question.
E. Statements 1 and 2 are not sufficient to answer the question - additional data is needed.

1. How many two-digit positive integers are multiples of a and b?

(1) Both a and b are odd integers that are less than 10
(2) Both a and b are greater than 6

2. Jenny's monthly budget includes $600 for rent, $300 for her car payment, $100 for insurance, $300 for utilities, and $300 for groceries. How much does she have left for discretionary spending?

(1) Jenny's monthly take-home pay is $3,000.
(2) Jenny pays 20% of her gross income in taxes.

3. X college students were asked to name their favorite color. 250 said red, 225 said blue, 150 said green and Y students each said yellow, orange and white, respectively. What percentage of students chose white?

(1) X = 775
(2) No student chose black

4. Six hundred guests will either eat shrimp or roast beef at a wedding reception. How many of the guests will eat roast beef?

(1) Ten percent of the guests are allergic to seafood
(2) The ratio of shrimp eaters to roast beef eaters is 6:4.

5. A chef has a wonderful recipe for meatloaf, which uses 8 oz of garlic. How much garlic will she need to make enough meatloaf to serve 48 people?

(1) For every ounce of garlic she uses, the chef must reduce the amount of onion by one-half
(2) The original recipe requires 4 ounces of onion

6. What are the values of X and Y?

(1) The difference between (X + Y) and (X – Y) is 10
(2) XY is 120.

7. What is the average of five integers: A, B, C, D, and E?

(1) The sum of A, B, C, D, and E is 850
(2) A, B, C, D, and E are consecutive odd integers

8. On a snowy Sunday night, Sam, Joe, and Pete decided to compare CD collections. How many CDs does Joe have?

(1) Joe has 10 fewer CDs than Sam
(2) Pete has 12 less than four times the number of CDs that Joe has

9. Joe borrowed $25,000 from the bank. How much will his monthly payments be?

(1) The term of the loan is two years
(2) The interest rate is fixed at 4.9%

10. Nancy is three years younger than her brother Cane, who is eight years older than Jake. How old is Nancy?

(1) Jake is 27
(2) Cane is 35

11. Gary and Bill decide to work together to mow a two-acre lawn. How many hours will it take them to complete the job?

(1) Gary can mow a one-acre lawn in 3 hours
(2) Bill works half as fast as Gary

12. Eighty students are attending summer school courses at Beaver Falls High School. X have registered for Spanish, Y have registered for Math, and Z have registered for neither Spanish nor Math. How many have registered for BOTH Spanish and Math?

(1) Thirty students are not taking Spanish
(2) Y = 40% of X, while Z = 75% of Y

13. At a church raffle, the pastor will award a single cash prize to one lucky winner. What is the probability (in percent) that any one ticket will be selected for the prize?

(1) There are 40 tickets in the bowl
(2) One person bought 10 of the 40 tickets

14. Jill's boyfriend asked her to bring X DVDs from her collection of Y to a weekend party. How many different possible combinations could she bring?

(1) Y = 20
(2) Two of the DVDs were destroyed during the long car ride to the party

15. What is the next term in the series?

(1) The first five terms are 1, 1, 6, 36, 41
(2) The series continues indefinitely

16. What is the median number of on-time flights into and out of the Miami airport during the week of January 1 – 7?

(1) Delta Airlines had 1,250 flights into and out of Miami during the first week of January
(2) No other airline flew into or out of the Miami airport during this timeframe

17. What is the area of triangle V?

(1) The longest side length is 15
(2) The perimeter is 20

18. For triangle FHG, what is the value of x?

(1) One angle equals 60 degrees and the second angle equals x
(2) The third angle is equal to 3x

19. What is the new area of the circle?

(1) The radius is decreased by 18%
(2) The original diameter was 18

20. What is the area of the square?

(1) The side length is 13
(2) The perimeter is 52

21. How many tiles will the decorator need to cover the entire living room floor?

(1) The perimeter of the living room is 240 feet
(2) Each individual tile measures 6 inches by 9 inches

22. A cube and a rectangular solid are equal in volume. What is the length of an edge of the cube?

(1) The lengths of the edges of the rectangular solid are 8, 9, and 24
(2) The surface area of the rectangular solid is 960

23. How old is Shawn?

(1) Shawn is 30 years younger than Dawn
(2) The product of Dawn's age and Shawn's age is 175

24   If Tina splits her lottery prize evenly with her two parents and three siblings, how much money will each person receive?

(1) The prize was $2,880 after taxes
(2) The prize was $3,600 before 20% taxes were deducted

25. What is the measure of the final internal angle of enclosed figure X?

(1) The other internal angles in X total 825
(2) X is an octagon

Answer Key: Sample Word Problems: Data Sufficiency

1. When taken together, Statements 1 and 2 provide enough information for us to learn that a and b are 7 and 9, respectively. Choice C is correct.

2. In this question, all we need to know is Jenny's take-home pay, which is given in Statement 1. Statement 2 allows us to calculate her gross pay, which is extraneous information. Hence, Choice A is correct.

3. To answer the question, we need to know the values of X and Y. Statement 1 gives us X, which is enough for us to calculate Y. Statement 2 is extraneous information. Choice A is correct.

4. To answer this question, we need to know the ratio of shrimp eaters to roast beef eaters, which is provided in Statement 2. The information in Statement 1 is interesting, but extraneous. Choice B is correct.

5.   To answer this question, we need to know the amount of people that the original recipe served. Neither statement gives us this information. Choice E is correct.

6. Statements 1 and 2, if taken together, will allow us to write an equation to solve for both X and Y. Neither is sufficient on its own. Choice C is correct.

7. To answer this question, we need to know the sum of the numbers and their relationship to each other. Statement 1 provides the sum, while Statement 2 defines their relationship. If taken together, they allow us to answer the question. Choice C is correct.

8. To answer this question, we need to know the exact number of CDs that one of the boys owns AND enough information to write an equation to solve for the number that belong to Joe. Neither of these statements gives us an exact number for any of the boys; additionally, there is insufficient information to write an equation to solve for the unknown. Choice E is correct.

9. To answer this question, we need to know the principal, the rate, and the time. Statement 1 tells us the time,

Statement 2 tells us the rate, and the question stem tells us the principal. Choice C is correct.

10. Either statement is sufficient to answer the question. Hence, Choice D is correct.

11. To solve this problem, we need to know the individual rates for Gary and Bill. Statement 1 gives us Gary's rate, while Statement 2 gives us Bill's rate. Choice C is correct.

12. We can only solve this problem if Statements 1 and 2 give us values for X, Y, and Z (or a way to determine them).   Statement 1 allows us to determine the value of X, which is 80 – 30 = 50. Statement 2 allows us to determine the values of Y and Z as 20 and 15, respectively. Thus, Choice C is correct.

13. The question asks us to determine the probability of any one ticket being selected. The only information we need is the number of tickets in the bowl, which is given in Statement 1. The information in Statement 2 is misleading – and extraneous. If one person holds 10 of the 40 tickets, then his/her overall odds of winning are 1 out of 4. However, this does NOT influence the odds of any *single ticket* being drawn, which remains 1 out of 40. Choice A is correct.

14. To answer this question, we need to know the values of X and Y. Statement 1 tells us Y, but not X. Statement 2 is extraneous information that does not tell us anything about X (only that the number of viewable DVDs will be X – 2). Therefore, we do not have sufficient information to answer the question. Choice E is correct.

15. To determine the next term in a series or sequence, we need twp pieces of information: (1) the pattern that the terms follow, and (2) whether or not the pattern will continue. Statement 1 gives us the first five terms of the series, which follows a definite pattern: the terms are squared, then increased by 5. Statement 2 provides the second essential piece of information, which is that the series or sequence will continue indefinitely. Therefore, Choice C is correct. With both statements, we can determine the next term in the series.

16. This problem includes a single phrase that totally changes its meaning: it asks for the number of *on-time flights*. Between Statement 1 and Statement 2, we know the total number of flights into and out of the Miami airport during the first week in January. However, neither statement tells us how many of those flights were on-time (or how many flights there were each day). Therefore, Choice E is correct.

17. Neither statement gives us enough information to calculate the area of the triangle. Hence, Choice E is correct.

18. If taken together, Statements 1 and 2 give us enough information to calculate the value of x. Choice C is correct.

19. If we take the two statements together, we have enough information to calculate the new area of the circle. Choice C is correct.

20. To calculate the area of a square, we simply need the length of a side, which Statement 1 provides. Choice A is correct.

21. The two statements, when taken together, provide enough information for us to determine the number of tiles the decorator will need. Choice C is correct.

22. Each statement, on its own, provides enough information to answer the question. Choice D is correct.

23. The two statements, if taken together, provide enough information for us to calculate Shawn's age. Choice C is correct.

24. We can find the answer using either Statement 1 or 2, which convey the same information. Choice D is correct.

25. To answer this question, we need to know the number of sides in the figure and the sum of the remaining angles. Statements 1 and 2, when taken together, provide this information. Choice C is correct.

Chapter 29: Final Exam

Now that you have practiced the different types of word problems on standardized tests, it's time to test your skills under simulated testing conditions. Sit down in a quiet place where you can work without interruption. Then, tackle the following problems as quickly and accurately as possible.

To keep pace with the actual exam, you should give yourself between one minute and three minutes for each problem.   Refer (as necessary) to the standard information that is presented at the beginning of the quantitative section of the test, which we have copied below.

When you are done, check your answers against our answer key, which presents a detailed solution to each problem. If you need additional help, we have also indicated the chapter in which each topic is covered.

These problems are difficult, but "doable." Take whatever time you need to review and practice the concepts and strategies for each type of problem. Ultimately, that is the key to getting a top score.

Good luck!

Directions: For each problem, decide which answer choice is best. Fill in the corresponding circle on the answer sheet. You may use any available space for scratch work.

Reference Information:

  7.   Circles. Area $= \pi r^2$, Circumference $= 2 \pi r$
  8.   Rectangles: Area $=$ Length X Width
  9.   Right Triangles: Area $= \frac{1}{2}$ (Base) (Height)
  10. Cubes: Volume $=$ Length x Width x Height
  11. Cylinders: Volume $= \pi r^2 h$
  12. Pythagorean Theorem: for right triangles $c^2 = a^2 + b^2$

1. The mean of nine numbers is 85. If 5 is subtracted from each of six of the numbers, what is the new mean?

      a.   81.67
      b.   82.50
      c.   83.50
      d.   83.67
      e.   84.07

2. A car salesman receives a commission of W% on a sale of B dollars. What is his commission?

      a.   1/WB
      b.   WB/100
      c.   W/B
      d.   WB
      e.   100WB

3. Circuit City reduced the price of a Sony laptop from $1,200 to $750. A month later, the store reduced the sales price by an additional 20%. What was the new price for the Sony laptop?

      a. $510
      b. $550
      c. $600
      d. $610
      e. $650

4. The ratio of professors to students at a private college is 1:8. If 56 new students are admitted, there will be 12 times as many students as professors. What is the new number of students at the college?

    a.   112
    b.   128
    c.   148
    d.   154
    e.   168

5. If $x + 11$ is an even integer, what is the sum of the next two even integers?

    a. $x + 4$
    b. $x + 15$
    c. $2x + 4$
    d. $2x + 15$
    e. $2x + 24$

6. If 50 less than twelve times a number is equal to 34, find the number.

    a.   7
    b.   8
    c.   9
    d.   11
    e.   14

7. Kelly has $100,000 invested at 5%. How much must she invest at 7% to earn $20,000 in interest from her investments annually?

    a. $114,285.71
    b. $178,571.42
    c. $214,285.71
    d. $285,714.28
    e. $357,142.85

8. The typical tire for a mini-van has a radius of 36 inches. How many feet will the tire cover in 3,000 revolutions?

    a. $1,080\pi$
    b. $9,000\pi$
    c. $10,800\pi$
    d. $18,000\pi$
    e. $36,000\pi$

9. The average of two numbers is 100. If the difference between the numbers is 18, what is the product of the two numbers?

    a.   8,464
    b.   8,888
    c.   9,600
    d.   9,800
    e.   9,919

10. What number is 1,500% greater than 20?

    a. 30
    b. 300
    c. 320
    d. 3,000
    e. 3,200

11. Francesca can type a manuscript in 30 minutes. If she works with Melanie, they can complete the job in 20 minutes. How long would it take Melanie to type the manuscript alone?

    a. 35
    b. 45
    c. 40
    d. 55
    e. 60

12. A wholesale coffee distributor wants to blend a Brazilian coffee bean that costs 50 dollars per pound with a Colombian bean that costs 75 dollars per pound to make 1000 pounds of a mixture that costs 60 dollars per pound. How many pounds of the Columbia beans can the company use?

    a. 200
    b. 250
    c. 400
    d. 600
    e. 750

13. Students at Miami Dade Elementary School either study English, Spanish or both. Seventy percent of the students study English, while ten percent study both Spanish and English. What percentage of the students only study Spanish?

    a. 10%
    b. 15%
    c. 20%
    d. 25%
    e. 30%

14. If the following series continues in the same pattern, what will the next term be?

    5, 9, 6, 11, 7, 13, 8, 15…..

    a. 7
    b. 9
    c. 11
    d. 12
    e. 13

15. A pizza is divided into slices of equal size, each with a side length of 8. Assuming that each slice meets at the center of the pizza, what is the pizza's circumference?

    a. 4π
    b. 8π
    c. 16π
    d. 64π
    e. 128π

16. In a class of 75 students, the average weight of the 30 girls was 50 lbs, while the average waistline of the 45 boys was 70 lbs. What was the average weight for the entire class?

    a. 55
    b. 58
    c. 60
    d. 62
    e. 65

17. If a wholesale dealer can buy K HD-TVs for V dollars, how much will P HD-TVs cost (in dollars)?

    a. 1/PVK
    b. (100/K)PV
    c. PK/V
    d. PV/K
    e. PVK

18. In Triangle X, the length of one side is 5 and the other side is 14. Which of the following could possibly be the length of the third side?

    a. 6
    b. 8
    c. 14
    d. 21
    e. 28

19. If the radius of a circle is decreased by 40%, by what percent is its area decreased?

    a. 36
    b. 40
    c. 45
    d. 60
    e. 64

20. If Jill's bank balance is 60% of Dawn's bank balance and Ginny's bank balance is 55% of Dawn's bank balance, what is the ratio of Jill's balance to Ginny's?

    a. 3/12
    b. 1/3
    c. 11/12
    d. 12/11
    e. 3/1

21. Olivia purchased carpeting for her family room, which measures 12 feet x 24 feet. If the carpet she selected costs $14 per square yard, how much will it cost Olivia to purchase enough of this carpet to cover her entire family room?

    a. $448
    b. $896
    c. $1,344
    d. $2,016
    e. $4,032

22. If the surface area of a cube is 1,350 square feet, how many cubic feet are there in the volume of the cube?

    a.   225
    b.   1,350
    c.   3,375
    d.   6,750
    e. $(1,350)^3$

23. A researcher pumps 100% argon gas into an experimental chamber at a rate of 90 cubic inches per second. If the chamber's dimensions are 12 inches by 36 inches by 18 inches, how many minutes will it take the researcher to fill the chamber with argon?

    a.   0.867
    b.   1.44
    c.   86.7
    d.   144.0
    e.   7,776

24. A cube and a rectangular solid are equal in volume. If the lengths of the edges of the rectangular solid are 9, 9, and 72, what is the length of an edge of the cube?

    a.   9
    b.   12
    c.   18
    d.   36
    e.   81

25. At Yankee Stadium, there are two places for fans to park. Lot 1 charges $10.00 for the first hour of parking and 50 cents for each additional half hour. Lot 2, on the other hand, charges a flat rate of $32.00 for an entire day of parking. Assuming that a fan will park her car for 8 hours that day, what will be the *additional* cost of parking in Lot 2?

    a. $13.50
    b. $15.00
    c. $17.00
    d. $18.50
    e. $22.00

26. How many positive integers less than 80 are evenly divisible by 4, 5 and 6?

    a.   1
    b.   2
    c.   3
    d.   4
    e.   5

27. A rectangle with sides of 24 and 36 inches is completely inscribed in a circle. If all four corners of the rectangle touch the circumference of the circle, what is the area of the circle?

    a. 43π
    b. 468π
    c. 864π
    d. $1,296\pi$
    e. $1,872\pi$

28. Lisa has 160 coins that are worth $31.00. If the coins are all quarters and dimes, how many fewer dimes than quarters does Lisa have?

    a.   15
    b.   25
    c.   40
    d.   60
    e.   100

29. Lila weights twice as much as Brenda. Monica weighs 20 pounds more than Lila. If their combined weights are 420 lbs., how much does Monica weigh?

    a.   80
    b.   100
    c.   160
    d.   180
    e.   200

30. The mean of eighteen consecutive integers is 111-1/2. If the integers are arranged in increasing order, what is the mean of the largest nine integers?

    a.   115
    b.   116
    c.   117
    d.   118
    e.   119

31. What is the least positive three-digit integer that is divisible by both 3 and 14 and leaves a remainder of 1 when divided by 5?

    a.   112
    b.   128
    c.   141
    d.   156
    e.   176

32. The denominator of a fraction is four times as large as the numerator. If 6 is added to both the numerator and denominator, the value of the fraction is 7/8. What was the numerator of the original fraction?

    a.   1/12
    b.   2/9
    c.   3/10
    d.   2/7
    e.   4/9

33. A hotel depletes its supply of laundry detergent every 65 days. If its use increases by 60%, how many days would the same amount of laundry detergent last?

    a.   35.0
    b.   36.0
    c.   39.0
    d.   40.6
    e.   45.6

34. At a political rally, 40% of the participants were Democrats and 65% of the Democrats were female. What percentage of participants at the rally were female Democrats?

    a. 15%
    b. 18%
    c. 20%
    d. 25%
    e. 26%

35. Jake has $1,800 dollars left over after spending 5/7 of his summer earnings. How much money did Jake earn over the summer?

    a. $1,985
    b. $2,250
    c. $2,520
    d. $2,750
    e. $2,850

36. Kyle invested an unknown amount of money in an account that pays 12% annually. Later, he invested an additional $50,000 for the same amount of time at 6% interest. If Kyle's two investments earn a total of 8% annual interest, how much was his original investment?

    a. $25,000
    b. $30,000
    c. $35,000
    d. $40,000
    e. $45,000

37. A vendor at Yankee Stadium sells two products: hot dogs and beer. Altogether, the vendor earned $45,000 in profits last year on the sale of 7,500 products. If the profit on a hot dog is $5.00 and the profit on a bottle of beer is $8.00, how many hot dogs did the vendor sell?

    a. 1,500
    b. 2,000
    c. 2,500
    d. 3,500
    e. 5,000

38. If Beverly's age eight years from now minus her age six years ago plus ten times her age ten years ago is equal to 150 years, how old will Beverly be in fifteen years?

    a. 20
    b. 21
    c. 35
    d. 36
    e. 38

39. On New Year's Eve, a limousine driver traveled from Philadelphia to Pittsburgh at an average rate of 75 miles per hour. On his return trip to Philadelphia, he encountered a heavy snow storm, which reduced his speed to 45 miles per hour. What was the limousine driver's average speed for the entire trip, in miles per hour?

    a. 55
    b. 56
    c. 58
    d. 60
    e. 62

40. If @, #, and & represent three numbers in which # = @ + 6 and & = # + 9, what is the result when the mean of the three numbers is subtracted from their median?

    a. -3
    b. -1
    c. 3
    d. 6
    e. It cannot be determined from the information given

41. A scientist has a 32-ounce solution that is 8% citric acid. If 3 ounces of pure acid are added to the solution, what percentage of the resulting mixture is acid?

    a. 2.56
    b. 5.56
    c. 15.89
    d. 17.38
    e. 18.00

42. At a talent agency with 250 performers, 150 are male and the rest are female. If 200 of the performers are over 18 and ten percent of the female performers are under 18, how many of the male performers are over 18?

    a. 10
    b. 40
    c. 90
    d. 100
    e. 110

43. Baskin Robbins offers five possible toppings for their ice cream sundaes: chocolate syrup, butterscotch syrup, nuts, whipped cream, and sugar sprinkles. If you choose three of these toppings, how many possible combinations are there?

    a. 3
    b. 9
    c. 15
    d. 20
    e. 30

44. What is the probability of getting a black jelly bean from a dispenser that contains 90 red jelly beans, 68 green ones, 46 purple ones, 36 white ones and 160 black ones?

    a. 1/4
    b. 1/5
    c. 1/3
    d. 2/5
    e. 3/5

45. For the repeating decimal 0.975634975634975634......, what is the 75th digit to the right of the decimal point?

    a. 3
    b. 4
    c. 5
    d. 6
    e. 7

46. Jim and Steve left the Raleigh airport at the same time and travelled in opposite directions. If Jim travelled at an average rate of 70 miles per hour and Steve travelled at an average rate of 55 miles per hour, how many hours will it take Jim and Steve to be 500 miles apart?

    a.   2
    b.   3
    c.   4
    d.   5
    e.   6

47. If the base of a parallelogram decreases by 25% and the height increases by 90%, by what percent does the area increase?

    a.   37.5%
    b.   42.5%
    c.   55.5%
    d.   65.0%
    e.   75.0%

48. A web site sells two types of picture frames: a gold frame that costs $25 and a wooden frame that costs $20. On a busy weekend, the site sold 500 gold picture frames and collected a total of $45,000 in revenues. Assuming that no other products were sold, and that the web site collected no sales tax on any of the items, how many TOTAL picture frames did it sell that weekend?

    a.   1,125
    b.   1,250
    c.   1,625
    d.   1,825
    e.   2,125

49. A hotel bathtub can be filled in 30 minutes and drained in 45 minutes. How many minutes will it take to fill the tub if a maid forgets to close the drain valve?

    a.   40
    b.   45
    c.   60
    d.   75
    e.   90

50. The first term in a sequence is -50. Every consecutive term is 25 greater than the term that immediately preceded it. What is the value of the 75th term in the sequence?

    a.   1,750
    b.   1,775
    c.   1,800
    d.   1,825
    e.   1,850

Answer Key: Final Exam

1. For the original numbers, (9)(85) = 765 = the sum. The new sum= 765 – (5)(6) = 735. 735/9 = 81.67. Choice A is correct. *This topic is covered in Chapter 17.*

2. For students who are uncomfortable working with variables, the easiest way to solve this problem is to plug in numbers and see what happens. Let's assume that W = 5% and B = $100. The salesman's commission would be

($100)(0.05) = $5.00. At first glance, this may seem like answer Choice D, which is WB, but it is not. When we converted the 5% to 0.05 we divided the 5 by 100; hence, the solution was actually WB/100, which is Choice B.

For students who are comfortable working with variables, you can obtain the same answer by simply plugging the letters into the formula. If the salesman receives a W% commission, then:

W% = W/100
(W/100) (B) = WB/100. *This topic is covered in Chapter 18.*

3. The trick to this question is to ignore the initial reduction from $1,200 to $750, which is extraneous information. What we are being asked to calculate is a 20% reduction in the price of a computer that is marked at $750. Our answer is 750 - (750)(0.20) = 750 – 150 = $600. Choice C is correct. *This topic is covered in Chapter 5.*

4. In this scenario, the # of professors (x) remains the same. We also know that the original number of students is 8 times this number, or 8x. Therefore, the number of new students is 8x + 56. Finally, we also know that 8x + 56 = 12x. Solving for x, we find that the number of professors (x) = 14. Therefore, the original number of students = (8)(14) = 112 and the new number of students = 112 + 56 = 168. Choice E is correct. *This topic is covered in Chapter 6.*

5.   In this case, we are asked to find the sum of two consecutive even integers. If (x + 11) is even, then the next consecutive even integer is (x + 13). The following consecutive even integer is (x + 15). Therefore, their sum is (x + 11) + (x + 13) = 2x + 24. Choice E is correct. *This topic is covered in Chapter 7.*

6. This can be solved by a simple equation: 12x – 50 = 34, so 12x = 84. x = 7. Choice A is correct. *This topic is covered in Chapter 7.*

7. In this problem, the interest payments from both investments must equal $20,000 per year. To solve, we will let x = the amount of money that Kelly will invest at 7%. Our equation becomes:

5%($100,000) + 7%(x) = $20,000
(0.05)($100,000) + (0.07)(x) = $20,000
5000 + 0.07x = $20,000
0.07x = $15,000
x = $214,285.71. Choice C is correct. *This topic is covered in Chapter 8.*

8. The tire is a circle with a radius of 36. The distance it covers in one revolution is simply the circumference of the tire. Since the circumference = $2\pi r$, we know that the tire covers $2\pi(36/12) = 6\pi$ feet in one revolution. Therefore, for 3,000 revolutions, the tire covers $(6\pi)(3,000)=18,000\pi$ feet. Choice D is correct. *This topic is covered in Chapter 23.*

9.   In this case, we can write one equation for the first condition and a second equation for the second condition. As always, we must first define our variables. We will let = x the one number and y equal the other number.

The first equation, which defines the first condition, is (x + y)/2 = 100
The second equation, which defines the second condition, is x – y = 18

First, let's re-write both equations in a clearer manner.

If we multiply equation 1 by 2, we get x + y = 200
If we re-write equation 2, we get y = x - 18

To solve the problem for x, we must combine the equations in a way that eliminates y. When we do, we get:

x + (x – 18) = 200
2x -18 = 200
2x = 218

x = 109
y = 109 - 18 = 91.

The question asks us the *product* of these numbers, which is (109)(91) = 9,919. Choice E is correct. *This topic is covered in Chapter 19.*

10. 20 + 15.0 (20) = 320. Choice C is correct. *This topic is covered in Chapter 5.*

11. To solve, we will use the equation, Work = Rate x Time. Our unknown (x) is Melanie's individual rate for typing the manuscript.

Francesca + Melanie = 1
20/30 + 20/X = 1

To simplify, we must multiply each side of the equation by our least common denominator, which is 30x:

20x + 600 = 30x
10x = 600
X = 60.   Melanie would require 60 minutes to type the manuscript alone. Choice E is correct.   *This topic is covered in Chapter 12.*

12. First, we must draw a table with the information that we know.

Bean Type	Quantity	Price/pound	Total Cost
Brazilian	1000 – x	50	50(1000 – x)
Colombian	x	75	75x
Mixture	1000	60	60,000

Since the problem asks us to calculate the amount of Colombian beans the company can use, we will let that value = x. Therefore, the amount of Brazilian beans = 1000 – x. Once we label our variables, we can write the expression for the total cost of each ingredient. We can also calculate the cost of the final mixture.

Since the cost of the Brazilian beans plus the cost of the Colombian beans equals the total cost of the blend, our equation becomes:

Colombian beans + Brazilian beans = Total Cost
75x + 50(1000 – x) = 60,000
75x + 50,000 – 50x = 60,000
25x = 10,000
X = 400 pounds of Columbian beans. Choice C is correct. *This topic is covered in Chapter 13.*

13. In this case, we have three distinct groups, which must add up to 100%. Since the original two groups are 70% and 10%, the remaining group must be 100 – 70 – 10 = 20% of the total. Choice C is correct. *This topic is covered in Chapter 14.*

14. This problem is a combination of two sub-series. In the first one, each number increase by 1 (5, 6, 7, 8); in the second, each number increases by 2 (9, 11, 13, 15). The next number would be 9. Choice B is correct. *This topic is covered in Chapter 16.*

15. Circumference = π times Diameter   If the radius is 8, the circumference= 16π. Choice C is correct. *This topic is covered in Chapter 23.*

16. Because the number of boys and girls is not the same, we must take a *weighted average* for each of the two groups.

Average for entire class =(Sum of Girls' Weights + Sum of Boys' Weights) / Total # Students
Average = {(30)(50) + (45)(70)} / 75
Average = (1500 + 3150)/75 = 4650/75 = 62. Choice D is correct. *This topic is covered in Chapter 17.*

17. To solve, let's plug in random numbers for each variable. In this case, let's assume that the dealer bought 20 HD-TVs (K) for 100 dollars (V). The cost for a single HD-TV is therefore 100/20 or V/K or 5 dollars. The cost for any value of P will simply be that number times 5, which, in symbols, is PV/K. Choice D is correct. *This topic is covered in Chapter 18.*

18. According to the triangle inequality theorem, the length of one side of a triangle must be greater than the difference and less than the sum of the lengths of the other two sides.

Therefore, in Triangle X, the length of the third side must be greater than 14 – 5 = 9 and less than 5 + 14 = 19. The only answer choice between 9 and 19 is Choice C. *This topic is covered in Chapter 22.*

19. If the radii of the two circles have a ratio of 10:6, their areas have a ratio of 100:36. Therefore, the decrease is 64 out of 100, or 64%. Choice E is correct. *This topic is covered in Chapter 23.*

20. For simplicity, we will let J = Jill's balance, D = Dawn's balance and G = Ginny's balance. Therefore,

J = 0.60D. G = 0.55D. Thus, J / G = 0.60/0.55 = 12/11. Choice D is correct. *This topic is covered in Chapter 6.*

21. First, we must convert our room measurements into yards: 12 feet = 4 yards, while 24 feet = 8 yards. Therefore, the area of Olivia's room is (4)(8) = 32 square yards.   (32)(14) = $448.   Choice A is correct. *This topic is covered in Chapter 24.*

22. The surface area of the cube – 1,350 square feet - is composed of 6 equal sides. Thus,

1,350 = $6x^2$, where x= a side of the cube.
x^2 = 225, or x = 15

The volume of the cube is 15^3 = 3,375 cubic feet. Choice C is correct. *This topic is covered in Chapter 25.*

23. Volume = (12)(36)(18) = 7,776 cubic inches /90 = 86.4 seconds = 1.44 minutes. Choice B is correct. *This topic is covered in Chapter 25.*

24. Volume of rectangular solid = 9 x 9 x 72 = 5,832 = also the volume of the cube. So, the length of an edge of the cube is the cubic root of 5832, or 18. Choice C is correct. *This topic is covered in Chapter 25.*

25. To solve, simply calculate the total amount to park in Lot 1 vs. Lot 2 for 8 hours. For Lot 1, the cost is $10.00 + (0.50)(14) = $17.00. Lot B, on the other hand, costs $32.00. The difference is $15.00, which is Choice B. *This topic is covered in Chapter 2.*

26. The question asks us to determine how positive integers less than 80 are divisible by 4, 5 and 6. First, we will list the integers that are evenly divisible by our largest number, which is 6: 6, 12, 18, 24, 30, 36, 42, 48, 54, 60, 66, 72, 78.

In this group, we must then select the numbers that are ALSO evenly divisible by 5, which are 30 and 60.

Finally, we must determine if either of these numbers is ALSO evenly divisible by 4; only 60 is. Hence, Choice A is correct. There is only one positive integer less than 80 that is evenly divisible by 4, 5, and 6. *This topic is covered in Chapter 3.*

27. In this situation, the diagonal of the rectangle is equal to the diameter of the circle. Because the rectangle can also be viewed as two triangles that share the diagonal as a common side, we can use the Pythagorean theorem to calculate its length.

Accordingly, the square of the diagonal is equal to $(24)(24) + (36)(36) = 576 + 1,296 = 1,872$. This means that the diameter of the circle is the square root of 1,872, or 43.27; the radius is therefore 21.63.

Now, we can calculate the area of the circle, which is $(21.63)^2(\pi)$, $= 468\pi$. Choice B is correct. *This topic is covered in Chapters 22 & 23.*

28. First, we must define our variables. In this case, x = the number of quarters. Therefore, $160 - x$ = the number of dimes. Since the total value of these two coins is $31.00, our equation becomes:

$25x + 10(160 - x) = 3100$
$25x + 1600 - 10x = 3100$
$15x = 1500$
$x = 100$ quarters, $160 - 100 = 60$ dimes. There are $100 - 60 = 40$ fewer dimes than quarters. Choice C is correct. *This topic is covered in Chapter 9.*

29. We can write and solve an equation to determine Monica's weight. First, we must define our variables: We will let x= Brenda's weight. Lila's weight = $2x$. Monica's weight = $2x + 20$.

Since the sum of the three weights is 420, our equation becomes:
$x + 2x + (2x + 20) = 420$
$5x = 400$

$X = 80$ = Brenda's weight. Therefore, Lila weighs $(2)(80) = 160$ and Monica weighs $160 + 20 = 180$. Choice D is correct. *This topic is covered in Chapter 10.*

30. If the mean of eighteen consecutive integers is 111-1/2, then nine of the integers are less than 111-1/2 and the other nine are larger. The nine largest integers must be 112, 113, 114, 115, 116, 117, 118, 119, and 120. The average of these nine numbers is 116. Choice B is correct. *This topic is covered in Chapter 7.*

31. We can start the problem by listing the three-digit multiples of 14. When we reach one that is *also* a multiple of 3, we can check to see if it meets the second criterion in the problem.

128 is the first three-digit multiple of both 3 and 14. But, it leaves a remainder of 3 when divided by 5.
156 is the next three-digit multiple of both 3 and 14. It leaves a remainder of 1 when divided by 5.

Hence, the correct answer is Choice D. *This topic is covered in Chapter 3.*

32. First, let x be the original numerator. The original fraction is therefore $x/4x$. The new fraction is $(x + 6)/(4x + 6)$, which equals 7/8. We must solve the equation for x. When we cross-multiply, we get:

$8x + 48 = 28x + 42$
$6 = 20x$
$x = 6/20 = 3/10$. Choice C is correct. *This topic is covered in Chapter 4.*

33. The laundry detergent would be used 1-3/5 (or 8/5) times as fast, which would deplete the supply in 5/8 the usual amount of time. $65 (5/8) = 40.6$ days. Choice D is correct. *This topic is covered in Chapter 5.*

34. In this case, we simply multiply the numbers together to find the percentage of participants in both groups: $0.40 \times 0.65 = 26\%$. Choice E is correct. *This topic is covered in Chapter 5.*

35. 5/7 of Jake's earnings = $1,800. Thus, we can set up a ratio to determine the original whole: 5/7 = 1,800/X. Hence, X = $2,520, which is Choice C. *This topic is covered in Chapter 6.*

36. To solve, we must first define our variables. In this case, we will let x = Kyle's initial investment. His second investment $50,000, which makes his total investment = x + $50,000. Next, we must write expressions to describe the interest that each investment earns:

The first investment earns $(0.12)x$
The second investment earns $(0.06)(\$50,000) = \$3000$
The total investment earns $(0.08)(x + \$50,000)$

Therefore, our equation becomes:

$(0.12)x + \$3000 = (0.08)(x + \$50,000)$
$0.12x + \$3000 = 0.08x + \$4000$
$0.04x = \$1000$
X = $25,000. Choice A is correct. *This topic is covered in Chapter 8.*

37. Let x = # of hot dogs and 7500 – x = the # of bottle of beer

The sum of their individual profits equals the total annual profit, or:
$5x + 8(7500 – x) = 45,000$
$5x + 60,000 – 8x = 45,000$
$-3x = -15,000$
X = 5,000 hot dogs. 7500 – 5,000 = 2,500 bottle of beer. Choice E is correct. *This topic is covered in Chapter 9.*

38. For age problems with a single person, our chart is:

Beverly Now	Beverly plus 8	Beverly minus 6	Beverly minus 7

Now, let's fill in our values. As always, we will let Beverly's current age = x.
Her age 8 years from now will be x + 8
Her age 6 years ago was x – 6
Her age 7 years ago was x - 7

Beverly Now	Beverly plus 8	Beverly minus 6	Beverly minus 7
x	x + 8	x – 6	x – 7

By definition, our equation is:
$(x + 8) - (x – 6) + 10(x – 7) = 154$
$x + 8 - x + 6 + 10x – 70 = 154$
$10x = 210$
x = 21 = Beverly's current age. In 15 years, Beverly will be 36. Choice D correct. *This topic is covered in Chapter 10.*

39. Since the driver traveled different speeds on each part of the trip, we must use the following formula to determine his average rate: Average Rate = Total Distance / Total Time

In this case, the test writers did not give us any specific numbers, so we are free to pick any value for the total distance. In this case, we will use 100 miles for the total distance, which makes each leg of the trip (the distance from Philadelphia to Pittsburgh) equal to one-half of 100, or 50 miles.

For the trip from Philadelphia to Pittsburgh, the Average Rate = 50 miles/75 miles per hour = 0.67 hours.

For the return trip from Pittsburgh to Philadelphia, the Average Rate = 50 miles/45 miles per hour = 1.11 hours. Hence, the total time was 0.67 + 1.11 = 1.78 hours

Going back to the original equation, for the total trip, Average Rate = Total Distance / Total Time = 100 miles/1.78 hours = 56 miles per hour. The correct answer is Choice B. *This topic is covered in Chapter 11.*

40. By definition, # = @ + 6 and & = @ + 6 + 9. The median of @, #, and & is simply the middle value, which is #, or (@ + 6).

The mean of the three numbers is their sum divided by three, or

{@ + (@ + 6) + (@ + 6 + 9)} / 3 = (3@ + 21)/3 = @ + 7.

The difference between the mean and the median is (@ + 7) – (@ + 8) = -1. Choice B is correct. *This topic is covered in Chapter 17.*

41. First, we must draw a table with the information we know.

Solution	Quantity (oz)	Percent Acid	Amount Acid (oz)
Original	32	8	32(0.08) = 2.56
Added	3	100	3(1.0) = 3
Final	35		2.56 + 3 = 5.56

In this case, the tabulated data tells us the entire story. The final 35-ounce solution contains 5.56 ounces of acid. 5.56/35 = 15.89% acid. Choice C is correct. *This topic is covered in Chapter 13.*

42. The best way to attack this type of problem is to summarize our data in a simple table.

In this case, the performers are either male or female. Some are over 18, while others are under 18. When we put the information into our chart, we get:

	Male	Female	Total
Under 18	40	10	50
Over 18	110	90	200
Total	150	100	250

From the table, we can answer the question; the number of male performers over 18 is 110. Choice C is correct. *This topic is covered in Chapter 14.*

43. Use the factorial formula to solve: 5! / 3! = (5 x 4 x 3 x 2 x 1) / (3 x 2 x 1) = 20. Choice D is correct. *This topic is covered in Chapter 15.*

44. First, we must determine the total number of jelly beans in the dispenser, which is 90 + 68 + 46 + 36 + 160 = 400. Then, we must calculate the probability of getting a red jelly bean, which is 160/400 = 2/5. Choice D is correct. *This topic is covered in Chapter 15.*

45. In this decimal, the repeating pattern is 975634, which is a string of 6 digits. The first 72 digits will be 12 repetitions of this pattern. Then, in the *thirteenth* repetition, the 75th digit to the right of the decimal point will be the *third* number in the series, which is 5. Choice C is correct. *This topic is covered in Chapter 16.*

46. The first step for this type of problem is to draw a quick chart of what we know. In this case, we will let x = the time it takes for Jim and Steve to travel 500 miles. We can also enter the rates for each man and write an expression for their respective distances. Next, we must use this information to solve for x.

Driver	Distance	Rate	Time
Jim	70x	70	x
Steve	55x	55	x

Jim and Steve each travelled *a portion* of the total distance, which is 400 miles. Our equation, therefore, is: Jim's Distance + Steve's Distance = Total Distance

70 x + 55x = 500
125x = 500
x = 4 hours Choice C is correct. *This topic is covered in Chapter 11.*

47. The area of the original parallelogram = Base X Height. Let B = the length of the base and H = the height of the original parallelogram.

If the base decreases by 25%, it becomes 0.75B. If the height increases by 90%, it becomes 1.90H. The new area is therefore: (0.75)(1.90) = 1.425, which is 42.5% bigger than the original area. Choice B is correct. *This topic is covered in Chapter 24.*

48. In this problem, we know the total revenue, which is based on the sale of two products, a gold picture frame and a wooden one. We need to know how many TOTAL picture frames were sold.

First, we must determine the amount of the total revenue came from the gold frames. In this case, the vendor sold 500 frames at $25, for a total of $12,500. Therefore, the rest of the $45,000 in sales – which is $32,500 – came from the sale of the wooden frames.

Since the wooden frames sold for $20 each, we can simply divide to determine the number of wooden frames that were sold: $32,500/$20 = 1,625 wooden frames.

Finally, the TOTAL number of picture frames sold that weekend was the sum of the two types: 500 gold frames and 1,625 wooden frames = 2,125 total frames. Choice E is correct. *This topic is covered in Chapter 2.*

49. In this case, the rate to fill the bathtub is x/30, while the rate to drain it is x/45. Since the drain is emptying the tank, our equation becomes x/30 – x/45 = 1.

To solve, we must multiple both sides by 90, which is our least common denominator:
3x – 2x = 90
x = 90 minutes to fill the tub. Choice E is correct. *This topic is covered in Chapter 12.*

50. For an arithmetic sequence in which the first term is A and the difference between the terms is D, the *nth* term is: An = A1 + (n – 1)D.

In this case, the first term in the sequence is -50. The difference in terms is 25 and n = 75.
The 75th term = -50 + (75 – 1)25 = -50 + 1,875 – 25 = 1,800. Choice C is correct. *This topic is covered in Chapter 16.*